TELEVI$ION

Les Brown

TELEVI$ION

The Business
Behind the Box

A HARVEST/HBJ BOOK

HARCOURT BRACE JOVANOVICH

NEW YORK AND LONDON

ISBN 0-15-688440-2
Library of Congress Catalog Card Number: 77–153684
Printed in the United States of America
D E F G H I J

For Jean
and Jessica, Joshua, and Rebecca

Foreword

On West Forty-sixth Street in Manhattan, some fifty or sixty paces from Broadway, there is a dingy, narrow, and antiquated five-story structure squeezed between the stage door of the Lyceum Theatre and the rear emergency exit of Loew's State. Built originally as a millinery shop around the turn of the century, it has retained the original façade, complete to the split-level display windows. In the upper window two men sit at their desks; in the lower stands the blow-up of a newspaper's front page. On the windows, in fading green paint and in old-style lettering of eccentric flourish, is the legend: *Variety*.

It is the home of the venerable show business journal, published weekly since 1905, and it will play a part in this book because it is where I work, as editor of the television and radio section. A depressing place to most outsiders, it scorns all the niceties of white-collar life and most of the modern conveniences, including fresh air. The hard environment seems to breed a brash, independent kind of journalist with a deep skepticism about press handouts, who delights in uncovering news stories that companies and government agencies are not eager to make known. Since this book's primary source is *Variety*, it owes certain reportorial debts to various broadcast beat reporters, but particularly to Bill Greeley, Larry Michie, and Steve Knoll. Others on the paper, including Bob Knight, Leonard Traube, and Jack Pitman, and numerous persons in the broadcast industry who would probably not want to be identified helped in providing information.

The interpretation and viewpoint, however, are one man's only, and the esteemed newspaper on which he has schooled for seventeen years must not be held answerable for his opinions.

More responsible for this book than any other person—save perhaps the author—was William B. Goodman, my editor at Harcourt Brace Jovanovich, Inc., who not only initiated the project and guided its course but asked the pertinent questions, as a consumer and layman, that helped to shape its purposes. Without Milton Slater's kindness this book would not have been begun, and without the abidance of the two men in *Variety*'s upper-level window, its publisher, Syd Silverman, and editor, Abel Green, it would not have been completed. I am also indebted to such good friends and colleagues as Richard Burgheim, Robert Bernstein, Ben Kubasik, and Richard Kellerman for their aid and moral support.

I set out in January 1970 to write on how the American television system works, and about the men who work in it, using as a framework the events that would take place in that calendar year. My expectation was that, whatever occurred, it would be in most respects a typical year.

It proved to be a kind of Abraham Zapruder experience. The late Zapruder, with his simple home movie camera, thought he was filming a presidential motorcade in Dallas and instead recorded the assassination of John F. Kennedy. While far from comparable in historic importance, my experience was to chronicle not the average year I had expected, but a chaotic twelve months for the television industry, full of change and portents of greater upheavals ahead—without doubt the harshest and most uncertain year in two decades of the Beautiful Business. But as it developed, the trials of 1970 served to put a sharper than normal focus on the structure of the system and the mentality of American broadcasting.

Looking back, it was not an untypical year. The events were inevitable, and the men in television dealt with them most typically. Bless them.

Contents

1

The Three Rocks

Along the steel-and-glass canyon that has become Sixth Avenue midtown, with façades so sober and businesslike they could pass for brokerage houses, stand the three rocks of American broadcasting—30 Rock, Black Rock, and Hard Rock. The visitor to New York riding uptown along the Avenue of the Americas (still Sixth Avenue to the natives) might catch sight of the illuminated ABC cube outside the entrance at Fifty-fourth Street; otherwise, he would have no sense of passing through Television Row, that unique quarter mile where most of what appears on his and 83 million other home receivers is ordained.

Except for ABC's lighted sign, the buildings seem to strive for anonymity. Beyond a plaque identifying it as the RCA Building and small marquees on the side streets, the home of NBC is unmarked on the row; and CBS, with a fastidiousness about contemporary design, has placed its letters where they will neither offend nor attract the eye. The three rocks are substantial members of the business landscape on Sixth, which includes the Burlington, Equitable Life, Time-Life, Sperry Rand, J. C. Penney, Amax, McGraw-Hill, Uniroyal, and Standard Oil buildings. That is considered fortunate. NBC, CBS, and ABC would rather associate with big business than with any other kind, least of all show business.

Sensible, Stable, and Prosperous is what the buildings say. The message is for the investment community.

More glamour and theatricality surround the mercantile Penney or Burlington buildings than the three great centers of entertainment and communications.

No stars or producers mill about their entrances, no television monitors or other symbolic hardware betray the craft in the outer lobbies, no signboards tell what *TV Guide* says about the day's programing. NBC's ground level is a mall for clothing shops, toy and shoe emporia, newsstands, and a pharmacy with a lunch counter. CBS's tenants are a bank and an expensive restaurant with a name as blunt as a checkbook, The Ground Floor. ABC's are a bank, a Loft's candy shop, and the entrance to an underground parking garage.

Only NBC produces television shows on the premises—*Today, Tonight,* the daytime games and panels, and newscasts—and invites tours to the studios and the engineering operations. The other two have their actual broadcast plants in factory buildings in seedy West Side streets, and it is from there that films and video tapes—most of them transported from Hollywood, where they were produced—are fed out over the air. These annexes also house the news divisions and are the origination points for the newscasts; the more pretentious shows are done from old midtown theaters that have been converted to television studios.

But if they are not among the wonders of New York or bedazzling to the tourist, the three rocks are worth some examination for what they reveal of their network occupants.

To most of the television audience the national webs are differentiated only by their trade-marks: the CBS eye, the NBC peacock, and the ABC lower-case monogram. It is no wonder they are hard to tell apart on the home screen. They imitate each other feverishly, buy their programs from the same sources, interchange their personnel, and operate not only from the same city but from the same neighborhood. Yet there are natural character differences between the three companies, stemming from their different origins, management philosophies, and status in the business world; and the buildings that house them are emblematic of some of these differences.

The National Broadcasting Company operates under the

wing of its parent, RCA Corporation, and has never left the nest. The Columbia Broadcasting System built its own skyscraper, a masterpiece of the high-rise architecture of the fifties. The American Broadcasting Companies, Inc., rents.

There are four street-level accesses to the NBC building, but two are the principal entrances, the one on Sixth and the other on a short parallel street between Sixth and Fifth Avenues, Rockefeller Plaza. Just the name implies its ambiance. It is a limousine-lined street in the Rockefeller Center complex, at the foot of the promenade, graced with shops for the carriage trade and the sunken ice rink festooned with flags of all nations and a perpetual hedge of spectators. A canopy over the building's entrance tells that important persons regularly pass through. In the main lobby, the architectural accents bespeak the streamlined opulence of the 1930's.

But the Sixth Avenue side is miles away. It is for the foot and taxi traffic. Hurley's Bar and a Whalen's drugstore flank the entrance on either corner, and the shops between are distinctly for the working classes. Grown sooty and hardly noticed by passers-by, a mosaic mural titled *Thought* arcs above the doors to the main lobby as the one concession to grandeur on the building's west side.

Quite understandably, the company officially identifies with the east side and has the formal address of 30 Rockefeller Plaza—hence the sobriquet, 30 Rock—but that does not necessarily make it the more typical side of NBC. The network's personality swings between the two poles, as if marked by the environment—patrician and pedestrian, caring for appearances and not caring, having a sense of luxury and a taste for the vulgar.

CBS is much more consistent. There are two entrances to the building, and they are identical. On all four sides and from every view the structure is handsome and imposing, and it is landscaped with thin spartan trees that are given miniature lights for foliage in winter. Appearances are not everything at CBS, but few things count for more. So obsessed is management with the looks of CBS that it has become a company neurosis.

The building, designed by Eero Saarinen and completed after his death in 1961, is in some ways a monument to the perfectionism and fastidiousness of corporate president Dr. Frank Stanton ("Dr." because he has a psychology doctorate from Ohio State in the field of statistics). If it expresses anything peculiar to CBS, it is the Stanton values of balance, symmetry, precision, and antiseptic good taste. As an architecture buff and the man who cultivated and nurtured the CBS image (that inflated institutional view of itself the company projects to the public), Stanton settled for nothing less than a building majestic among the towers of New York, and Saarinen gave him a soaring sculpture in black granite and glass, clean of line and unadorned, suggestive of power and poetry. That it is a cold poetry, all rhythm and no melody, is somehow consistent with CBS.

Form has always seemed to count more than content in the CBS mind, and this was reflected in a rule established when the company moved into the building in 1965, a rule that depersonalized the offices to preserve their orderliness and beauty. No one was permitted to add to the decor of his office, whether a painting from his own collection or a piece of bric-a-brac, without approval from Lou Dorfsman, then director of design and responsible for all graphics and wall hangings. Until the rules were relaxed a few years ago—but only relaxed—the prohibition had held for family photographs, children's art, and the sentimental items common to most offices. The entire building conformed to a single standard of taste.

Maintenance of 51W52 (as the address is stylistically rendered) is compulsive. Few hospitals in New York are cleaner. The walls show no scuffing, no handprints; their stark whiteness is counterpointed by a scheme of walls covered in a charcoal gray fabric reminiscent of the flannel suits that used to be the uniform of the advertising man. A Japanese woman who is perhaps a genius at flower arrangement produces floral bouquets daily for the top executives and twice a week for the reception areas. Each secretary's desk bears a single rose. The company's annual bill for fresh flowers surely runs into the thousands.

Company pride and narcissism, and a caution for good taste, have become part of the fiber of the CBS executive. At a black tie company party given by the chairman, William S. Paley, one of the lesser executives was appalled at the obesity of a colleague's wife, whom he had met for the first time. "Seeing him with his wife made me realize why I felt S—— never really belonged," he said. "He was never my idea of CBS. Together they were so out of place in that group that I felt embarrassed for Mr. Paley."

Another rising young man declined to use Sixth Avenue as his route to the office, choosing to walk up Fifth and cutting over at Fifty-second Street. There is a clear class difference in the foot traffic on the two avenues.

The brevity of Tom Dawson's tenure as president of the television network (which encompassed about a year in 1968 and 1969) has been attributed by insiders at least partly to his unwillingness to assume the identity of a CBS president. Dawson insisted upon wearing a suburban jacket to work, never realizing that the jests made about it were really warnings, and he frequently excused his chauffeur early so that he might drive his presidential limousine up to his home in Greenwich, Connecticut, himself. He was even known to commute by train while president. Such unaristocratic behavior embarrassed not only his superiors but those who worked under him.

It was the color of the granite that gave CBS the name Black Rock—that and the aptness of the allusion to a Spencer Tracy film, *Bad Day at Black Rock*. CBS is a formal and tense place—as any place with rules of deportment and decor is bound to be—and it follows that such an atmosphere will produce many more crises, more deeply suffered, than comparable companies less anxious about image and appearance. There are many more bad days at Black Rock than at 30 Rock. At Hard Rock the bad days are of another kind.

If moving from 485 Madison Avenue to 51 West Fifty-second Street, at Sixth Avenue, was a step down in prestige for CBS, as an address change from the East Side to the West Side might be, ABC's move to 1330 Avenue of the Americas was a step up. Completed within a year after the CBS move, ABC not only brought all its divisions together under a single roof for the first time, but elevated many of them from shabby office space in peripheral midtown buildings to a brand-new steel-and-glass structure. The height of prestige, however, was that it became the next-door neighbor to CBS, just across Fifty-third Street.

Blandly modern and totally undistinguished as a building, ABC's quarters, rented on a long-term lease, signify up-to-dateness and a sort of residential equality with the rival networks. But the nondescript architecture inspired the taunt that ABC moved into the crate the CBS building came packed in.

Was it coincidence that ABC moved just after CBS, and right nearby? To know the company and its long adoration of CBS is to doubt it. ABC has had a history of acting like CBS. Its organizational plan is almost an exact parallel, and one of the company's greatest coups in the fifties was to spirit away the head of CBS spot sales and his entire staff to set up spot sales and owned-stations divisions for ABC in the manner of CBS. Where programing is concerned, ABC's forms and philosophies have always been closer to those of CBS than of NBC.

In network society, ABC is the parvenu, wealthy as a company through its vast chain of motion picture theaters and its ownership of television and radio stations in the largest markets, but as a television network somewhat out of its class. ABC is the climber, and it has been a hard climb. It is hard to catch up with network leaders who are entrenched, hard to beat them at the game they invented, hard to convey a public impression of respectability without a history of it, and hard to win the full co-operation and support of affiliated stations which, through the lean years, have operated from short-range goals. Therefore Hard Rock.

It is not an honest nickname, however, but really a tag to complete the idea of three rocks. When CBS became Black Rock and there were two, it became natural to include ABC in the scheme. Little Rock was an early choice, validated both by the network's third-place standing and the fact of a drawling Southerner, Tom Moore, as its president. Moore lost the job in 1968, and Little Rock was disqualified. Hard Rock works in the motif and is appropriate for the additional reason that the ABC radio stations have been champions of rock 'n' roll music, but it is not in regular currency, and people still tend to refer to the ABC building as the ABC Building.

Stanton could have wished for such luck. Black Rock distressed him; it was anti-image. But there is no quashing a nickname that comes naturally and delivers truth with humor. He apparently had hoped to promote 51W52 as a catch name, indeed was so struck by the rhythm of the address that he took it for his internal phone number, the license number of his limousine, and the number of the company jet.

The will of Paley and Stanton and their standards of rightness have always prevailed at CBS. Their men readily conformed. Only in latter years have they been challenged and even frustrated; the subversive element in the company is Woman.

In January of 1970, a memo from the personnel department expressed the wish of management that female personnel refrain from wearing slacks or pants suits. The rule prompted a defiant "slack-in" at the West Side broadcast center's cafeteria, a pants parade in the tray lines by the women employed there. The Paris bureau of CBS News threatened nudity in protest, wiring the following day:

"The girls of the Paris bureau, which is the fountainhead of CBS fashion, stand united with their fellow workers in New York in favor of slacks, pants suits, and whatever the mode should decree. Rather than have anyone tell us what to wear, we would prefer not to wear anything at all."

The "slack-in" made the papers, and the memorandum, while never recanted, was never enforced. Significantly, the victory of the distaff side emboldened some of the younger men to grow beards and longer sideburns, never formally outlawed in the company but taken for granted by the department heads as undesirable.

Then came the female complaint about the art collection on the corporate floor. *Variety* received the following unsigned letter, which it chose not to publish:

PORNOGRAPHY AT BLACK ROCK. ATT: Messrs Agnew, Pastore, Burch!

Secretaries on 35 are all atitter about art recently hung in public corridor between Chairman's suite and Board room. Title: "Bless its pointed little head" (Artist: Avedisian) Subject: a sizable erect red penus [*sic*]—aimed toward the Board room. Most outside directors of CBS too old to remember their last erection; most inside directors too beat.

(Note: Paley is President of Museum of Modern Art; CBS director Ralph Colin is VP of Modern Museum; CBS director Ambassador Burden is Trustee of Modern Museum).

The CBS thirty-fifth floor is like a plush wing of the Museum of Modern Art, which is just a short distance away, down Fifty-third Street. The works are exhibited rather than hung and are so boldly avant-garde as to be a spectacle. It is an awesome suite of offices, calculated to humble, if not intimidate, the visitor. NBC's art (except that of RCA chairman Robert Sarnoff, a trustee of the Whitney Museum) is not a collection and encompasses a broader range of genres and price value than CBS's. Except for some personal acquisitions, they are little more than pictures on the wall. At ABC there are a few striking contemporary canvases in the reception areas, but they hang more out of obligation to decor than from a collector's conviction. In the ABC corporate offices the emphasis is on artifacts rather than art, presumably because it is easier to comprehend the value of relics.

There is no scheme or consistency to the office decor at NBC; at its best it has the feel of old rich, at its worst it is "decorated," but for the most part the suites are merely furnished. The casualness about the looks of things carries over to the NBC peacock and the snake sign of the NBC initials. Stanton, who is graphics-minded, would never have tolerated anything so ugly for CBS.

An important difference between the two companies is implicit in this, and it is one that extends to the consequential decisions the companies make in broadcast matters. CBS as a company expresses the legendary leadership chemistry of two unlike men, its chairman and president, whose standards and values are all-pervasive. Authority descends, in the CBS bureaucracy, in concentric circles, narrowing as the corporate executive vice-president, the group president, the division president, and the departmental vice-presidents impose their separate leadership cachet on what originally has been circumscribed by Paley and Stanton. The further down the line he is, the narrower an executive's operating compass.

NBC, by contrast, expresses an essentially faceless committee of company elders serving the business purposes of parent RCA, a sprawling conglomerate engaged in electronics manufacture, computer technology, real estate, frozen foods, automobile rentals (Hertz), and book publishing (Random House), as well as phonograph recordings and broadcasting. NBC corporate president and chief executive officer Julian Goodman is so insulated with advisers that he could not, if he chose to, personalize the company to make it an extension of his own value system. Nor did Sarnoff, when he headed NBC, bind up the broadcast company in hallowed traditions.

Goodman maintains such low visibility as head of the company that he frequently passes unnoticed among the people who work for him. At an NBC banquet for its affiliated stations one year, he spent the better part of an hour in conversation with comedian Don Adams, who was then the star of an NBC hit series, *Get Smart*. When Adams got up to leave, he told Goodman how enjoyable it was speaking to him, and then asked, "What station are you with, again?"

Authority is diffuse at NBC. Goodman is part of a triumvirate which includes two partriarchs, NBC chairman Walter Scott and executive vice-president David Adams, and virtually all policy decisions are filtered through a president's council made up of other senior members of the organization. No prescribed operating style or rules of deportment are handed down the line from above. There is a high degree of departmental autonomy on most matters extraneous to fulfilling the vital business objectives.

The net effect of the organizational differences is that CBS in general is rigid in its standards of what may go out over the air and NBC more venturesome.

As a program of topical and political satire, *The Smothers Brothers Comedy Hour* was a source in 1968 of constant concern at CBS since it frequently flouted the Paley-Stanton criteria of taste and balance; but at the same time, *Rowan and Martin's Laugh-In*, which practiced new forms of irreverence every week and was often more direct with its political shafts than *The Smothers Brothers*, was flourishing at NBC.

When *Laugh-In* producer George Schlatter sought to make a running joke of "Look *that* up in your Funk & Wagnalls," the NBC censors tried to block it since the phonetics flirted with profanity. But Schlatter pressed the issue, arguing that Funk & Wagnalls was not a fictitious but a company name and that its use was justified in the show because it was a funny name. Whether the name is so innocently funny may be moot, but the NBC censors gave in on the point with one condition: that the ampersand be pronounced very distinctly as *and* and not as *'n'*. There would have been no such discussion at CBS; the line would have been struck from the script the first time, once and for all.

The National Broadcasting Company was formed as a radio network to create programing that would make people want to buy radio sets, which RCA was selling, and in television NBC remains an extension of RCA's manufacturing interest. This was why NBC was broadcasting in color years before the other networks, and it is why the five-second "living color" announcement with the symbolic peacock was retained long after the other networks dropped their color logos as superfluous.

The Columbia Broadcasting System was built up by Paley from the Columbia Phonograph Broadcasting System, which had been a failing business when he acquired it in 1928. Paley had become enchanted with the commercial possibilities of radio when, working out of Philadelphia, he was buying advertising time in the medium for his father's business, the Congress Cigar Company. His real success with CBS began with the piracy of Jack Benny, *Amos 'n' Andy*, and later other stars from NBC, and it has been a Paley precept at the network ever since, and fundamental to his showmanship, that stars are the heart of the program schedule and are to be pampered and kept happy.

Stanton, who became president of the corporation in 1946, from the first maintained a safe distance from the entertainment functions of the broadcast properties, which were Paley's domain, and gave himself to the more cosmic questions of communications freedom and government-media relations. His keen intellect, coolness under fire, and well-ordered presentations before congressional committees projected him as the spokesman for the broadcast industry—its most eloquent and effective witness. And so with Paley as impresario and Stanton as statesman, CBS assumed the leadership role in ratings and in broadcast affairs.

Broadcasting remains the primary business of CBS, although through a series of acquisitions it has been diversifying into a number of other fields, both in the interest of corporate growth and as a hedge against a possible stock crisis in the event of a severe advertising recession or some technological threat to the television business as it is practiced today.

ABC evolved from the old Blue Network of NBC, when it was divested (and the Red Network retained) under government decree. Later it was acquired by the Paramount Theatres chain, and Leonard Goldenson became president of the new theater-broadcast complex. From the earliest days the company labored for an equal footing with the other networks, against the handicap of weak station affiliations. CBS and NBC had already secured the more powerful and well-established local stations for their television webs, and ABC had to build upon the newer stations and the leftovers. In small markets of one or two television stations, CBS and NBC were the primary networks and ABC all but excluded. Its circulation tended to be confined to the larger population centers. Making the climb more difficult was the fact that Goldenson and his executive vice-president, Simon B. Siegel, were theater-oriented men and not intuitively broadcasters. Their approach to the business was to keep an eye on what CBS was doing.

CBS had been first in total circulation since the beginning of television's three-network competition, and ABC perennially ran third. ABC's people experienced few triumphs and little glory in the company's history, and the network seemed hounded by hard luck—another justification for the Hard Rock appellation. CBS would have a plan and it would work; ABC would have a plan and suffer a power failure that night.

In spite of the company's aspirations, Hard Rock is a friendly place and somewhat ingenuous in its striving for the formalities of big-time business. Black Rock betrays the regimentation within the company, and the corporate idea of image has afflicted the building with an atmosphere of emotional constipation.

Like the NBC peacock, 30 Rock is varicolored—stuffier than the others at the one extreme, more given to humor at the other. Perhaps because of the retail commerce on the ground floor, and the presence of network news and studio operations on the premises, the building conveys a greater cosmopolitanism than the newer rocks.

Across Sixth Avenue, in the Burlington Building, are the New York offices of the Corporation for Public Television and its network, Public Broadcasting Service (PBS). Public television has encamped in the same quarter mile as the commercial networks.

Not surprisingly, so has the fourth great force in American broadcasting—after ABC, CBS, and NBC—the A. C. Nielsen Company, the Chicago-based research firm whose New York quarters are in the Sperry Rand Building, in a line between the CBS and NBC headquarters. The Nielsen Company, which produces the television ratings that influence nearly every program decision made by the networks, is not only the scorekeeper of network television but the score itself. There are other rating services, but only the national Nielsens are considered to be official by the advertising industry. One trusts the score; there is no other way. Nielsen is the gospel.

By extension, the Nielsen numbers are the real product of American television. They are what the networks sell to advertisers and what the programs are designed for. A show has a 20.0 rating at 8:30 at night. That's 12 million television homes, or 25,200,000 people, and Nielsen breaks that figure down to young, old, and in between. This is what the advertiser buys, the numbers and the breakdown; conceivably, he may never learn the name of the show.

The game of television is basically between the network and the advertiser, and the Nielsen digits determine what the latter will pay for the circulation of his commercial. The public is involved only as the definition of the number: so many persons 18–49, so many others, all neatly processed by television.

In day-to-day commerce, television is not so much interested in the business of communications as in the business of delivering people to advertisers. People are the merchandise, not the shows. The shows are merely the bait.

The consumer, whom the custodians of the medium are pledged to serve, is in fact served up.

2

A Sprig of Hollywood

It was a minor event of scant informational reward, but as the first industry meeting of the year it had a certain ritual value. More than 400 practitioners of broadcasting and advertising, as though of one fraternity, turned out for the January 6, 1970, luncheon meeting of the International Radio and Television Society, the feature of which would be the Mort, Mike, and Marty Show, a panel quiz in news conference form with the three network program chiefs, Mort Werner of NBC, Mike Dann of CBS, and Marty Starger of ABC. They would be careful, characteristically, not to divulge state secrets in an open forum, particularly not to each other on the eve of that most secretive time in television, the drafting of the new fall schedules. Alongside them at the head table were nineteen New York advertising men whose buying power at the networks gave them influence over the life and death of television shows. This was reveille for the executioners.

Others may have been more newsworthy or closer to the centers of power, but Mike Dann made the news in network television, even when it seemed there was no news to be made. He had the talent for it and with that an insatiable desire to make print. Those who paid $10 for the Senegalese soup and beef Bordelaise would not leave the Grand Ballroom of the Waldorf that day without a soupçon of history.

Werner and Starger held to the script; they were amiably noncommittal in answering written questions from the floor. So was Dann, in the main, until it came upon him to make the prediction, almost casually, that movies would diminish to four a week on the networks in the 1972–73 season. The remark was to have repercussions from Wall Street to Hollywood that very afternoon.

Dann was not projecting for the next month or the next year but for a distant three years hence. Television talk is often about the future: things will be different then, perchance better. Television people tend to live in the future. It may be that they have to.

The television season was at the halfway point, and for ABC, running a poor third in the ratings for the fourth consecutive year, January provided an opportunity to cast out failing programs and rebuild. Five new series were going into the schedule the week of January 19, and seven others would move into new time periods on different nights. Such an extensive revision was made at great expense, but unless ABC closed the considerable rating gap that existed between it and its rivals there was no chance of reducing its operating losses.

Heralding it again as a "second season," as it had done the three Januarys previous, ABC used the selling power of its own medium to stir an anticipation for the five new premieres, saturating its schedule with promotional spots for *The Johnny Cash Show, The Engelbert Humperdinck Show, Nanny and the Professor, Pat Paulsen's Half a Comedy Hour,* and *Paris 7000.*

The pressure was on the network's president, Elton H. Rule, to move ABC back into the prime-time race, where it would effectively challenge NBC and CBS for supremacy in the circulation numbers. Rule's network was delivering approximately 5 million *fewer* viewers per average minute of prime time than the competitors, and as a result was forced to sell its commercial time at considerably lower rates. In 1968, while its rivals were enjoying profits, the ABC television network showed a loss of nearly $20 million, and the disparity in fortunes was largely a condition of a four or five rating-point span that separated the two front runners from the hindmost.

NBC was well ahead in the seasonal numbers and, although there were some weak spots in its schedule, its leaders elected to ride out the existing contracts, making no changes in January. It was the economical thing to do, and only the network running first was privileged to do it.

CBS had done some minor retooling in December and would make another alteration on January 30, replacing *The Good Guys* with another half-hour situation comedy, *The Tim Conway Show*. The December shift might have been a straight substitution of one show for another, but there was a complication, so it involved two moves.

Dropped from the schedule was the *Leslie Uggams Show*, and to replace it CBS brought back the hit of the previous summer, *Hee Haw*. This was the problem: the *Uggams Show* was a variety series with a black star and predominantly black supporting cast, while *Hee Haw*, a country-bumpkin version of *Laugh-In*, produced in Nashville, was by definition a white show, and Southern white, at that. The implications were delicate. And so although *Hee Haw* had occupied the Sunday night period before Leslie Uggams had it, and had proved its rating capabilities in that time slot, CBS elected not to risk what some might take as a racial affront and instead moved the Wednesday night *Glen Campbell Goodtime Hour* into that period. *Hee Haw* then became Campbell's replacement.

The rating improvement from the December changes was slight and left CBS still running well behind NBC in total circulation. As there were no high expectations for the Tim Conway entry on January 30, CBS seemed to have one last chance of catching NBC: ABC's mid-season moves would have to succeed, and primarily at NBC's expense.

Realistically, neither Rule nor his program lieutenants hoped to close the gap with the new January shows. All five would have to be rather substantial hits to accomplish that, and that was improbable. New shows historically had a high mortality rate; one success for two or three failures was a typical ratio. All Rule could reasonably hope for was some competitive improvement. One new hit would suffice, something to inspire interest in ABC's future season, a talking point for ABC's salesmen who in March would be on the street trying to tempt advertisers with the network's new September line-up of shows.

Four years earlier, ABC had received the mid-season popularity burst it needed from *Batman*. Its big hope now was Johnny Cash.

Mike Dann of CBS received two phone calls from Hollywood that afternoon, one from Stanley Jaffe, the young new president of Paramount Pictures, the other from David Gerber, an executive with 20th Century-Fox Television. Both said they needed to know whether his statement on the future of movies in television was a lark or whether it revealed the thinking of the higher councils at CBS. Dann assured them it was made in seriousness and that it reflected a top-level attitude in the company. For Gerber and his boss, Bill Self, that was good news. The elimination of three movies from prime time, which Dann had predicted for the 1972–73 season, meant there would be six more hours per week for TV production companies to shoot for.

Jaffe had another reason for asking. Paramount, like the other major film companies, operated in the belief that each motion picture made was virtually presold to television and could expect a minimum of a million dollars from domestic TV rentals, derived from two runs on the networks and subsequent local station syndication. Advised by Dann that the market for movies was now uncertain at the television networks, and that the future did not necessarily guarantee a million dollars per film from television, he was going to reconsider a number of film projects he had inherited from the previous Paramount regime. Some of those films would not be made, he said.

It would be reasonable to suppose that someone with governing powers over ABC had heard a recording, seen a concert, read an article, or in some other way came upon the thought, studied it, and then called a meeting to announce, "We're going after Johnny Cash for a series." That's not at all how it happened.

Like many another series on the networks, this one originated by a kind of commercial accident.

In the spring of 1969, ABC programers needed a summer replacement for *The Hollywood Palace,* and were looking for another variety show rather than a film to keep the audience conditioned to musical entertainment in that Saturday night hour, 9:30 Eastern Time. If the summer substitute had the potential for a full-time series which could begin in January, so much the better.

The word went out to the various network program suppliers that ABC had a summer vacancy and would consider their proposals. Normally, Screen Gems, the TV subsidiary of Columbia Pictures Corporation, would not have been asked since its specialty had always been filmed programs, but ABC was Screen Gems' best customer and its president, John Mitchell, was broached probably more out of courtesy than expectation.

As it happened, Mitchell was just then in the process of expanding the company's horizons to the kind of video-taped shows that are used in daytime television—soap operas, game shows, and panel quizzes—and had just enlisted Harold Cohen to develop such properties for him. Cohen, a former talent agent with General Artists Corporation, had left the agency field to establish his own business, Halcyon Productions, which under the agreement with Mitchell would serve as a subcontractor for Screen Gems. And in Cohen's employ as his principal aide was a man with wide experience in the video-tape game-show field, Bill Carruthers.

For several years, Carruthers had been a producer or director for the most successful company then in the TV game-show business, Chuck Barris Productions, working on such programs as *The Dating Game, The Newlywed Game*, and *Operation Entertainment*. It was on a producing assignment for the latter, in a segment featuring Johnny Cash, that Carruthers became interested in building a series around the country singer. When he joined Cohen, this was one of the projects he wanted to pursue.

Mitchell was excited about the opportunity to get a tape show on the air and called Cohen immediately. Cohen mentioned Carruthers' idea for a Johnny Cash hour. By incredible luck, Cash was giving a concert in Anaheim that week. Mitchell, Cohen, Carruthers, and Jackie Cooper, then head of production for Screen Gems, drove out to it and decided on the spot that this was the show they'd pitch to ABC.

Mitchell, one of the super salesmen in the TV program business, went to work to get the network interested. Carruthers, meanwhile, had the assignment of convincing Cash that Halcyon Productions and Screen Gems would do right by him in presenting the show. When he told Cash he would not want to do it anywhere but Nashville, he had a deal. Cash's manager, Saul Holiff, was amenable.

If the Nashville idea sold Cash, it made the package harder to sell to ABC. The networks found it hard to imagine programs of professional quality coming from anywhere but New York, Hollywood, or London; besides that, they had resident executives on the scene in the first two cities who could control what was happening in a show. But Mitchell pointed out that the Cash show would be cheaper to produce in Nashville than in Hollywood, because of the differences in the craft unions, and where summer shows are concerned economy is desirable. Within a matter of days Mitchell got an acceptance from ABC and worked out the terms of the contract in Hollywood with Dick Zimbert of the network's business affairs department. It provided the network with options to resume production in December for January and for the program's continuance over a period of years.

Carruthers was to be executive producer. Brought in to be the operational producer for the summer show was Stan Jacobson, a Canadian who had been free-lancing in Hollywood. His producing credits in Toronto included a CBC-TV special, *The Legend of Johnny Cash.*

The whole transaction, from Mitchell's enlistment of Harold Cohen for program development to the signing of the contracts with ABC for Johnny Cash, took place in three weeks.

E. Jonny Graff had pictures to sell, one of them *The Graduate,* and he was in a stew over Mike Dann's remarks at the IRTS luncheon the previous day that the networks were losing interest in movies because the new ones had become too gamy.

"People do things in these pictures—boys and girls, boys and boys, and girls and girls—that are naughty," Dann had said. "The film companies are going to be in for a surprise when they come to the networks with them." And then, in listing a number of recent films he felt were too sexually liberated, too outspoken, or too limited in appeal for television's mass audience, he included *The Graduate.*

(That film would someday be the top title in an Avco-Embassy feature package for TV and, as the third highest-grossing picture of all time in theaters, it would be priced out at about $2.5 million for two plays when offered to the networks.)

"What does he know about pictures?" Graff said. "*The Graduate*'s a work of art, and Dann's got it in a list with trash."

"Maybe Mike is trying to shake up the market to create some panic-selling at lower prices," I said.

"When I told Joe Levine how he slandered the picture he wanted to sue."

"Take it as a good sign," I said, "that Werner and Starger didn't seem to agree with him."

"One of these days we're going to sell pictures to the cable companies and pay TV and forget the networks," Graff said. "Mike Dann won't know what hit him. When the networks cut down to four a week it won't be because they don't want pictures but because they can't get them."

During the summer series the stage of the Ryman collapsed several times from the weight of the cameras and the sets. Lacking air conditioning, and with the lights intensifying the Tennessee heat, the old auditorium brutally punished the staff and crew. The Ryman was not meant for the television age, but the building had a symbolic and inspirational value, and Johnny Cash wanted his show to come from there. It was probably typical of him to put meaning before convenience.

A summer show is only a filler, but a winter series on the networks is big business and not to be trifled with, so something had to be done to get the Ryman into shape. Built in the late nineteenth century as a tabernacle, it had been used for more than four decades, with few concessions to modernity, by radio station WSM for its weekend country music presentation, *The Grand Ole Opry*. The original bench pews were still used for seating, and it was said that the paint on the walls and the dirt were also original. What the Palace was to vaudeville the Ryman was to country music, and more. To the musicians and singers it was the mother church, and such was Cash's devotion to the *Opry* that when he thought of doing his show from his home ground it had to be not just Nashville but the old Ryman. No one at ABC or Screen Gems disputed his decision, although it was clear to all that as a television facility the house was a nightmare.

One of the things Cash insisted on was distinctive lighting. Fine, except that the Ryman auditorium, as it was wired, barely lent itself to taking a television picture. Lighting designers, Imero Fiorentino Associates, were brought in to do what was necessary, and that entailed the installation of permanent electrical pipes, a dimmer board, follow spots, and other paraphernalia of a sophisticated system. The equipment had to be trucked in from Hollywood, since very little of it was available locally. The lighting consultant assigned to the show, Jim Kilgore, who lived in the Los Angeles area, had to commute to Nashville every week.

A reverberation problem, tolerated during the summer, was corrected by Dr. Charles Bonner of the University of Texas. From an audio standpoint, the house was like a barrel, and Dr. Bonner, who is credited with developing sonar, was equal to deadening the antiquated show place for television.

Finally, there was the matter of the stage. The *Opry* was still the Ryman, or vice versa, and the Cash show but a boarder. So whatever had to be done to adapt the auditorium for the television rehearsal and taping on Wednesdays and Thursdays had to be undone to restore the house for the first *Opry* concert on Friday. Engineers devised a system of portable steel supports to hold a temporary stage ranging over two-thirds of the orchestra floor. The pews had to be carried out, the supports mounted in place, the stage laid upon it and the sets installed for the Wednesday rehearsal. Two days later the whole thing had to be struck and hauled away, so that the *Opry* could have full seating for its performances.

It took a crew of twelve men eight hours to set up and eight more to tear down the temporary stage.

The Johnny Cash Show would have a difficult birth week after week.

Dann's augury that movies had a limited future on the networks was not echoed by his colleagues on the IRTS panel, but it was not disputed, either. Since neither NBC nor ABC had reason to be disenchanted with movie programing so far as the ratings were concerned, it was supposed by industry professionals that both would continue to think in long-range terms of the motion picture as a television staple. At the same time, it was understandable that neither NBC's Mort Werner nor ABC's Marty Starger would challenge Dann's assertion that pictures were getting too raw for television. To have joined the argument might have suggested that either network was prepared to show X-rated films, and this would have been sure to set off an explosion with legislators, PTA groups, clergymen, hinterland station operators, and others determined to keep television a wholesome, family medium.

The networks had bought sophisticated pictures in the past, and always with the trust that they could be edited into reasonably acceptable form for TV (often with the snipping of one or two objectionable scenes that were only box-office embellishments in the first place) or, more important, that by the time they were televised, morality in the medium would have relaxed sufficiently so that they no longer shocked.

Old pictures such as *The Moon Is Blue* and *The French Line,* which were moral issues in their time, had become tame and even innocent by the 1970's. Late in the sixties, NBC flouted an old taboo with *Never on Sunday*, the story of a prostitute, and created only a small and harmless stir.

Werner and Starger ducked the subject of theatrical movies and spoke instead of movies made expressly for television, to which each had a heavy commitment. The ersatz movies were going well in the ratings. It was suggested, if need be, that they could be the product to sustain the networks' various *Night at the Movies* showcases.

ABC signed Johnny Cash at a time when he seemed on the verge of becoming a major name in show business. In country music he was the super star, but in the universe of general entertainment he was only at the threshold, as others had been who never made it across.

It would have been CBS's way to wait until he was further along. Although the price would have been richer, CBS was always glad to pay more for less gamble. Not that ABC was looking for a bargain in this instance; but it had become an accepted truth in television that ABC, as chronically the third network, was usually the third place an agent would go with a proven star who was available for television. Denied the pick of the field, ABC was trying to build a stable of stars from performers on the rise—Tom Jones, Engelbert Humperdinck, and the Lennon Sisters as cases in point.

So far Cash was the network's best prospect. There was no denying he was giving off strong vibrations in show business, although not everyone understood why. He did not meet the usual requirements. He was not known for his wit, versatility, glycerine charm, or outgoing manner, and his handsomeness was, for women, very much a matter of taste. He seemed to belong to Sunday daytime television, either football or the religious ghetto. He rarely smiled, he looked tough, and he dressed in black. In another time, he might have done Westerns and played the heavy. As for his voice, it was manly and attractively deep but unmitigatedly countrified. Those who came into television from the country field before him played the bucolic either with a wink, as did Tennessee Ernie Ford, or, like Glen Campbell, in a manner that seemed suburban rather than grass roots. Cash's music was pure country; the saving grace was that it was not hillbilly.

Adding up the demerits, by New York and Hollywood standards, he was not the type to host a TV musicale. On the other hand, he had a certain antihero quality in a time when that was marketable. The rest of his qualifications were these:

He had a string of recording successes over a period of fifteen years, had achieved absolute stardom in the limited but growing country music field, and in the lore of show business had become one of the good new myths: a sharecropper's boy who had felt the full abrasion of poverty, hit bottom in a reckless young manhood, conquered the habit of pills, and never forgot where he had been or who had suffered with him. The songs he wrote were of the downtrodden and the imprisoned, and he had forged a musical style that was bringing commercial country music closer to the culturally approved folk idiom. If the hard core of his following was the rural working class, he was not disregarded by the young idealists of the cities who saw him not as another red-neck singer but as one of the latter-day social poets.

The Cash phenomenon was not really new; it was new only to the television and advertising professionals in New York, who were more aware of a performing triumph on the Broadway stage recognized by a few thousand theater enthusiasts than of any national entertainment phenomenon that managed to miss Manhattan.

Two years prior to his ABC series, Cash, his wife, June Carter, and their troupe recorded a TV special in Toronto for the Canadian Broadcasting Corporation in the *O'Keefe Center Presents* series, and while the Canadian system is not tyrannized by ratings in the way of the American, although it, too, is a commercial system, CBC offered the program without expectation of special audience dividends. It was a revelation, therefore, when the Cash special attracted the largest audience for all shows during the rating period in Canada, surpassing even ice hockey, the national sport, and was also the leading program in the Canadian enjoyment index.

Soon afterward, with the rating data as entree, the program was screened for CBS. It was rejected as too regional in appeal.

Canada has a two-network system of its own, the state-owned CBC and the independent CTV web, but its major population centers also receive American television beamed over the border from cities such as Buffalo, Seattle, and Detroit. So it cannot be said that Canadian viewers are insulated from the mass culture of the States, and persons who have worked in both the United States and Canadian industries have testified that viewing tastes are about the same on both sides of the border. This would seem to belie the CBS verdict on Cash.

The truth is that Cash was ideal for CBS, and CBS ideal for him, in point of maximizing the chances for his show's success. Of the three networks, CBS has the best penetration into the rural communities and ABC the poorest, and of course Cash's known audience base was in the provinces where country music flourishes. Up to the time of Cash's premiere, CBS's rating average in the rural areas was 21.2 while for ABC it was 13.7. Moreover, at CBS, with its quantity of hit shows, Cash would have been favored with a winning environment and very likely positioned behind an established series of similar audience components to feed viewers into his show.

But successful series were a scarcity at ABC, and as for being positioned behind a compatible show it was more like the opposite. Cash's lead-in in January was to be *Room 222,* a good freshman series which had been struggling to catch on and one whose leading character was a sophisticated black high school teacher, hardly the ideal conveyor for Southern viewers, who were the prime prospects for the Cash hour. But if ABC did not provide him with what the trade calls audience flow, it did serve Cash with some logic. His competition at nine o'clock Wednesdays would be NBC's *Kraft Music Hall,* the musical anthology which Cash had several times hosted. His ratings had been the best for the year in the Kraft series, and that seemed to show that there was a Wednesday evening audience disposed to watching Johnny Cash. The programs he would inherit his rural audience from were on the other networks, *The Virginian* and *The Beverly Hillbillies,* both of which ended at nine. ABC was counting on a massive switchover.

Cash had come along both too soon and too late for CBS —too soon with respect to the stage in his career and too late for the long CBS romance with rural America. For many years CBS had programed to its hinterland advantage, and that was nearly always its winning edge over NBC. The proliferation of its bucolic and small-town shows had actually brought into being such urban dramatic series as *The Defenders, East Side, West Side,* and *Slattery's People* for balance, to maintain the network's sophistication and its credibility in the cities. As it developed, the country-slanted entertainments were immensely popular and the city shows were failing.

With NBC continually challenging its long-held leadership in total circulation, CBS began to meet virtually every emergency with a new, and yet another new, rural-appeal program. By January 1970 the list had grown to *Mayberry R.F.D., The Lucy Show, Red Skelton, The Beverly Hillbillies, Gunsmoke, The Jim Nabors Show, The Good Guys, My Three Sons, Green Acres, Petticoat Junction, The Glen Campbell Goodtime Hour, Lancer, The Doris Day Show,* and *Hee Haw.*

CBS had an excess of corn, and the company's top executives were concerned about it. Moreover, as the CBS hit shows grew older so did their audiences, and advertising agencies were courting more vigorously than ever the young consumer in the 18–49 age range. Programs attractive to persons over fifty were becoming increasingly hard to sell to sponsors. NBC, with its schedule of programs that was neither distinctly urban nor rural, was delivering ample numbers of what the advertising media experts were seeking, the "young marrieds." Bulk circulation, which once had been all-important to the networks, was becoming irrelevant.

Not only was there a reluctance to take on more shows of countrified flavor but CBS was about to begin the process of deruralizing its program schedule. And so if there had been the opportunity to sign Johnny Cash in 1970, CBS probably would have spurned it.

Cash's television future became linked with ABC's the night of January 21.

One of Mort Werner's arguments in behalf of the quasi-movie made for television was that the moral level could be kept in line with what was acceptable for television. As it proved, however, NBC was using the *World Premiere* films to explore the new boundaries of permissibility in subject matter.

Two weeks prior to Werner's statement, during Christmas week in 1969, NBC had telecast a custom-made movie titled *Silent Night, Lonely Night,* based on the Robert Anderson stage play. It was about two married people, cut off from their spouses, who were dying to go to bed with each other and played no games with the viewer about it. There were scenes of partial nudity and one with the adulterers under the sheets after the act. The complaints to the network were negligible.

Less than a month later, NBC carried the film version of another stage play, *My Sweet Charlie,* which concerned a white Southern girl and a black Northern rights worker who, having taken separate refuge in an abandoned lighthouse, came to love each other in an explicit but platonic sort of way. The girl is unmarried, pregnant, and high school age; the man has murdered a white man. Far from causing trouble for NBC, the film scored a 53 share in the ratings and went immediately into theatrical release.

At just about the same time, on the Walter Cronkite evening news at CBS, two news-clip interviews of persons under great emotional stress recorded them using the word "Goddam." This rocked the Bible Belt, brought threats of disaffiliation by local stations, and drew more angry mail to CBS News than did its coverage of the 1968 Democratic Convention.

About eight minutes into the program my wife said she thought she could hear the dials clicking all across the country. She had picked up my senseless way of trying to count the house nationally.

The network had not created a program for the special talents and idiom of Johnny Cash, but had instead made him host of another variety show, a fairly typical variety show,

with guest stars and stilted patter between the numbers. If it
came from Nashville, it looked like Hollywood. All the special ingredients were compromised and pressed into the
stock mold of TV vaudeville. My wife was sure there was a
massive exodus of audience.

"He's not a TV host, and he can't be," the lady said,
"and what he does that's so special has gotten lost. People
who don't know him must be wondering why he's supposed
to be good. No, they're not even wondering. I can feel them
tuning out."

"He doesn't need the whole audience, you know. Just
33 per cent to make it," I said.

"It's still wrong to present him as Andy Williams," said
the critic.

I could only agree.

In the theater or at a movie the audience is captive, more
or less; its choice is the show or the exit. With television
there are multiple choices on the dial and any number of
other possible diversions about the house. Television producers are always mindful of a viewer's options. Haunted
by a sense of unfaithfulness across the screen, of an audience that is always on the verge of deserting, television people have developed a fear of boring the beholder to an extent
that over the years has become phobic. This accounts for
many of the sins of the medium and many of the clichés of
production.

It is why action melodramas are trusted and character
dramas are not; it is the reason people are always stumbling
over chairs in situation comedies to keep the laugh track
busy, and it is probably why Cash had to have a succession
of guest stars unrelated to his idiom, and a change of setting
for each musical number.

Bobbie Gentry, José Feliciano, and Arlo Guthrie were the
guests for the premiere, and while remotely they had something in common with Cash, as popular singers tending to
social realism, it was clear that they were on the bill to give
the program a big-time aura rather than to produce any kind

of musical chemistry with the star. Each performed about as he would on any program that required two numbers of him.

It was not until the closing moments of the hour, when Cash performed with his wife and other members of the regular cast he liked to call his "family"—his mother-in-law, Mother Maybelle, and the Carter Sisters, Carl Perkins, the Statler Brothers, and the Tennessee Three—that the show struck the Nashville sound and played as inspired rather than as contrived.

As we watched, sophisticated little boxes attached to TV sets in 1,200 homes across the country were recording minute-by-minute impulses on the slow-crawling 16-millimeter film within, indicating which channels were being viewed at any time of the day. These were the Nielsen Audimeters, the fateful electronic counters which, abetted by a system of daily viewing diaries, were keeping the television score.

At the end of the week, a householder removed the film, put it in a metal cylinder, and sent it off to Nielsen headquarters in Chicago. There the film would be developed and fed into a data-processing machine, which would read the information and punch it out on cards. Those in turn would be fed into a computer that, after putting all the data together, would print out the numbers that are life or death to television shows and which swing millions of dollars in the television market place.

The numbers come in a variety of demographic breakdowns that are useful in buying and selling, but the two sets of numbers that are the prime indicators of success or failure are those known as *rating* and *share*, terms whose use cannot be avoided in any discussion of the American television system.

The rating is a percentage of the total possible audience, based on households.

If there are 60 million TV households in America, the rating number indicates the percentage of those tuned in for a national program. (In local ratings, if there are 500,000 households in a TV market the figure represents a percentage of that universe.) In network television, a national score of 17.0 is generally satisfactory in prime time, and expensive programs which fall below that level rarely are able to produce a profit. The rating indicates that 17 per cent of the homes equipped with television are tuned in to the program, and although the demographic breakdowns are more specific, the rule of thumb during the prime-time hours of 7:00 to 11:00 P.M. is that each household represents approximately 2.3 viewers.

The share (short for share-of-audience) is a competitive evaluation, denoting how a given program is performing opposite others on the dial at the same time.

It is a percentage of the actual sets-in-use audience, and it says, "Of all the people who had their sets on in a given hour X per cent watched this one." In other words, it is a share of the pie; and in a three-network competition a program failing to receive one-third is not sufficiently competitive.

Given the other factors, such as independent, UHF, and educational stations—all of which make some claim on portions of the audience—it is considered reasonable to require a 30 share from a network show as the lowest measure of success. Most that fall below that mark are summarily canceled.

The validity of the Nielsen ratings (and shares) is taken for granted in the television and advertising industries, and although I no less than others have maintained a skepticism about a sample of 1,200 Audimeters and 2,200 diaries as representative of the viewing patterns of nearly 200 million Americans able to receive television, I am assured by researchers and statisticians whom I respect that the sample size is perfectly adequate for the laws of probability to operate correctly.

At the same time, because I'm not a statistician, I would not argue with Art Buchwald's wry observation that if one Audimeter family should go off to visit grandma that would mean 50,000 households had left the set to visit grandma.

Like the Audimeters, the Nielsen diaries are scientifically placed in what is said to be a cross section of American homes, representative of the different income and educational levels (although necessarily excluding the illiterate) and carefully apportioned according to regional density. The 2,200 diaries are assigned to four teams of 550 families, each of which submits viewing data one week a month on a rotating basis, taking turns in this manner because of what has come to be recognized as diary fatigue. Ideally, the diary keepers (who keep separate books for each working television set in the household) provide a detailed account of actual viewing by all members of the household throughout each day of the week assigned them, noting the time (by quarter hours), the program, the channel number, the number of persons viewing in any quarter hour, and the age and sex of each. No qualitative responses to the programs are solicited.

Since Audimeters can only report electronic impulses and never reveal how many are watching in whatever age groups, demographic research is possible only through diaries. The Audimeter results are collated with the diary information, and from the combined data derived from 3,400 television homes the Nielsen computers project the probable viewing for 60 million households.

Every year Nielsen has to move 20 per cent of those little Audimeter boxes to new homes so that the same 1,200 families will not become the television rulers who set the tastes for the whole country. No home is an Audimeter home for more than five years. In payment for their co-operation, the Nielsen sample families receive 50 cents a week for cooperating and periodically a gift which they select from a catalogue. Nielsen also helps with their television repair bills, paying 50 per cent of repairs for black-and-white sets and 10 per cent for color sets.

Although there are other rating services used for special

surveys—Trendex, Hooper, Sindlinger, Simmons, and TvQ, to list a few—Nielsen has a virtual monopoly on keeping the score in network television. One reason is that it is the only research company of its kind which can afford to do so. Network ratings are not the Nielsen Company's great profit center; its most lucrative research is in the retail products field, where it measures how rapidly and in what quantities given foodstuffs and drug products are sold in the stores. Its television service, while profitable, has had the particular value of publicizing the Nielsen name in market research.

Since the price of audience research is high, networks and advertising agencies are content to rely on a single service for the vital national data, rather than invest twice the amount in duplicated research that might create serious problems when the results disagreed. It is a convenience to have a single score.

The only rating service, particularly at the local level, to rival Nielsen with any degree of credibility among those who purchase television time is the American Research Bureau (ARB). For a national service, ARB has an instant rating tabulation, known as the national Arbitrons, which uses meters hooked up to a central computer. Overnight it produces a national nose count which some networks, CBS in particular, subscribe to early in the season for fast reports on the new shows.

Nielsen also has an instant report on a similar principle of meters feeding impulses to a computer over AT&T lines, but until 1970 it confined that overnight count to the New York market. In the middle of the year, Los Angeles was similarly wired.

The over-nights are not definitive, but they are trusted indicators of the trends in viewing. There would be a reading on *The Johnny Cash Show* the morning after the premiere.

The picture business was in a nervous state even without Mike Dann's help. Unknowns were turning out big box-office features on flimsy budgets, while the established professionals with all the skilled craftsmen and proven stars at hand, and supported by the exploitation skills mastered over four decades, were finding it difficult to put over expensive pictures that used to be naturals. The studios were in upheaval, brought about partly by their absorption into nonentertainment conglomerates whose managements had no emotional preparation for the vicissitudes of show business. Money was tight, financing hard to come by, the audience changing, the market place uncertain. Dann's remark that movies might lose network television as a regular customer in the future was distressing to studios and added caution to financiers.

With movies in demand by all three networks, the average price per title could escalate from the $850,000 standard to more than a million dollars in time. But if one network were to withdraw, the value of pictures to the webs would depreciate by nature of its becoming a buyer's market.

Dann had made it clear that television wanted the kind of pictures that Hollywood used to make. The problem was that the new theater patron, on whom the film industry's real economic dependence was fixed, did not.

The New York ratings for the Cash premiere were terrible, a 12 share. That was only New York, of course—10 per cent of the country in television marketing terms—and Cash was not expected to do well there. Neither, however, was he expected to do that badly. A 12 share meant that 88 per cent of the homes with their sets on at the time were looking at another program.

But with five shows premiering that week, ABC's strategists did not despair over the bad news about Cash. *Nanny and the Professor* and *The Engelbert Humperdinck Show,* the variety hour from England, slotted right behind Cash, made a hopeful showing in the over-nights. And although reviews count even less than over-night ratings with regard to the prospects for a show, ABC executives were heartened by the notices for Humperdinck that morning, particularly the favorable one in the *Times*.

As for the Cash show, which had carried ABC's highest hopes, the matter of ratings was far from settled. Losing in New York but winning throughout most of the rest of the country had been the pattern of his summer show, and he would surely look sturdier when the national ratings arrived a week later. Furthermore, NBC had thrown a tough show against Cash's January 21 debut, a Friar's Club Roast for Jack Benny, which was carried as an edition of the *Kraft Music Hall*. The show featured, along with Benny, such formidable television names as Johnny Carson, Ed Sullivan, Alan King, George Burns, Milton Berle, and Vice President Spiro Agnew. It was pure strategy, of the sort NBC excels at. The Friar's Roast could have been scheduled for almost any week, but NBC was going to use its best shot to hobble the Cash premiere, knowing it was the ace card in ABC's mid-season shuffle.

When a new program does not get off to a booming start, if its premiere is not such an event that it becomes a matter of conversation the next day, its chances of catching on with the viewership are considerably diminished. Passed over the first week, it tends to get passed over the next. CBS played a regular episode of *Medical Center* against the premiere. In New York, the Friar's Roast was the easy winner.

ABC had four more irons in the fire. If the nationals held the same good news for *Nanny* and *Humperdinck* that the New York over-nights reported, Elton Rule's second season might surprise the industry, himself included. Pat Paulsen, one of the school of lugubrious comics who came into prominence on the CBS *Smothers Brothers Comedy Hour* in one of those mock candidacies for the presidency, had a show archly subtitled *Half a Comedy Hour*. There's no predicting the television audience; they might go for this one, even though it was a bad idea from the start. Paulsen practiced a one-note kind of humor, persistence in the face of certain failure. The repetition of that premise from week to week promised to wear thin, but that had also been the outlook for the one-joke *Beverly Hillbillies*, which was in its seventh year. Paulsen's show was up against CBS's *Family Affair*, and that was perilous.

Paris 7000 was the other Thursday night entry, a hasty foreign intrigue series which was created in the first place because ABC was under firm contract to Universal Television to produce a full season of *The Survivors*, the 1969–70 season's one real fiasco. The case history of that is worth a digression.

The Survivors began on bravado. It was one of those announcements for the future—when ABC was at a particularly low point in the standings—that seemed to say: don't lose heart in ABC, great things are ahead, the network is on the move with a spectacular sure-fire idea for the season after next. Why the long delay to bring it off? Because it is such a perfect idea involving such an enormous investment that it must not be rushed. The pieces have to be put together carefully.

The idea was born in a meeting between ABC corporate president Leonard Goldenson and one of the most commercially successful writers of trash fiction in this century, Harold Robbins. An operator of theaters before he came into broadcasting, Goldenson was convinced that motion pictures were the most reliable barometer of public taste in mass entertainment, and he was determined to give the ABC television network the benefit of the ABC theater chain's experience with the paying public. The movies based on the novels of Harold Robbins were nearly always powerful at the box office, so it seemed to follow that a television series written by Robbins could not help but be a hit.

The project was trumpeted as the first television novel, each chapter to be a complete TV drama in itself but at the same time advancing the continuing central story. Robbins would write the pilot episode and outline the remaining chapters for the first season, and those would be scripted by

Hollywood writers. Ostensibly he was to oversee the development of the basic story.

Robbins was the first sure-fire element; the second was money—it would be about wealthy and powerful jet-setters. The third was glamour and foreign locales, almost all of it to be shot on location, and the fourth stars—Lana Turner and George Hamilton, with Ralph Bellamy playing a temporary role as their father, who would die in one of the early episodes. Fifth, it would have the time slot that launched *Peyton Place* a few seasons earlier on the network, Monday night at nine, perfect for the target audience, which was women. And finally, the most important element of all, implied in the involvement of Robbins: sex.

Sex, money, glamour, exotic scenery, big stars, Robbins' name, proven time slot—ABC executives confided they did not see how it could possibly fail. No less confident was Universal Television, which agreed to produce it, although that would involve deficit financing of $50,000 per show.

The Survivors premiered as ABC's great expectation of the season in September 1969 and never drew enough audience to have the faintest hope of succeeding. For all the supposedly sure-fire elements, the public gave it a massive rejection. Possibly the cynicism behind its creation showed.

The series was in trouble before it left the author's head. Robbins had prepared a story about the spoiled and headstrong progeny of an American business tycoon, who disliked each other and their father, and were sure to be disliked in turn by the audience. There were three protagonists, none of them sympathetic. The only sure-fire thing in that, for a simple-minded melodrama, is noninterest.

If as a star of yesteryear Lana Turner epitomized glamour, the series received precious few benefits from her beyond that. There was clearly the miscalculation that she was a strong draw. Further, in the production of the series, there was the discovery that she had not lost the star temperament that was indulged in the picture business during the thirties and forties but was an embarrassing anachronism in television of the sixties. It drove three producers off the project.

The next blow to the series was Senator John O. Pastore of Rhode Island, who, as head of the Senate Communications Subcommittee, had been conducting hearings on television violence. The networks were quickly reforming at his behest, clearing their schedules of programs that depended on acts of brutality and ordering scripts about mental conflicts rather than physical. Then without warning, triggered apparently by the Noxzema "take it off" shaving commercial, Senator Pastore extended his war from violence to sex and violence, holding over the broadcast industry a bill he proposed to introduce which would safeguard their station licenses against challengers promising to do better programing for the community. Nearly every station operator in the country was anxious for the bill to be passed, so the networks were forced to comply with the Senator's wishes for all-round cleaner television. Sex had to go, and *The Survivors* went in for a rewrite. The series lost one of its selling points.

During the summer of 1969, while the series was in production, word of strife on the set of *The Survivors* spread throughout the business. It began with Miss Turner's refusal to wear paste jewelry. She couldn't get into the mood of her part, as a person of enormous wealth, unless she wore the real symbols of opulence. The diamonds had to be rented from a jewelry dealer in the south of France, with guards hired to move them back and forth. Then it developed she would not wear the same jewelry in any two scenes, and so the logistics of the jewelry was added to a production that was otherwise not going well.

For assorted reasons, the producers left, one after another. After the premiere show, Bellamy could not wait to be written out of the story. By December Miss Turner was out of it, too, the story drastically changed, and all that remained of the original scheme was the title and George Hamilton.

The dying enterprise was costing Universal Television

$50,000 an episode, and there was clearly no point in continuing it. But Hamilton had a firm twenty-five-week contract that had to be honored, and so a new and far less costly series, *Paris 7000*, was devised for him. On January 23, it became Dean Martin's new competition on Thursday night. The series was not really expected to run beyond the duration of Hamilton's contract, but there was always the chance that it might be a sleeper. Although hastily produced on a modest budget, it was at least an improvement on *The Survivors*.

Joe Levine, president of Avco-Embassy Pictures, had Dann on the phone and wanted him to answer for slandering *The Graduate*.

"No, no, you misunderstand. I didn't put it with the dirty pictures; I mentioned it as a specialized picture for the young people who go to the movies but don't watch television," said Dann. "*Georgy Girl* and *Tom Jones* were big box office and nice artistic pictures, but did you see the numbers they got on television? Lousy. These pictures are great, I love them, but they're for the kids, not the mass audience."

"This is news," said Levine. "Since when is television not interested in young people? From what I hear that's all they're interested in, those agency guys."

"That's absolutely right. But here's the thing—the kids are going out to the movies and not staying home to watch TV. The guys at the agencies want young demographics, but they also want volume—numbers, people," said Dann.

"I would like to know how you think you're going to get the kids to stay home and watch television if you got nothing to show them but the same old crap. Anyway, I'm not worried about selling *The Graduate* to TV. When I'm ready—"

"When you're ready," said Dann, "be sure to let me know. I want the picture. I want to bid on it."

Forewarned that Cash was shy and not an easy interview, I expected worse. Possibly what made him mildly talkative over our dinner of fried chicken at Nashville's Ramada Inn were some of the negative points in my review of the show for *Variety*. As it happened, he and his manager, Saul Holiff, had similar reservations about their own program. My main quarrel with it was that for a country show it smacked of Hollywood. I had also questioned the necessity for guest stars from the popular music field.

"You said you didn't know why we had to have these pop names on a country music show. I didn't know why we had to either and still don't, but they told me there had to be four guests a week on a network variety show," Cash said. "They let us cut it down to three finally, but the network people said it was important to have popular names to build up the audience. This show—it's very important to me, and we have very good producers who know how to put on a television show, but I wanted to do more country music with the people down here. We're doing part of the show the way we want and part the way the network wants it. I'd say it was fifty-fifty.

"There were three things I wanted in the show that had to be mine, the 'Ride This Train' segment, the concert with June and the family, and then the closing talk and song. If they gave me that I'd go with their judgment on the rest.

" 'Ride This Train' was something I first did in an album ten years ago and thought it would make a good television show at the time. I've got my wish now, even though it only runs eight to ten minutes, or from commercial to commercial, as Joe Byrne says."

The segment was a nostalgic look at rural America from the railroad tracks, told through song and sometimes illustrated by still photographs.

My review had criticized certain production aspects of the show, its excessive concern with settings, its lighting effects that were perhaps too grand for a country music offering, and all the changes of costume that made the program look spliced together and manufactured.

Cash was not defensive about it. "The costume changes

were my idea," he said. "I like clothes. So was the lighting. I wanted the show to have a look of its own that everyone would know it by. I didn't want it to look bush league, coming from Nashville. But someday, if everything goes right, I want this to be a family show with just me and my family on it. I hope we can get away from using the name singers and comedians. The show is a country show, and I want it to be totally that way."

Bob Hope was to be the guest on the program Cash would tape that week, a top-drawer name for the television marquee, consistently the highest rated performer in the medium. Hope came to Nashville in a swap of guest appearances. He would be headlining a benefit for the Eisenhower Hospital in New York, a show that would be televised, and he wanted Cash to be on the bill.

Hope was not at the rehearsal. He would do a run-through with Cash just before the taping; it is the prerogative of the big stars and the old pros who are 100 per cent dependable at the moment of truth. For most of the afternoon, Cash rehearsed his musical numbers and the "concert" with his troupe, and to my mind it was better than any show he would ever do for television—easy, informal, and true to the music he champions. Neither would the audio on the home TV sets do justice to the exquisite live guitar playing that backed Cash. The rehearsal was a disciplined, gorgeous experience.

It was Wednesday, a long day for the company. Following rehearsals and the dinner break, taping began for the "Ride This Train" sequences, two or three recorded in advance every week. Production stopped at eight o'clock, Nashville time, so that everyone could watch the broadcast of *The Johnny Cash Show* on ABC. It was this week's show to the viewing multitudes but to the people who were working that night, it was a fortnight old.

Afterward I had a drink with the producers. Joe Byrne and Stan Jacobson were not much alike and did not select each other, but they seemed to work well together, dividing the administrative, planning, and extra-artistic chores without apparent conflict. Jacobson was a free-lancer who had worked with Cash before, in Canada, and Byrne had been on the ABC programing staff in Hollywood until Screen Gems hired him away to co-produce the Cash show. They were earnest young men who seemed to have in common the determination to make the series work by the accepted professional standards and to express Johnny Cash. The two aspects of their mission, it seemed to me, were possibly contradictory.

They seemed good men who were going to give their full talents and all the necessary time to the enterprise. Jacobson's sensitivity to Cash's temperament particularly impressed me. During the taping, after Cash had done four or five retakes of the opening, a musician miscued at the start of the medley, and it all had to be done once again. Cash seemed about to explode, but Jacobson appeared, put his hand on the singer's shoulder and spoke to him awhile, and then Cash went into the wings to start it over again. I was told by members of the staff that Cash had had frequent rages during the summer show but now he had a better grasp of the ways of television and took the frustrations more calmly. Jacobson, who had worked on the summer series, undoubtedly figured in Cash's adjustment.

But taming a star is not a conspicuous credit for a young producer. Jacobson and Bryne would be going back to Hollywood for their next jobs, and if they were going to make their mark with this assignment it would be through producing a slick and elaborate variety hour of the sort the Hollywood circle could appreciate. Anything less would be a poor advertisement for themselves. And so the best personal interests of Cash and his producers were at some variance.

In Dann's own analysis of the state of the ratings, NBC's lead over CBS since the start of the season could be traced to the differences in their movies. The NBC two-hour features were scoring substantially higher numbers than those on CBS. Since NBC had three movies a week and CBS had two, a total of ten prime-time hours were affected.

Why were the NBC movie ratings higher? Partly because that network had a greater supply of potent titles. Because of the differences in management philosophies regarding what was morally acceptable for air play, NBC was able to buy pictures CBS rejected. NBC had greater latitude with adult themes, and this was proving a distinct rating advantage. Dann made an appeal in his company for a liberalizing of the standards but was rebuffed.

They were not making the CBS kind of picture in Hollywood any more—not the blockbusters, at any rate—and so it appeared to Dann the best competitive course would be to fold one of the movie showcases. But that decision could not be made immediately, since CBS had contractual commitments for pictures previously purchased which booked the network's two showcases tight through 1971. If the network failed to play them off by the contract date, it would have to pay for them just the same.

When the national Nielsens arrived for the week of January 19, Cash had won his time period with a 33 share, compared with 32 for the Friar's Roast for Jack Benny and 27 for *Medical Center* on CBS. That Cash had been able to make up the deficit from New York indicated an unusually heavy tune-in from the rest of the country.

This was network television's official score, and the country singer was well above the 30-share danger zone. So Johnny Cash was a winner in his premiere week, but that was not necessarily proof of his acceptance. New programs frequently do well in their premieres and then trail off, suggesting that they had aroused audience curiosity but were unequal to sustaining a lasting interest.

Furthermore, CBS and NBC would threaten Cash's survival on ABC with a raft of specials, first a Danny Thomas hour, *Make Room for Granddaddy*, on CBS; then a *Kraft*

Music Hall featuring Desi Arnaz and his (and Lucille Ball's) offspring, on NBC; next *Ice Capades* on NBC; and finally the Anne Bancroft special, *Annie—Woman, and the Men in Her Life,* on CBS.

Danny Thomas and the *Ice Capades* both outscored Cash in the ratings, but in both cases he held above a 30 share, and in each instance it was the third program in the competition which suffered. Cash bested the other two specials with shares of 34 and 36, respectively.

Over that same period of weeks, *Nanny* held satisfactorily against the competition, but *Humperdinck,* Paulsen, and *Paris 7000* all failed. ABC's second season was moderately effective, the changes serving to diminish somewhat the point spread between that network and the leaders.

Cash's own rating history established that his show was the commanding one at nine o'clock on Wednesday nights. He was no Batman, but ABC had a new star.

Ed Montanus and Bob Wood were working out at their club in Greenwich, playing paddle tennis. In their other life, Montanus sold for MGM-TV and Wood was president of the CBS television network, Mike Dann's immediate boss.

In a breather, Wood said, "Sell me some pictures. You have a package of, say, about twenty big ones?"

"You buying?"

"I'm buying."

Wood had found a way to play off some of the lesser films before their 1971 deadline. He would add a third night of movies during the summer.

3

The Six-Minute Hour

It could not be said that Robert D. Wood was in the tradition of CBS television network presidents, if one remembers such cool, patrician executives as Jim Aubrey, Louis Cowan, Merle Jones, John Reynolds, and Jack Schneider. Energetic, he seemed to put a physical effort into his desk job and often, even on social occasions, had a harried appearance. Although his suits were tailored, the careful fitting and cutting seemed somehow wasted on him. Baldish, in his early forties, with his gray horseshoe rim cropped close to the skin, Wood gave the impression of someone not above settling an argument with his fists.

Unlike the presidents before him, Wood was a talkative man who was disarmingly direct in answering for himself or his company. He displayed little talent for, or patience with, the diplomatic arts of innuendo and sarcasm. He spoke his mind in a rhetoric that tumbled plain speech with malapropisms and pretentious clichés.

"It's my turn to bite the bullet," Wood said on the occasion of formulating the new program schedule for CBS. "I can either reverse back to our old 'I' formation, which our opponents are onto by now, or I can send out a split end. I think we'll opt for the split end."

The poverty of Wood's language belied his intelligence. He was a quick study who learned his job, with all its complexities, in an astonishingly brief time, and in his year in office demonstrated his ability to make sound decisions and to argue a point forcefully and cogently if not always elegantly. If he was aware of his verbal shortcomings, they seemed not to trouble or even inhibit him. Wood was out-going and unreserved, accessible to the press and ingenu-ously confident—a new kind of CBS network president.

He was Schneider's choice for the job, his first key ap-pointment in his gradual succession to corporate authority, and Wood knew that with the company's executive vice-president and heir apparent to Paley behind him he had not only the title of network president but the power that went with it if he chose to use it.

He grew up in Beverly Hills—the poorer section of it, he once told me (I've searched for it ever since)—and left his heart in Southern California when he came to New York. If there was an institution that commanded his allegiance more than CBS it was probably the University of Southern Cali-fornia, his alma mater (class of '48), of which he had be-come a trustee, and he would probably never outgrow his undergraduate zeal for its football team. As one of many network officials to give up a happy residence elsewhere for the indignities of New York to further his career, Wood at least had a network president's privilege to return frequently to his home town as a person of extraordinary importance, one of the biggest customers of the film industry there. Hav-ing spent much of his life as a townsman of the stars and celebrated film entrepreneurs, he was now a member of their spiritual community and had the credentials to mingle with the biggest. That would matter, in its way, in the future of CBS.

A president might take a greater or a lesser part in the network's programing function, as he chose. The glamour of television was concentrated in that activity, but it was as treacherous as it was gay. A president who elected a deep involvement in the programing decisions ran the risk of be-ing fired for a poor schedule; one who did not could spread the blame for failure. Three presidents before Wood left the development and scheduling of programs largely to the com-pany's resident expert, Michael H. Dann, senior vice-president for programing. So had Wood throughout his first year, but that was the breaking-in period.

He had not yet been the author of a CBS program schedule, having inherited from Tom Dawson the one he presided over during the 1969–70 television season, and he felt now he had some ideas of his own to offer.

During the chill weeks between the middle of January and the end of February, more network program decisions are made than in all the rest of the year; for this is deadline time on series options—do the performers and production unit stay together for another season or does the company disband?—and the networks must, in this period, make their determination of what is expendable for the next fall season and what, for competitive purposes, should be continued.

In a feverish five weeks at the three rocks, rating histories are scrutinized and analyzed, while pilot programs representing prospective new series are screened by committees, tested, studied, and rescreened. Network committees in daily meetings debate the merits of the potential program supply for September, choosing finally what the consensus—or a leader—decides will best gain the network a larger share of the audience, and consequently of the market, than it had the previous year. In the dead of winter television programs are born and die.

They die, almost without exception, from rating anemia. For a program series to be worthy of a network berth it must earn numbers suitable for the prime-time economy and, at the same time, make a contribution to the over-all strength of the schedule. Quality may make its argument, but it is rarely persuasive in a competitive arena in which more than $500 million is staked annually by the three networks for program fare, against the $1.3 billion that advertisers aggregately spend.

Programs come into being to attract an audience. Not to feed their minds, or to elevate them morally or spiritually, but to deliver them to an advertiser. Just as it understandably costs more to rent a billboard on a busy street than on one where the traffic is light, so it costs more to buy a minute of television time in a program that dependably draws more viewers to the set than the programs opposite it. The difference between billboards and TV is that television shows can generate traffic while the billboard cannot.

The importance of winning the ratings (*i.e.*, beating the competition) is why—to the embarrassment of latter-day executives who want the business to appear more business-like—television in America resembles a game.

In game terms, programs must be eliminated that do not perform adequately for the team, either by not holding up at their assigned positions or by not performing at the economic requirements. As baseball teams cut players from their rosters and bring up new ones in a constant rebuilding process, so the television networks reposition and replace their shows as a means of gaining a larger share of the advertising market.

A network that is far ahead of its rivals in popularity numbers will make sizable profits, one that lags too far behind will lose money, and if all three are at approximately the same rating level, all three, in a robust economy, should make money. But as in any business, the heads of the organizations are measured by their ability to show larger profits every year, and a chief whose profit center shrinks rather than expands will be replaced faster than a low-rated show. Thus, network administrations do not play the game casually, and network presidents and their lieutenants have too much at stake personally to be good sports. There have been exceptions, but the average tenure for a network president is three years; and at CBS the turnover in recent years has been even more rapid—five presidents within five years—but that was partly an effect of the parent corporation's haste in overhauling the management cadre to saturate the second echelon with young men.

Given the consequences of a program schedule that loses

rather than gains ground for the network, the decisions made in January and February are momentous for an administration, for they involve not just its own alterations but those of its rivals as well. There is no improvement unless it is at a competitor's expense, and program schedules are blocked out with a mind to winning in each half-hour period, or at least to diminishing a rival's long-held dominance. Decisions, therefore, are based partly on what may be known or surmised of a competitor's plans, and adding to the frenzy of the moment are the intelligence reports, real or rumored, of rival strategies, transmitted usually by the advertising executives, television agents, or studio executives encamped on Television Row throughout the ordeal of schedule-making.

In January 1970, eight programs that had premiered with the rest of the field the previous September were either already off the air (having been replaced at mid-season) or had received notice of cancellation. Thirty-one others were in danger of being terminated, most of them on the borderline of the survival standard, their prospects for renewal depending in most cases on a marked uptrend or downtrend in the few remaining rating reports until deadline. New shows which premiered in January, as replacements, had only three or four weeks to prove themselves.

It calls for no special expertise to sort out the winners and losers at the extreme ends of the rating scale, but it is the programs in the gray area between which pose the difficulty and require analysis. A series that has been high on the popularity scale for many years may be showing clear signs of attrition, indicating it may flop if renewed one more season. Conversely, careful study of rating histories may reveal that certain program series which performed indifferently during the season had the potential of becoming hits if placed on a different evening, or at a different hour.

Each evening of the week, as well as each half hour of the evening, has its own peculiar audience characteristics.

In earlier years, it was all but automatic that a program whose season average was under a 30 share was canceled.

But as rating analysis grew more sophisticated, it was perceived that certain shows with shares of 28 were building audiences while others with shares of 32 were slipping. More important, in a time when the advertising community prized a young audience, a 28-share program series with favorable demographics might be of more benefit to a network than a 32-share show that appealed to viewers who were too young or too old to interest Madison Avenue.

Nine series were definitely up for cancellation and seemed beyond redemption in the January Nielsens, their collective failure signaling the end of two program cycles—fantasy comedy and Westerns. Not only would they be eliminated, but the new series prospects of their genre would in all probability be rejected as well.

Get Smart, I Dream of Jeannie, Land of the Giants, The Flying Nun, and *The Ghost and Mrs. Muir* all had gone into a steep decline during the season in progress, and to the networks that meant that mass interest in fantasy had waned. Similarly, the failure of *Daniel Boone, Lancer,* and *Here Come the Brides* marked the end of the Western vogue, and no new Westerns were purchased by the networks, although several older ones such as *Gunsmoke* and *Bonanza* would continue. The Western, which had been a mainstay of American film entertainment since the silents, had apparently lost its appeal to *young* people, and that was fatal in a medium that operated to accommodate the desires of advertisers. Furthermore, with the prohibition against overt violence in television fiction, the sagebrush sagas were reduced to a form of period drama, a program type that has had no history of success in American television.

The ninth series that was doomed was *The Debbie Reynolds Show,* one of NBC's more expensive attempts to duplicate the long-running Lucille Ball series at CBS. Debbie Reynolds was thought to be a comedienne who was irresistible to mid-America, and she was packaged for television with Jess Oppenheim as producer, he being the original producer of *I Love Lucy.* All the elements seemed right, and

NBC had such confidence in the project that it accepted high terms, which included a firm two-year contract for Miss Reynolds. It was a show that could not fail, except that it did, and NBC was dropping it after the freshman season because there had never been a sign that it would become popular enough to justify the cost. It was more economical for the network to buy up the contract than to go into a second year of production.

Along with the lesson learned concerning fantasies and Westerns, there was an added caution from the Debbie Reynolds experience against silly comedies.

Of the twenty-two other shows whose fate the Nielsens would help to decide in January, seven were the mid-season entries and six others were series of marginal popularity that were faced with cancellation because the new January program shifts had put them in new competitive circumstances. Those were *The Virginian, Kraft Music Hall, Medical Center, That Girl, The Brady Bunch, Let's Make a Deal,* and *It Takes a Thief.*

The remainder were in doubt because they had been receiving less than the necessary 30 share in the Nielsens: *My World and Welcome to It, The Governor and J.J., The Courtship of Eddie's Father, Then Came Bronson, Jimmy Durante Presents the Lennon Sisters, To Rome With Love, Tom Jones, Bracken's World,* and *Love, American Style.*

It was Mike Dann who engineered the CBS program schedules under presidents Schneider, Reynolds, and Dawson, because he knew from long experience how to implement the philosophies of the chairman of the board, William S. Paley. Dann was the disciple, but Paley was the network's master showman, and until he retired he would always be the final authority on the level and quality of its light entertainment.

Paley's instinct for programs to please the masses was demonstrated soon after he bought the CBS radio network in 1928, and after four decades there was no reason to question the keenness of his programing judgment. When in 1967 the Nielsens indicated that *Gunsmoke* was finished and it was replaced in the schedule while Paley was vacationing in Nassau, the chairman, learning the news by telephone, ordered the show reinstated.

Gunsmoke had always been a Saturday night show, even in its radio days before it was carried over into television in 1955, and when its ratings began to plunge, CBS's analysts took it as clear evidence that the series had finally worn out. Paley didn't think so, no matter what the ratings showed, and his instructions were to move the program to Monday nights at 7:30. This was eccentric scheduling that defied all the principles of prime-time make-up at the time, but the program was reborn in the new time period and has been in the Nielsen top ten, the television hit parade, ever since.

Having Paley's ear and trust gave Dann power at the network beyond his rank on the table of organization, and he used it lavishly to push past Wood's two predecessors, Dawson and Reynolds, not only his schemes for program maneuvers that would win for CBS but also his own exemption from their authority. He enjoyed a peculiar kind of autonomy within a system that did not normally permit it.

Confident of his power, Dann went into the program meetings with the new schedule in his pocket. He would eliminate the shows with the poorest shares and replace them with the strongest prospects from his program development. That his plan would meet opposition from sales vice-president Frank Smith, with whom he had informally discussed it, troubled him not in the least. Smith wanted to get rid of certain popular shows that he believed advertisers had lost interest in. Even if Smith were to persuade Wood that a winning schedule was no good if the sales department could not sell it, what real authority did Wood have against the Paley-Dann nexus? Paley would rule, and the chairman had always demanded that CBS be Number One. He liked to think of the network as the Tiffany of broadcasting, commanding the highest prices because of its leadership.

Smith had told Wood all season that sales were becoming increasingly difficult in some of CBS's highest-rated series, because with every year of their continuance their audiences grew a year older. Although they were winning their time periods in total audience, they were not delivering enough viewers in the 18–49 age range to command the rates for hit programs. With its long-running series, CBS was beginning to fall victim to its own success and was developing a reputation as an old person's network. In a time of demographic consciousness on Madison Avenue, NBC's salesmen were making the most of CBS's deficiencies in the youth market.

Two of the hardest programs for CBS to sell during the 1969–70 television season were Red Skelton and Jackie Gleason. A few seasons earlier, when only the mass viewers counted, both were among the first to sell out completely for the year. Conscious now of the quality of audience—on age, income, and education levels—the media buyers of advertising agencies considered the two CBS comedians overpriced for the kinds of people they delivered.

It was traditional to grant raises of approximately 8 per cent to the star every year that a series was renewed. Thus, on a compound-interest basis, old programs in general are far more expensive than new ones. So, paradoxically, as a series grows older and costs more for a network to maintain, its attractiveness to advertisers diminishes. Red Skelton, on a $4 million program investment by CBS, returned a profit for the network in the 1969–70 season of only $25,000. Jackie Gleason represented a loss of $300,000.

The lawyers for both Skelton and Gleason were negotiating their renewals in January, hitherto always a routine function. Don Sipes, vice-president of business affairs for CBS, reported back to his management that although confronted with the new realities of the market place and with the figures showing they were no longer profit-makers for the network, both comedians were insistent on firm three-year contracts at the usual 8 per cent escalations each year.

Wood had his own plan for the CBS fall schedule. Taking it up through channels, he gained for it the support of both broadcast group president Richard Jencks and corporate executive vice-president Jack Schneider, his patron saint. Wood proposed that CBS not only deruralize but that it also begin to divest itself of the aging programs that were imposing an economic drain. The company had to begin building for the future, he argued, and could not hope to win the young new audience with the materials of the past.

Now it was Smith, Wood, Jencks, and Schneider against Dann.

"Mr. Paley," Wood said at the critical meeting of the year for CBS, "you can sit on your front porch on a rocking chair collecting your dividends on what you've created. A parade will be coming down the street and you may watch it from your rocking chair, collecting your dividends, and it will go by you. Or you might get up from that chair and get into the parade, so that when it goes by your house you won't just be watching it you'll be leading it. Mr. Paley, CBS is falling behind the times, and we have to get back in step."

The proposal was to drop three hit shows of long duration on the network—Skelton, Gleason, and *Petticoat Junction*—as but the first stage in a thorough reordering of program priorities leading to a rejuvenation of CBS. Wood conceded that the network would in all probability lose rating ground in the fall, but it had become necessary to take some steps backward in order to begin to move forward.

"What we need to begin the rebuilding," said Wood, "are programs that are relevant to what is happening today, instead of the make-believe. That's what will get us looking young again. The old shows may still get audience, but are they relevant?"

Jackie Gleason? Red Skelton? *Petticoat Junction?* To Mike Dann they were relevant—not socially relevant, but competitively. Winning the Nielsens was relevant. In all his twenty-one years at CBS and NBC it had been. It was the game, it was how you stayed alive, how you kept the job. Losers got fired, not winners. Winners are who Madison Avenue's high-rollers had always bet on.

Wood was proposing to discard two and one-half hours a week of proven hit programing for two and one-half replacement hours that were at best speculation. The odds were heavily against bringing in three new hits in a season. One out of three was asking a lot. If you worked in the business a long time you knew things like that; if you were new at it you let yourself get carried away by wishful thinking.

Skelton, after eighteen years on the air, was still in the top ten. You built whole evenings around shows like these, because they could be counted on to bring audiences to the set. Tuesday was built around Skelton; he drew the crowds, and the adjacent shows fed off him. If the show itself did not make much of a profit, the neighboring programs did because of their contiguity, and the competition meanwhile was held at bay.

Wood's proposal, Dann felt, was insulting to Mr. Paley in that it flew in the face of all his precepts as a showman. The chairman had built the network on star power and sustained its success on the careful treatment of stars. If Lucille Ball threatened to quit, Paley himself met with her to convince her to stay. If Jackie Gleason wanted a circular house built for him in Peekskill, New York, CBS obliged at $150,000 and later sold it at a loss when Gleason decided he wanted to live in Miami and originate his shows from there. There being no network studios in Miami, CBS had to construct and staff them and, to oblige Gleason further, they were built on the periphery of a golf course.

Dann strenuously opposed his president's plan and promised Paley CBS would be Number One again by consolidating its established hits to buttress the new programs.

Paley had not only heard Wood's evangelistic appeal but also the assent by Schneider and Jencks, his next generation of management. He would someday have to let them steer the company, and he agreed to the proposal.

Skelton, Gleason, and *Petticoat Junction* would go. CBS would seek an urbanized, up-to-date pattern of programing in prime time. The old rules no longer applied.

Wood, who up to that point had been one of the invisible presidents at CBS, had broken the Paley-Dann axis. That established him as a president of authority, reducing Dann to a subordinate who would have to serve his aims.

"After we did it and it was all agreed," Wood confided to a friend, "Mr. Paley called me several times from the islands to ask if I were sure we were doing the right thing. Hell, I didn't know any better than he if we were right, but I knew I couldn't waver with Mr. Paley so I stood my ground, I answered in my most positive voice, 'I'm sure we are, Mr. Paley. This is what we must do.' If I'd shown the least sign of indecision or doubt, Skelton and Gleason would have been back in the schedule the next day."

To the critic, television is about programs. To the broadcast practitioner, it is mainly about sales. This explains why most critics have nothing important to say to the industry and why, among all the critics in show business and the arts, the television reviewer is probably the least effective.

In television only one notice matters, that from the ultimate critic, the A. C. Nielsen Company.

The knowledge of this terrifies the conservative businessmen who run the rating service, since it tends to implicate them in the destruction of television shows. Any suggestion to that effect brings forth a nervous representative of the company to explain that it is not the Nielsen ratings that kill programs but the persons who order the service and interpret the numbers at the networks and advertising agencies. The Nielsen reports have neither point of view nor soul; they are merely static data dispassionately presented. One program gets a low score, another gets a high score, and beyond that Nielsen is not involved. The networks are responsible for what happens next, and how they act—whether they cancel a show, renew it, alter it, or reposition it in the schedule —largely depends on the peculiar requirements of the advertising industry that year.

Over the five decades since the beginning of commercial radio the advertisers' role in broadcasting has changed radically, but their influence remains essentially what it has always been. They are the customers, collectively the market place, and the programs exist in reality for them, as shills for their "messages," rather than for the general public.

As in the other forms of show business, artistic decisions in television are ruled by the box office; but unlike the stage, motion pictures, concerts, and recordings, television's box office is not comprised of people but of advertisers, and what is sold to them is not the program but the audience. Nielsen's numbers are not about television shows but the people who watch them and it is they who are the real product of the wonderful electronic picture machine.

Under the camouflage, the viewer is not the customer but only the consumer of television. He is what the advertiser buys like herds of cattle—$2.50 per thousand bulk, $4 to $8 per thousand select (young men, young women, teenagers, depending on the product marketed).

One of the myths about American television is that it operates as a cultural democracy, wholly responsible to the will of the viewing majority in terms of the programs that survive or fade. More aptly, in the area of entertainment mainly, it is a cultural oligarchy, ruled by a consensus of the advertising community. As it happens, television's largest advertisers—the manufacturers of foodstuffs, drugs, beverages, household products, automobiles, cosmetics and, until 1971, cigarettes, among others—have from the first desired great circulation among the middle classes, so that the density of viewers has become the most important criterion in the evaluation of programs. This emphasis on the popularity of shows has made television appear to be democratic in its principles of program selection. In truth, programs of great popularity go off the air, without regard for the viewers' bereavement, if the kinds of people it reaches are not attractive to advertisers.

It was not through oversight that the networks, and local stations, did not for years produce programs of specific interest to the black population. The ghetto Negro was not a target audience for most advertisers because, generally speaking, he was a low-income citizen with scant buying power. It was not that advertisers did not want to reach Negroes but that they did not want to reach them *especially*, and it was assumed that the poor black, as a heavy viewer of television, would be part of the audience composition of programs aimed at other segments of the audience.

So little valued has been the black man as a consumer of nationally advertised products that he was not properly represented in the Nielsen sample of the American television audience. Although this was generally known in the television and advertising industries there was no outcry, no move to set it right, no show of conscience that the ghetto black did not have a representative "vote" as a member of the viewing masses. The Nielsen Company, as well as the other, lesser, rating services, explained that it was difficult to place their hardware in ghetto homes, difficult to get representative families to keep viewing diaries adequately because of the high rate of illiteracy, and even a problem in the telephone methods of audience research because of the shortage of telephone homes in the ghetto.

This sound explanation, given conventional advertising priorities, seemed fair enough to everyone until it became desirable to count the audience for *Sesame Street*, the non-commercial children's show which had been designed for the culturally underprivileged of the ghettos. The real success of *Sesame* was not to be told in the total number of persons reached but specifically in the total number of slum children reached.

At approximately the same time, moreover, station WTOP-TV in Washington, D.C., complained that its black-oriented programing in a city whose population was predominantly black was receiving no advertising support because the rating numbers were slight for them, and they were slight, the station charged, because black households were not adequately represented in the rating samples. Thus, it became a matter of one station's economic interest and one conspicuous program's social value that the ghettos be adequately surveyed, and so far as is known corrective action then began to be taken.

No one created the American television system. It evolved in a series of patchwork progressions, affected variously by government regulations, corporate aims, technological advances, advertising and marketing requirements, and to some degree by public reaction. It probably did not start out to put commerce before communication, but if that was the inevitable result of the medium's great penetration into American life, its sweeping embrace of rural and urban households everywhere, the industry calmly accepted it. Product salesmen, who would be turned away at the door, were admitted into every household through the small electronic screen; and the world of business came to know that nothing could sell as well as television.

There was so much money to be made in television that a network or a station was remiss if it did not make the most of it. The industry's present system of values is descended from that pattern of easy affluence.

American television is a business before it is anything else, and within the broadcast companies the sales function is pre-eminent. That is as true at the local station level as at the networks and is indicated, if in no other way, by the top sales executive having a voice in the design of the program schedule, comparable perhaps to a sales manager taking part in the editorial decisions of a newspaper or magazine. Often, at the local stations, it is the sales director and not the program director who buys the syndicated programs and, at one network, NBC, the head of sales controls the selection of specials, rarely accepting one that is not already presold to a sponsor. A good program schedule is not a critic's schedule but a salesman's—one that will sell rapidly at the prices asked.

If that smacks of avarice, consider the problems inherent in the system. The television networks and a large number of the stations they serve are subsidiaries of public corporations and as such have obligations to their stockholders. And since stockholders in a broadcast corporation do not ask for better programs every year but rather for larger profits, it becomes clear where the priorities must be.

There is no other course but for broadcast managements to dedicate themselves to profit growth; their executive survival depends upon it. They must at the same time convey the impression of being stable and sturdy in the face of the speculative and volatile nature of show business, and so to whatever extent possible they divorce themselves from the impresario risks and behave as companies engaged in the manufacture of goods. They deal, therefore, in programs that will be instantly accepted by the audience, rejecting new and experimental forms that might take weeks or months to catch on, if at all.

Television's new generation of leaders did not rise because they had vision or imagination but because they were realists.

Don Durgin, president of the NBC television network, made a suggestion to his staff a few summers ago which typified where the broadcasters' priorities lay relative to consumer-viewer and customer-advertiser.

In a meeting to discuss new ways to promote that year's fall schedule over the air, Durgin solicited ideas to augment the existing techniques. Seemingly, to the staff, every on-the-air resource had been tapped. Promotional spots filled the unsold commercial minutes, theme music was silenced over the credit crawls of most programs for an audio "Be sure to watch—" pitch by the announcers, and the lead players of the forthcoming NBC prime-time series were interviewed on the morning *Today* show as a summer-long feature. None of Durgin's executives came forth with a new idea.

The network president made his own proposal. During the programs that were in summer repeat, the horizontal crawl at the bottom of the screen normally used for news bulletins could be superimposed upon the action to publicize the September premieres.

In that way, the programs would carry the promotional message while they were in progress without technically being interrupted.

Durgin's staff received the suggestion in mournful silence. He was recommending one more assault on the viewer's pleasure before the set. After a moment, one executive spoke up:

"Good idea, Don. And we'll bust in with the crawl on the commercials, too."

"No, no—not the commercials!" Durgin cautioned before he recognized the sarcasm.

And then, in a moment of epiphany, the idea died.

Consumer groups, citizens committees, critics, the Federal Communications Commission, and idealists working in the industry have all tried to change television in their separate ways, but no institution has really succeeded except the advertising industry. Sooner or later, through its economic power, its will is accommodated.

Although he is no longer the sponsor who, as in the past, selected and paid for a show and thereby assumed the right to exercise creative and editorial control over its production, the advertiser still creates a favorable or unfavorable climate for types of programs and plays a direct part in the kinds of audiences the networks choose to pursue.

When by consensus, advertisers determine that Saturday morning is a cheaper and more efficient way to reach young children than by investing money in early prime time, the juvenile-slanted shows vanish from 7:30 P.M., which had been the children's hour since the start of television. When the advertiser's need is to set his fall budgets six or seven months ahead of the season, the networks adjust their fall planning accordingly. When advertisers manifest an interest in sports, they proliferate on the home screen; an aversion to serious original plays, they evaporate. And when the advertisers spurn the viewers who are past the age of fifty and assert a preference for young married couples, the networks obediently disfranchise the older audience and go full tilt in pursuit of the young.

Golf receives more television exposure than some more popular sports, although its limited audience defies the usual economic criteria. Partly, one suspects, this is due to its being a favorite recreational activity of TV executives, agency men, and their clients. Here they are their own rating service. Since golf matters to them and to nearly everyone else they are associated with, it seems to follow that golf reaches quality viewers, the *right* people. This recalls the possibly apocryphal story of the sponsor who, in the early days of television, berated his advertising agency for buying Sunday afternoon programs. "No one watches television on Sundays," he argued. "They're all at the polo matches."

There are also, apparently, sporting events for the wrong people. The advertising manager of a major company instructed his agency to spend most of the advertising budget for 1969 on televised sports, but he ruled out basketball. That sport, he felt, appealed to elements of society with which it was probably best not to associate his product. He meant, the agency man told me with a helpless shrug, blacks.

Sponsorship—advertiser identification with specific programs—has been a passing thing in television and scarcely exists today outside of specials and sports, although Kraft Foods still controlled the Wednesday night *Music Hall* and Procter & Gamble the half hour between *Walt Disney* and *Bonanza* on NBC, occupied in 1970 by *The Bill Cosby Show*.

Until the early sixties the practice, carried over from radio, had been for advertisers to control time periods at the networks, to fully underwrite the shows presented there, and in many cases to own the properties. This gave them the authority over subject matter and intellectual content, and allowed advertisers to impose their standards of production upon the show. The network was no more than a conveyance. Chevrolet, as a sponsor, once scratched "fording a stream" from dialogue because the phrase spoke the name of its competitor. The American Gas Company blipped out of a drama the reference to the means by which Jews were exterminated by Nazis in the concentration camps. A curious example of sponsor sensitivity; the gas, after all, was not guilty of genocide, the Nazis were. Numerous acts of advertiser consorship were less petty.

Obviously unhealthy, the system gave way to one in which the network had full control over programing and sold the advertiser one-minute spots, just as magazines maintain an editorial independence while selling advertisers full or partial pages. ABC, running third in the ratings, initiated it as a way to compete for advertising dollars, and the Madison Avenue consensus found it such a comfortable arrangement that the other networks were given no choice but to adopt it.

As the magazine concept solved one problem, it created another: overcommercialization. When the advertiser was sponsor it behooved him to be sensitive to the frequency and length of his program interruptions. As a buyer of minute *packages* which disperse his message over an assortment of programs on various nights of the week, he is unburdened of that aesthetic decency as well as other responsibilities.

There are no half-hour programs on television. Most are filmed or taped in twenty-six-minute lengths, including titles, plugs for next week's show, and credits. The hour show has an approximate running time of fifty-two minutes, give or take a few seconds for extra-program matters. What remains is the real goods of television, time for sale—six minutes to the hour for the network, slightly less than two minutes for the local station.

To the viewer, prime time is three and one-half hours long, but to the keeper of the network books, it is twenty-one salable minutes per night.

If the commercial breaks sell for $60,000 a minute and the program costs the network $200,000 per one-hour episode, obviously there's quite a profit when all six minutes are sold. But if the ratings are such that the minutes fetch only $25,000 apiece and the expenses are at the same $200,000 level, the loss is substantial. Each network has some of the latter and some of the former in its prime-time inventory, and the successful network is the one with a preponderance of profitable shows.

The function of the television program is to make the commercial breaks valuable. A good show is one that is important enough to the advertiser so that he will pay a premium for the minute breaks within; a bad show is one that sells at distress prices. Accordingly, the system thrives on *The Beverly Hillbillies* and will not support a *Playhouse 90*.

Against the industry's code of ten commercial minutes an hour in prime time, the networks' allocation of six an hour seems almost civilized. Yet any viewer who has spent a full evening before the set will be certain that someone has cheated, for he will have been subjected to many more than six sponsor messages in any sixty-minute period. This is because the minutes are fractioned by advertisers into thirty-, twenty-, ten-, and even five-second "announcements," so that the three breaks in a half-hour program and the station's local minute following the show could add up to nine different commercials. In addition there may be "billboards" at the opening or close ("Tonight's episode is brought to you by—") and inevitably other brief nonprogramatic material such as station identification slides (some stations even sell that to sponsors), the network color logos, public service spots, network promotion, station promotion, program titles, and program credits (required by the unions), all of which are recognized by the industry as irritating clutter to the viewer.

Not just the quantity of "sell" but the maddeningly intensive imperative of the commercials (*buy . . . pick up . . . be sure to . . . you'll want . . . ask your grocer . . . get . . . pamper yourself . . . hurry*) serve to make an evening at the set insufferable. Aware of this as an abuse of the viewer even before advertisers found it possible to produce "drama" in thirty seconds, the heads of the networks nevertheless, after a feeble show of resistance, allowed Madison Avenue to subdivide its minutes so that two commercials could be had for the price of one, doubling the assault on the public and compounding the problem.

The networks capitulated because the management apparatus is designed for short-range decisions. Each had to make its yearly quota of sales or face the consequences, and each was aware that the first network to accept the double-thirty minute would enjoy a flush of business. There was no suspense. The two-for-one commercial (called variously the *piggyback*, the *split-thirty* or *matched-thirty*, depending on whether the two companion products were pitched contiguously or in separate commercial breaks) quickly became the standard. The networks, however, issued word that they would hold the line against the *triggyback*—three twenty-second commercials.

And how much did Madison Avenue appreciate the accommodation of the double-thirty?

In April 1970, at a seminar of the Association of National Advertisers in Absecon, New Jersey, the president of Grey Advertising, Edward H. Meyer, noted that there was a slight but discernible disaffection with television by national advertisers, and one of the reasons for it was the tremendous increase in clutter resulting from the thirty-second commercial, which was producing negative results.

To dramatize what he termed "the debasement of commercial television today," Meyer ran off a seven-minute film, an air check of a network, which spanned the actual end of one network show and the start of another. "That film," he said to fellow ad men, "is a dramatic example of where your television commercial is today. Allow me to do the counting for you. There were thirty-seven different messages during that brief seven-minute period. Is it any wonder that consumers are complaining and advertisers are restless?"

He cited *recall* research (noting how clearly TV consumers remember the advertisements they were bombarded with during an evening) which showed a significant drop from recall levels of previous years. "If we want to get the same number of homes recalling commercials in 1969 as we did in 1965," he said, "we have to pay a cost per thousand increase of 45 per cent over 1965."

There was one other interesting bit of comparative research in his presentation. During the early sixties surveys indicated that sponsors were losing 15 to 18 per cent of the audience during commercial breaks. The figure was now up to 50 per cent.

Dann would probably never understand his defeat. He had twenty-one years of network program experience behind him, and Wood, his adversary, had but one—if presiding over Tom Dawson's schedule counted as experience. Wood had never created a show for television, never even authorized one of any importance, and never really knew what it was to put a schedule together strategically, matching the program to the time period, at the same time mindful of the competition. It was tricky work and not to be entrusted to beginners. Surely Paley knew that, and Dann was puzzled.

Bob Wood had been a station man until a year ago. All his previous experience at CBS had been in sales, management, and administration in the company's television station division, where program decisions were relatively few and decidedly local. Nothing in his professional or educational background qualified him to take charge of a national programing plan for the peak viewing hours of television.

Steeped in sales, Wood's sensitivity was only to the market place. He knew advertisers, not programs.

That—Dann would probably never understand—was why Wood won.

4

Hatfields and McCoys

In spite of all, I came to like Mike Dann. That probably cast me with the minority. I bother to mention it because he is not the sort of person you can accept without making a pro or con decision. You have to have a reason to like him. He's that kind of knave.

Nearly three years after I met him I had my first experience with someone who felt genuine affection for him, a former secretary. There are few better references. That was in the winter of 1967, at the very time Dann and I were at war over several unsympathetic pieces I had written about CBS and one Bill Greeley wrote that had embarrassed Dann personally.

In a conversation circle at a party attended mainly by ABC and advertising people, the business gossip was interrupted by a young lady who had overheard Dann's name taken in vain. Defending him, she said, "I don't care what kind of person Mike is in business or what he means to other people, I don't care whether he brings good or bad shows to television—all I would say about him is that he is an exciting person, and he was very kind to me and fun to work for." She had been his secretary at CBS until her marriage to a salesman for ABC.

Mark now: we were at an ABC party, and the talk was about Mike Dann. Not unusual; no one in the business was more often discussed or written about. Why, it's fair to ask, with all the network presidents and higher-ranking corporate officers to choose from, did *New York Magazine* and *Business Week* single out Dann for a study? And why did *TV Guide*, which did not accord such treatment to the biggest stars, select him for a three-part profile?

It was because Dann was the complete child of the television system, a system he never made but one he never questioned. He was the thorough professional who measured life and death not in heartbeats but in Nielsen digits, who felt around for power, respecting the man who had it, and crapping on whoever did not. He was the perfect soldier of network television, the guy who mastered the manual, the best of the jungle fighters, the authority on the art of survival in the organization.

You did not go to Dann for better television. He was no theorist. He provided what was called for, what would keep him his job. At the time it was *Hee Haw* and *Green Acres*, but I suspect that if the system had called for Pirandello, Pinter, or Greek tragedy—if that was where the numbers were—Dann would have provided it on a scale never experienced in the history of audiences.

He was not in the CBS image. He lacked the tact, the reserve, the class. Exceptions were made in the vulgar reaches of the program department. The ideal CBS executive had the clubman's dignity and behaved as if he were dealing in stocks, but he required the aura of a winner, and it was Dann who provided that gilt-edged attribute. Dann was a chronic front-runner, a gut-fighter, a groin-kicker, a double-dealer, a publicity-seeker, a comedian, a show-off, a charmer, a pragmatist, a schemer, a good provider—insensitive, amoral, generous.

Unlike the others, he was highly complex and more honest than they in the basics of television commerce and organizational self-preservation. In a milieu of low-key executives, he had the temerity to be visible. In a communications industry that was passing into the cautious hands of sales-

men, lawyers, and accountants, Dann kept alive an old spirit
of gamesmanship. Largely through him and the news he generated, television business maintained, in the public mind,
a sparkle and a sense of action.

The first time I had audience with Dann in his office—
it was early in 1965—he sat yogi-like, feet tucked under him
in his expensive swivel chair, with his right forefinger in his
nose. It was, apparently, how he chose to make an impression on the new man from Chicago who was succeeding
Variety's noted television editor, George Rosen—as if to
show he was not one of those stamped out of an executive
machine.

I should have liked him then but did not. What struck me
during the meeting was that he manifestly lacked the cultural background, the intellectual depth, and the concern for
the people at the other end of the TV set to deserve the job
of programing one of the country's three television networks.
That was also to be my impression of Mort Werner at NBC.
The fellow at ABC, at the time, was Edgar Scherick, an edu-
cated man and undeniably bright, but nervous and, it seemed
to me, frightened. Since I was new to New York and the centers of broadcasting power, I found it an easy conclusion that
American television was in its miserable state because the
selection of its program matter had been delegated to inferior
men. I no longer feel quite that way. The requirements of
television do not begin in the program department.

Jim Aubrey, erstwhile president of CBS television, had
a brilliant mind and the formal schooling to go with it (B.A.
cum laude from Princeton), and he gave the country *The
Beverly Hillbillies, Petticoat Junction*, and *The Baileys of
Balboa*. Oliver Treyz, a man of some breeding with an astonishingly rapid and retentive mind, contributed *Surfside
Six, 77 Sunset Strip, Hawaiian Eye*, and *Bus Stop* when he
was running ABC. And Bob Kintner, a thinking man if ever
the networks had one, was a champion of television news at
NBC, but in the realm of light entertainment no more dis-

tinguished than the others. His deed was to abdicate the medium's own creativity for expedient secondhand material, old movies in prime time.

Treyz prefers to remember his administration at ABC for other things. His present office on Park Avenue, from which he operates a broadcast consultancy, contains such memorabilia as a letter from Winston Churchill thanking him for scheduling a Churchill series, a photograph of the third Kennedy-Nixon great debate on its origination from ABC, and a photograph of himself and his former boss Leonard Goldenson with President John F. Kennedy. No reminders, however, of the animated cartoons and potboiler adventure hours from Warner Brothers, which had predominated on his network.

The men who had run the networks in the past were not lacking in taste themselves, but were cynical about the tastes of the masses and ready at any time, in the interest of profits, to compromise their standards to deliver the mass audience.

Dann was not cynical, he was a technician. He allowed himself no vision for the medium and no philosophy of what it should be; such considerations were extraneous to his work. Not a maker of shows, he bought them and made sure they looked professional. He cultivated creative people who could turn out winners for CBS, and he indulged the performers who were valuable to the network. But he was proudest of his expertise in scheduling programs, believing the strategic placement to be half the difference between a hit and a flop.

Television, to him, was a continuous grind of weekly series in the evening, occasionally pre-empted by specials. By day it was soap operas, on Saturday mornings comic-book trifles. Sports on weekends, public affairs on Sundays, a talk show late at night. All of it subject to disruption by news. That was the grand design, and Dann was content to work within it.

I asked him some years ago why prime-time programs were always the same every year: action melodramas, situation comedies, and variety shows.

He answered, What else is there?

I said that surely television lent itself to other kinds of light entertainment.

He said, "Look, there are three basic forms. Well, okay, a fourth—anthology—but it doesn't sell. I'd like to do Shakespeare and symphony concerts, but where would I be?"

Dann had been a prize student of the old methodology. Every one of the skills pertinent to his job could be traced to an apprenticeship under an old master. He learned programing operations first from Pat Weaver at NBC, when he and Mort Werner were on the same team in a department that was exemplary for its boldness and inventiveness; and it was Dann's membership in the Weaver school that made him attractive to CBS when that network hired him away. There he was to learn, from Bill Paley, a reverence for the star system, and from Aubrey both how to schedule the shows strategically for ratings and how to aim for the network's peculiar audience advantage, its penetration into the rural communities.

One skill he acquired on his own, from his days in the NBC press department, where he was in charge of trade press publicity. It may be the only one of his skills that came intuitively, and it is the only one that was really irrelevant to his work as a programing executive. That was his ability to stir up the press, to keep it tuned to the idea of winners and losers in television, to make it care about competition between the networks.

His romance with the newspapers grew partly from his own exhibitionism and partly from the saga quality he gave to his work. Seeing the challenges of his job in terms of high drama, he could not enjoy his own heroism unless it was celebrated in print. It was not satisfying to earn $100,000 a year for knowing what most people want to watch on television most of the time. Dann lived his professional life in the press, and there it became real to him. He was forever creating imaginary crises in which he was at the center and his job in peril. He was given to saying, "Well, I bought the such-and-such show to put against Bob Hope on Thursday night. It was a big decision. My job is on the line."

With such melodrama he gave mock importance to insignificant decisions he had to make in the normal course of business. Whether they succeeded or failed never really affected his status with CBS.

Dann was on the phone with the New York press daily, Sundays, holidays, and even while vacationing with his family at Martha's Vineyard, but there was one out-of-town newspaperman who heard from him just as often. That was Frank Judge of the *Detroit News*, and for a particular reason. Dann's mother was in Detroit, and he always wanted to be sure she saw his triumphs in print.

Far from being pleased at having regular direct contact with one of the most important figures at the networks, which could have been productive of exclusive stories, Judge was annoyed by the calls. "The peg is always that Mike is a Detroiter," he told me. "He wants the 'Local Boy Makes Good' story every week."

As for news exclusives, Judge was convinced that Dann, never passing up a chance to make print, would confirm any rumor or tip.

"Once I trapped him," Judge said. "On a lark I asked him about a completely fictitious lead.

" 'Say, Mike,' I said, 'What's this about CBS and the Stratford Festival?'

" 'You heard about that?' Mike said. 'I can tell you this, you're on to something.'

" 'Well, maybe you can tell me which Stratford group it is—the one in Connecticut, the one in Canada, or the one in England.'

" 'You know us,' Mike said. 'We go for the original.' "

Pride never interfered with Dann's objectives. In a dispute over a program deal a number of years ago, producer Herbert Brodkin heaped such abuse on Dann that he might have burned his bridges to CBS. A more petty network executive would have been vindictive and never had further dealings with Brodkin. But when Dann was ordered by his management to organize an occasional series of original dramas to be offered two or three times a year as *CBS Playhouse*, one of the first producers of reputation Dann solicited was Brodkin.

I found myself admiring his shamelessness. Once, in an article for *Variety*, I reported that a CBS executive in Hollywood, John Reynolds, was next in line for the network presidency, to succeed Jack Schneider, who would be moving up to a higher post. Dann called me to say "You're out of touch. John isn't going anywhere. If I thought he had any chance I could have finished him off long ago."

But Reynolds did get the job, and he had hardly arrived in New York when Dann strode into his office and handed him a sheet of paper.

"What's this?" Reynolds asked.

"My resignation. You're going to fire me, aren't you? I thought I'd make it easy on both of us."

"I'm not going to fire you, Mike," Reynolds said.

Instead of thinking Reynolds was a swell guy not to hold old animosities against him, Dann took the fact that Reynolds kept him as a sign of weakness. He reasoned, perhaps rightly, that Reynolds was tempted to let him go but needed Dann's expertise in programing. Having sighted the weakness, Dann took every advantage of it, down to insisting that press releases on programing announcements be issued as *his* disclosures rather than the president's, which is *pro forma*. Reynolds was an ineffectual president, and Dann made sure it was obvious.

I admired him in the winter of 1968 when the ratings were going badly for CBS and Paley was known to have interviewed several studio executives for Dann's job. I stopped in on Dann, purposely to see what he was like as a loser. He was magnificent. I think that was when I really came to like him. He was like the good poker player who did not blame fate or curse his own miserable soul for a poor run of luck. Like the career soldier who lived by the manual, he was ready to be relieved of his post for failing to execute his duty. He lived so religiously by the rules that Win means Survive and Lose means Expulsion that he would have been upset and confused if he had been exempted.

He said to me, without gloom, "I've had a pretty good run in this spot. Better than most program veeps. I don't know what happened to our numbers. I guess Mort's schedule is just too good. He's got a winner, and you've got to recognize that. You've got to write that he did a helluva fine job."

That was in 1968, and in 1970 Dann was still in the job. What happened? Late in December, Dann made a couple of changes in the CBS schedule. He pulled out one loser and installed the Glen Campbell show. Then he switched two programs, *The Jonathan Winters Show* and *Hawaii Five-O*, and CBS began to win the weekly ratings. NBC, meanwhile, twice pre-empted its strongest show, *Laugh-In*, for specials that did not do as well in the ratings, and by the time the season ended CBS had squeaked ahead by 0.1 in the Nielsen averages for the season. Practically speaking, it was a tie; under standard statistical error an absolutely meaningless lead. Still, the basic arithmetic showed CBS ahead of NBC by the slightest margin—an estimated 120,000 more homes per half hour out of the more than 23 million that supposedly were tuned to one of the two networks—and that sufficed for a victory claim. Mike Dann, who had jockeyed the schedule home, was a hero again.

What made him unique among the professionals in network television was that he was *willing* to live or die by what he understood to be the rules of war. Others, some of them higher up the scale, busied themselves with running for cover. In the new manual, the art of survival is to stay out of the battle rather than to join it. There are executives who spend three-quarters of their working day figuring ways to take credit for favorable developments and to escape blame for the disasters.

Networks do not too often get their money's worth from high-salaried personnel. One who made the sudden jump from a staff position to a $50,000-a-year power post confessed to me over a drink one night, "It's a terrible thing, in a way. You begin to love the prestige and the authority, and the first thing you think about is how to preserve that and how to keep the money from stopping. Suddenly, every new idea becomes a threat to you. It means you have to act on it, one way or another. You can't afford to be reckless. So you try to push the ideas down, make them go away or, if possible, make them someone else's responsibility.

"Listen, there is a technique, and I got wise to it right away. You learn to say *no* to everything. 'No' doesn't get you involved, 'yes' does. The company doesn't appreciate that you try to do right by it. So many boners and you're out. So you don't worry about doing right by the company. First you worry about doing right by yourself."

Mike Dann had surely done his share of suppressing new ideas and resisting change, but he continually set himself up to take either the credit or the blame for CBS programing. Indeed, he had been known to shelter some of his superiors by taking the blame in their stead.

Werner was unlike Dann. Rarely seen or quoted, he was not particularly identified with every show on the NBC schedule. Some people who had been in the television business for years did not know the name of the man who headed programing for NBC.

One night, at a dinner, I was seated next to Werner's wife. She told me, "Mike looks for publicity, Mort runs from it. We don't care if he never gets his name in the papers. When you do, you become a moving target. People are out to get you. We feel that if nobody hears about Mort, and he keeps doing his job and staying out of trouble, he'll last longer where he is."

Privately, many important television executives have confessed to me that they rarely watch television, not, in any event, the prime-time series night after night. Dann had told me that he saw most of what he wanted to see in the screening room and otherwise spent little time before the set.

But Werner struck me as one who watched all the time. Not only watched but loved the stories, the comedies, and the variety shows. I do not know that for sure; it's just an impression. He always spoke of TV shows with the surrendered will of a connoisseur in a museum.

Werner was Dann's opposite number at NBC but not his opposite in vital respects. Mort and Mike performed similar functions as competitors and played the survival game, each in his own way.

Dann's opposite at NBC—his true rival and foil—was someone quite as bold as he, and a far more formidable adversary than Mort Werner.

From a small unpretentious office on the seventh floor of the RCA Building (on the Sixth Avenue side), Paul Klein directed the NBC audience research department, whose work basically was to compute and interpret the raw rating numbers and to evaluate the testing of pilots for new series. As possibly the best brain in broadcasting, Klein also had the character to be embarrassed by the business and was perpetually on the verge of quitting, although his salary was well above $50,000 a year and his job reasonably secure for all his personal peccadilloes.

Heavy-set and fortyish, he was a melancholy philosopher who displayed such an understanding of what rating research indicated of public taste and such intuition about the placement of programs that he became part of the network's high council in its programing decisions.

Klein, for instance, was responsible for *Julia*, the rookie hit of the 1968–69 season, which almost failed to make the NBC schedule. The pilot for the series arrived early in January of 1968 and was promptly rejected. In February, when the schedule was being drawn up, a half-hour period was open opposite Red Skelton on CBS, and the network's programing brain trust was trying to decide between two other pilots. The consensus was that neither was going to beat Skelton, but the question was which would fail more nobly against him. Klein, at this point, suggested that as long as the half hour was going to be conceded to CBS, NBC might as well select a show that would have value beyond the ratings.

Julia, he argued, may be saccharine but it had racial importance at a time when television was under heavy criticism as a lily-white medium. With Diahann Carroll in the lead, it would be the first situation comedy since the opprobrious *Amos 'n' Andy* to be built around a black person. Among other virtues, it would bespeak newness in a new season.

Klein sold his argument, and the program series paid an unexpected dividend. It was not only the talk of the season but a genuine rating hit.

Such triumphs gave him sporadic sustenance. In 1968 a colleague, Larry Grossman, gave up a vice-presidency at NBC and a prospectively comfortable future because he felt that television would never be more than an electronic comic book, and he couldn't bear to devote the rest of his life to promoting and advertising programs he could never admire. Klein was similarly afflicted, nearly always on the threshold of despair, dabbling avocationally in the field of education, and speaking frequently of abandoning television; but he remained because he, unlike Grossman, was in position to sway the network, occasionally, in new directions.

Like Dann, Klein was an incautious, visible executive— but for wholly different reasons. He believed that television could be better than it was under the system, that the audience could force a modification of the old programing formulas, and this gave him a mission.

In his own mind, CBS was representative of the old television and NBC of the new. The old saw the TV audience as a single mass, the means to which was programing for the lowest-common denominator. The new recognized the viewership as several different audiences, and it set out to capture the most desirable, from a commercial standpoint, for itself. Klein's mission (self-assigned) was to prove that CBS was out of date. His primary target was the living symbol of the old television, Mike Dann. It became his obsession to crush Dann.

As Dann's way was to work through the press, Klein's tactic was direct assault by mail. He habitually vented his competitive rage in insulting letters written on impulse, often to members of the press, and while those who knew him were willing to indulge that quirk, others reacted angrily. On one occasion he affronted Dick Doan, a columnist for *TV Guide*, and had to answer to NBC management for it. His friend Bud Rukeyser, head of the NBC press department, took him in hand and persuaded Klein to call him whenever he felt the urge to write a letter.

He made an exception of Klein's letters to Dann, and during the 1969–70 season Klein aimed a steady stream of missives at his CBS rival, all calculated to demoralize and harass him.

Get Smart was the symbolic program in the Klein-Dann joust. On Klein's recommendation it was discarded by NBC as played out; on Dann's it was salvaged by CBS to solve a particular Friday night scheduling problem. Before the season began, Dann, up to his absurd mock heroics, told *New York Post* columnist Leonard Lyons that *Get Smart* was the momentous gamble of the schedule and that his job could be preserved or lost with the success or failure of that series. Klein clipped the item and saved it.

When the early ratings arrived, *Get Smart* was painfully low in the standings. Klein pasted the Lyons item in a home-made funeral card and mailed it to Dann. Some weeks later the show made a strong surge in the ratings, and Dann went to the press with the new numbers as evidence that his decision to buy it for CBS had been a sound one. But Klein recognized that the rating spurt might be artificial, a one-shot hypo for the episode in which a baby was born to the comic secret agents in the series. Such gimmick "events" historically have lifted ratings for a single week but rarely have resulted in permanent rehabilitation of a program's popularity. He sent off the words: "Pray for Mike Dann's baby."

Missing the allusion, Dann wrote Klein not to worry about his ability to feed his children. To which Klein replied, "I wasn't worried about your feeding them but about your eating them."

The exchange of taunts was childish, of course, and not at all typical of how television executives behave, but it was indicative of a spirit of gamesmanship that had prevailed almost since the beginning of the networks.

Dann and Klein never met. I made an attempt to bring them together once, but Klein was unwilling to be introduced.

"I might like him," he said, "and that would ruin everything."

Early in February, NBC's lead over CBS was half a rating point, signifying about 600,000 more viewers per half hour of prime time, on the average for the season. CBS had made its mid-season changes, and they were not sufficient to disrupt NBC's winning momentum. For the first seventeen weeks of the season, NBC had been the weekly leader two-thirds of the time.

I wrote about it in *Variety* on February 4, in an article titled "NBC's Edge of Nighttime." It stated, "Theoretically, it's still possible for CBS to catch up and even overtake, but it's hard to imagine how."

That produced a call from Dann.

"You practically gave them the season, and there's still three months to go."

"Tell me what's inaccurate in the story."

"Nothing. But I'm not giving up."

"What do you have in mind? The numbers guys say there's no chance."

"I can't argue with them. But there's still three months left."

It's a silly game, the rating race, and one that would be a pleasure for me to ignore in my work, if it were not for one thing. The Nielsen decimal points have everything to do with what America receives as television fare. NBC's comfortable lead and Dann's unwillingness to accept defeat would have a definite effect on the television consumer's viewing for the next three months.

The same article in *Variety* noted: "The irony of it all is that winning the total homes ratings hardly matters to NBC —which is determined to prove that it's an out-of-date evaluation and that only the demographic break-outs, or 'people ratings,' count with the advertiser—while at CBS winning in total circulation is the essential mission, a matter of pride and an old tradition. CBS has been supreme in the prime-time nose count for fourteen years in a row, and if there were one great satisfaction for NBC in winning the prime-time numbers this year, it would be to break up the CBS winning streak."

Klein was planning a press conference, coincident with the last rating report of the season, to make a declaration that he hoped would end the old rating game forever and introduce a new one.

He would say: Well, we have *won* the season. Here are the books to prove it, and I am here to tell you that it does not mean a thing. It does not matter how many homes are tuned to a program, and it will never matter again. What matters is which *people* are watching, whether they are old people or young people. Old people want to watch the staples, Lawrence Welk and situation comedies. Young people will watch dramas, movies, and new program forms we have not gotten around to discovering yet. When we start thinking in terms of People Ratings instead of Homes Ratings, television is going to improve vastly.

On February 19 I received a call from Dann.

"You have anyone down for lunch on April 24? It's a Friday."

"I'm open that day," I said.

"Okay, put me down. We'll go to La Caravelle."

"How come you're booking me two months in advance?"

"For a story."

"If it's a story, tell me now."

"It's not a story now."

"Give me a hint."

"No hints. Keep the date open."

I marked it down on my calendar, although I was sure we'd never keep the date. April 24 was the week of the last rating report. If there was going to be a dramatic turn in the ratings I would know about it long before. Mike was up to something, and whatever it was, if he was having any success with it, he would not wait until April 24 to tell the world.

Two hours later his secretary, Madeline Katz, was on the phone.

"I'm calling," she said, "to confirm your lunch with Mr. Dann."

"Not the April one?"

"April 24."

"Madeline, this is comical."

"I'm just doing what Mr. Dann said."

"Tell him I've got a date but am going to break it for him."

"Thank you."

Later Bud Rukeyser called from NBC.

"Dann must be on the weed."

"What's going on?"

"You ought to check this. All of a sudden CBS is throwing in specials they never announced before. But I mean weird shows, like they're rerunning an old Andy Griffith–Jim Nabors special out of left field, and they just scheduled one on Eskimos. You don't think the poor guy is still trying to win, do you?"

"He does go down fighting."

"It's the dying gasp," said Bud.

"I guess."

I conferred with Greeley and Steve Knoll at the office.

We would keep track of the specials going in on short notice and would look for other signs of Dann's machinations in the CBS schedule. Meanwhile, several CBS affiliates complained to me about the rash of program pre-emptions by the network which barely gave them time to change the program listings in the papers and in *TV Guide*.

Could Dann possibly win? I consulted one of the network experts in statistics. He analyzed it this way. The average ratings for the season up to that point were: NBC 20.3 and CBS 19.8. With an 0.5 spread after seventeen weeks, the odds against catching up were very long. It meant that NBC was ahead by 0.5 (600,000 viewers) in every one of the forty-nine half hours of the prime-time week, not for any single week but for seventeen of them. Cumulatively, it was a total deficit of nearly 500 million viewers. In order to negate such a lead, CBS would have to beat NBC by about two full rating points every week for the remaining weeks of the season. CBS would have to attract 2.4 million more people than NBC, on the average, in every one of the forty-nine half hours each week for the next seven weeks. Given NBC's strength and momentum, the prospect was quite hopeless.

On Wednesday, March 4, Dann caught me at home.

"Hate to bother you on your day off, but this is major," he said. "Can you see me tomorrow afternoon?"

I said I would.

Dann was forty-eight, on the short side, and getting fleshy of jowl. He looked older that day and less carefully dressed than usual. His voice had the hoarse and uneven quality that signifies fatigue. Admitting me into his office, he shambled over to a piece of stationery which he had taped to a wall and, pointing to it, said, "This is what it's about. I'll brief you here, and then Jay Eliasberg and Arnie Becker are going to show you the presentation we'll be making to Mr. Paley on Monday. You'll be impressed, I promise you."

The stationery was a cream color and the letterhead red. It read: "Operation 100 (January 10–April 19, 1970)."

On the left side it said "New York" and listed the names Michael Dann, Irwin Segelstein, Fred Silverman, Paul Rauch, Philip Capice, Michael Filerman, Michael Marden, Ray McCullough, James Krayer. On the right side it said "Hollywood" and listed Perry Lafferty, Paul King, Alan Wagner, Henry Colman, Martin Dooling, Boris Kaplan, Ellis Marcus, Patrick Betz.

Dann hobbled to his desk, his eyes drooping suddenly, his mouth forming a stage grimace. This was going to be both a story and a performance.

"I've been working from seven in the morning to midnight every day since January 10th," he said. "I'm very tired. This may be my last roar. I just wanted you to know."

He opened the top drawer of his desk.

"Look in here—three kinds of pills. I've only been to the Coast twice this year. It's tough being on the line year after year, and I'm burning out. I don't know what I'll be doing next year. I may try for a corporate job—long-range planning in all fields CBS is interested in—or I might take some time off.

"But I wanted to tell you this. I've been with CBS for twelve years and in this job for six. And we have never, never, never been second in that time. I couldn't break the string my last year. I had to win this one, and you know it as well as anyone—you wrote it—that I didn't have a chance.

"You saw the stationery. You know what Operation 100 is? I gave my department one hundred days to catch up and overtake NBC. I told Wood I wanted to do it, and he gave me the go-ahead. He also came in to tell my people he hoped we could pull it off. I brought the New York group in here and laid it out. We needed every idea. We met every morning, and so did Perry's group on the Coast. We had to build up the regular shows wherever we could—like Sullivan, that's one you can hypo with special acts—grab some good specials where we could find them to replace our weakest shows, and somehow build up the movies. You know why we were losing? Mostly because we had lousy movie titles, and NBC had good ones.

"We had only one thing going for us. We knew that NBC was asleep, figuring itself the winner, and that we could counterprogram the shit out of them. You should see what those kids of mine did. They're beautiful."

"Are you telling me, Mike, that you have a chance of beating NBC now?" I said.

His voice rose to the high pitch it climbs to when he is excited, or ecstatic. "Chance? It's working. Everything is working. Jay Eliasberg—you know how conservative Jay is—believes it now. He thought I was crazy. Now he has a presentation, a calendar, to show Mr. Paley just how we're going to win. It's fantastic."

"This was what you were going to tell me over lunch a month from now?"

Dann handed me a letter. It was addressed to me, in care of him at CBS, and it was sealed. The postmark, he asked me to observe, was February 20. "I was going to give you this at our lunch," he said. "Open it." The letter read:

> Dear Les:
> Today I will tell you how it happened.
> Cordially,
> Mike.

Then in a large open scrawl, the postscript: "I hope you enjoy this lunch as much as I will."

He handed me a file of Operation 100 sheets on which the members of his programing staff had made their suggestions.

"This isn't all of them," Dann said. "But I don't want to give any secrets away for what's coming up. Take them for your story, but I want to have them back for keepsakes. The kids are beautiful."

This is how the suggestions went:

If we push, I think we can put together a special Sullivan show featuring the Beatles live or tape. We can also use the other stars doing Beatle material. —Irwin S.

Red Skelton likes the idea of Tiny Tim, and we have booked him. —Marty Dooling.

Although *Hatari* has been run twice on ABC, each time on a single night, I think with the proper promotion we can make it an excellent two-parter that will work on Thursday and Friday nights. —Mike Marden.

I think we should get Dick Van Dyke to host *Born Free*. His presence will get it a sense of importance that showing the film alone may not have. If not Van Dyke, Fred MacMurray. —Irwin Segelstein.

Let's make special promos for *Born Free* to be scheduled only in kid shows on Sat. morning block. We can use that great "cub" footage. —Paul Rauch.

Although *Peyton Place* was played out on ABC in the series, I still think with the correct promotion it would do well for us as a two-parter. Just remember we won't promote Lana Turner because that will remind people of *The Survivors*. —Mike Marden.

Buy *African Queen*. It was in syndication for seven years and played a dozen times on local stations. It has been resting for nine years, and I think we can get it cheap from Sam Spiegel. —Mike Filerman.

Use soap opera aspects of *Peyton Place* in all our daytime promos. —Fred Silverman.

The Power has great appeal for kids and families. Like *Mysterious Island*, we must schedule it on a holiday weekend. I'm checking Thurs., March 26, as best date and will let you know. —Mike M.

O.K., it's done! All in-season repeats for Gleason will be *Honeymooners*. —Tom Loeb.

Ice shows are doing well. Sullivan can do *Holiday on Ice*. Let's go. —Mike Marden.

I think I can buy Paul Newman & Joanne Woodward

feature *New Kind of Love* in time for use this season. I'll let you know in a day or so. —Bob Daly.

I just talked to Phil on the Coast. We think we can get Dick Van Dyke to plug *Campbell* and *Mission* in his *Born Free* wraparounds. —Jim Rogers.

Get *Lions Are Free*. —Mike Dann.

I talked to Glen Campbell and he promises to book a special show—big acts—following the *Born Free* showing. This could give him as big a share as he's ever had. —Perry Lafferty.

Robert Young's *Eskimo: Fight for Life* is great—I picked him for *J.T.* from that film. We can buy it from the National Science Foundation. —Mike Dann.

Why don't we use Expo 70 as an early evening special event? News dept. can do a helluva job on it. —Phil Capice.

Following *Cinderella* Friday 4/3 schedule two specials rather than Fri. night movie to make a special family evening by running Don Knotts special. —Fred Silverman.

Having learned, through ad agency sources, the dates of all the forthcoming NBC specials and the titles of most of that network's movies for the next three months, Dann and his people planned a counterprograming strategy that would make use of NBC's own weapons—the special and the "event" program. The latter is either live coverage of an actual event, such as the opening of the Expo 70 world's fair in Osaka, Japan, or an occasion created by television, such as an Ed Sullivan program given over to the ice-skating extravaganza, *Holiday on Ice*, or one honoring the Beatles.

The diagnosis was that almost anything presented as a special would do better than the four big losers in the schedule, *Get Smart, The Tim Conway Show, To Rome With Love*, and *Lancer*. Accordingly, the first two were pre-empted seven consecutive times, mostly with nonfiction programs of natural history or archaeology, and the other two three weeks out of seven. It was also recognized that CBS had a lackluster supply of movies, in terms of what would appeal to a large television audience, and that challenged the resource-fulness of Dann's program staff. The CBS Thursday and Friday night motion pictures had been averaging a desultory 30 per cent of the available audience all season, and in or-der for the plan to work these two movie showcases would have to improve their competitive performance to at least 35 per cent of the audience every week. That would call for both ingenuity in scheduling and a massive promotion effort by Jack Cowden's advertising, publicity, and on-the-air pro-motion forces. If the movie phase of the rating push failed, the entire campaign was lost.

One of Dann's New York lieutenants, Fred Silverman, recommended that the film *Born Free* not be shown in a regu-lar movie-time period but scheduled instead as a Sunday night special, early enough so that it would be available to young children. It played at seven o'clock on February 22, preceded by intense promotion in the network's children's shows.

Dann awakened early the following morning and before going to the office put in a phone call to learn the rating. Then, from his home, he phoned London to buy the rights to the sequel, *The Lions Are Free*, which had been made orig-inally as a special for NBC and played two years previously. Dann acted that swiftly because he knew the news had not yet traveled on the *Born Free* rating, and he suspected that most people in the business on both sides of the Atlantic were not yet aware of what he was attempting to do. He was able to secure *The Lions Are Free* at bargain prices, sup-posedly less than half of what NBC had paid for the orig-inal play. The ratings for *Born Free* were the highest movie ratings of the year and the third highest in the history of movies on network television, exceeded only by *The Bridge on the River Kwai* and Alfred Hitchcock's *The Birds*. It was a 34.2 rating, roughly equivalent to 40 million viewers, and for a two-hour period it commanded 53 per cent of the view-ing audience. Had that information circulated before Dann made his call to London that Monday morning, he might well have had to pay a good deal more for the sequel. *The Lions Are Free* aired March 3 on a Tuesday night, in place of *Lancer*, and pulled a smashing 26.4 rating and 40 per cent of the available audience, better than its initial showing on NBC.

Mike Marden's suggestion that *Hatari* be played as a two-part film, although it had already been shown twice on ABC, each time on a single night, was also inspired. Because its movie showcases were on successive nights, Thursdays and Fridays, CBS had a certain scheduling advantage over the other networks when long films were involved, being able to schedule them over two evenings. Films presented that way seem more important to the viewer than those which run their full length in one night. Also, in spreading a single picture over two movie periods, CBS was able to conserve on a number of strong picture titles it needed for its rating drive.

Hatari was long out of its theatrical run and never had been a box-office smash, but it had John Wayne as its star, an actor of great appeal in the CBS rural counties and, as Dann described it, it was promoted as though it were *Gone With the Wind*. It scored 38 per cent of the audience the first night and 41 per cent the second, better than its original runs on ABC.

The film adaptation of the book *Peyton Place* had been sitting in the CBS vaults for several years, held back from exhibition because of possible confusion with the ABC prime-time serial which had also been based on the Grace Metallious novel. Dann's film experts felt certain that enough time had elapsed so that it would not be tainted by the TV series. It, too, was offered as a two-parter, and it, too, fulfilled its mission. The ratings were far above average for the CBS movies during the season. Over the two nights it attracted 39 per cent of the audience watching television.

The African Queen was the biggest gamble of all. Two decades old, it had played dozens of times on local stations and then was reissued theatrically to the motion picture art houses for their Humphrey Bogart festivals. Having been out of television circulation for a number of years, it was the hunch of Dann's film experts that it might attract a big audience for a small investment. The producer, Sam Spiegel, surprised that a network would want it after its local station exposure, sold CBS the rights at $225,000 the first showing and $100,000 the second. Bad or good, the ordinary motion picture costs a network about $800,000 a play. At bargain prices, *The African Queen* proved to be one of the top-rated CBS pictures of the year, with an audience of 30 million viewers, or 43 per cent of those tuned to television that evening.

Dann's wild programing spree also involved the purchase of old specials: two with Andy Griffith that normally would never have been repeated, one with the Harlem Globetrotters, one out of the realm of the Saturday morning cartoons, and one with Dinah Shore that originally played on NBC—and a raft of new ones in the nonfiction field that were not normally considered programs of rating potential. CBS, however, had had extraordinary success with the National Geographic specials for several seasons, and Dann's hunch was that programs of that stripe would perform better on Friday nights than his losing combination of *Get Smart* and *Tim Conway*.

For six of the seven weeks he played documentary programs with titles such as *The Trail of the Feathered Serpent*, *Savage Waters, Savage Beast, The Incredible Auto Race, Eskimo: Fight for Life, Dive to the Unknown,* and *Sail Around the World.* Most barely outscored the programs they replaced, but some did rather well, and over-all the Friday night hour at 7:30 was an improvement on the scheduled programing, and that was the objective. The Eskimo program was a particular success, reaching nearly 28 million viewers and 37 per cent of the Friday night audience, a showing that was notable for the fact that the film was made for the National Science Foundation and was not even intended for either television or theatrical exhibition.

In Dann's office that day, as I expressed amused disbelief that anyone would be so enslaved by a number psychology as to attempt such a stunt, Dann snapped at me, "Who is hurt by this? The public? Are they better off with my educational Eskimo film or that Tim Conway crap that nobody likes? Are they better off with more jugglers and bum comedians on Sullivan or that show we're doing from the veterans' hospital? Tell me that we sold the kids short by giving them *Born Free* and *Lions Are Free*. Okay, so it's a repeat. The kids who saw it this time were sucking a tit the last time it played."

He opened his office door and ushered me down the hall to a conference room where Eliasberg and Becker were waiting. It was dimly lit except for a spotlight falling upon a large easel bearing a flip-card presentation, the top one of which read Operation 100. Eliasberg turned the top card back, presenting the month of February laid out in large squares, with blue ink entries indicating NBC's special programs and red ink the CBS ploys. Behind that were similar cards for March and April.

"Here you see what we have done in February to build up our ratings," Eliasberg said, "and now we are able to project week by week how our programing moves are going to overtake NBC."

"Listen to these projections," Dann interjected, "but bear in mind that he's conservative. You *are* conservative, Jay."

What Eliasberg's charts showed was that CBS had won the ratings against NBC for the last three weeks in February and that, through Dann's counterprograming, it was going to win the next seven weeks by margins ranging from half a rating point to more than three full points. By the week of March 16 to 22, according to his projections, CBS would have caught up with NBC and in the weeks thereafter would build its lead in the season averages to 0.3.

"We're going to do it," Eliasberg said. "There's no doubt now."

Mike floated out of the conference room, leaving me to

return to my office to write the story of his latest heroic triumph.

And then Rukeyser and Klein pulled a gorgeous stunt of their own.

Suddenly, NBC declared to the press that the television season would end a month early this year, on March 22. That was because nearly 40 per cent of its schedule would be in reruns. Several newspapers printed the story.

I was afraid Dann would go out of his thirty-fourth-floor window.

Dann was a wily fighter, but Klein had always managed to keep him unnerved through a single tactic: just as Dann appeared to have victory within his grasp, Klein changed the rules of the game. He did it with demographics against bulk ratings, and now he was doing it with an abbreviated season against Operation 100. His statement that the season would end on March 22, while patently a trick, was not altogether arbitrary. Nowhere is there a book of rules on how network television competition must be conducted. It is an essentially improvised game.

A television season, having no concrete definition, is thought to be the period between the premiere of the weekly series and the termination of their first-run cycle. It begins some time after Labor Day and ends some time in the spring. The boundaries are complicated by the fact that the networks do not always start their new shows in the same week. NBC began 1969–70 on September 14, while CBS and ABC were still in the summer reruns; the latter two began a week later, there being more money in a later start since audience levels increase week by week after Labor Day. But if NBC lost some business volume in being first to launch, it may have seized the competitive advantage that kept it running ahead of CBS through most of the season. For NBC's lead was attributed at least in part to its head start over the other networks, enabling it to establish its new programs before the others introduced theirs.

As to the *end* of the season, convention designated it as

mid-April, coincident with Daylight Saving Time, and that was still the logical boundary. The changing of the clocks sharply affects television tune-in, marking the beginning of the summer drop-off, and therefore it affects television's time rates. The $60,000-a-minute rate for a commercial in the winter months could drop to almost half after the time change. Also validating mid-April as the end of the season is that Nielsen publishes its last regular book at the end of April, covering the first half of the month. In 1970, the final Nielsen report surveyed the period up to April 19. Conventionally, that was the end of the season.

Yet Klein's argument did have merit. The earlier designations of a season were based in part on the competition between first-run episodes of regular series. In the fifties, a network bought thirty-nine episodes of a series and completed a full year by repeating thirteen of them during the summer months. Later, for economic reasons, the orders were trimmed down to twenty-six originals and twenty-six repeats. Even at that, it was extremely costly for a network to buy out of a weak program it wanted to cancel prematurely, since it would have to pay for every episode it did not use. And so it became feasible to cut back to seventeen original episodes, space them out with specials, repeat them, and then install a nine-week replacement show for the summer. Klein's argument was that NBC would be partially on a repeat schedule after March 22 because it started first, and therefore at a disadvantage in the competition.

After the ploy, the inevitable call from Dann. He was barely coherent.

"You're not going to believe them," he said. "You know it's just a trick. I can't beat them by March 22."

"I think it's wonderful, Mike," I said, needling him. "There'll be two winners this year."

He was crestfallen.

The day after *Variety*'s story on Operation 100, which was titled "CBS Turns It on in the Stretch," Jack Gould of the *New York Times* answered with an article interviewing the three network presidents, all of them denying the importance of a rating competition and scoffing at the idea of any network *winning* the season. It was a classic piece of textbook journalism—all facts and no truth. The facts were that the network presidents made the statements, as quoted, but it was not indicated in the story that their statements (*i.e.*, facts) concealed the truth. Network presidents make ratings their first order of business. They will arrive at the office and, before considering other matters, ask, How did we do last night? Gould knew that as well as anyone, but I suspect he wanted it to be true that the networks had grown up and that they no longer indulged in such demeaning and apparently fruitless activity.

The rating war embarrassed the network presidents. It was a little like street fighting, and they wanted to represent themselves as being above that. They denounced it and yet persisted in taking part. It was like a war being called a peace action. Klein and Rukeyser did not have the authority to declare the season's end on March 22; that required the approval of their president, Don Durgin, who surely knew the purpose of it. Nor could Dann risk CBS millions with his Operation 100 scheme on his own, or order Jack Cowden, who was of equal rank in the company and no friend, to lend his project the immense promotional effort it received. This required Wood's authority and in the end would be his deed.

Only Elton Rule of ABC was unable to resist being honest in his interview with Gould. In mildly deploring the industry's preoccupation with ratings, he inserted a plug for the gains his network was making in the numbers toward closing the gap between the two leaders.

The industry and most of the press accepted April 19 as the termination date, and Dann's Operation 100 succeeded in its objective, although it turned out that conservative Eliasberg was a bit liberal in his projections. CBS won not by three-tenths of a rating point but only by two-tenths, and then by ruling out the two premiere weeks, on the basis that they were not typical competitive weeks. As it happened, NBC had won both those weeks. Given the ratings' margin for error, the two-tenths of a point lead was at best only theoretical and really equal to a tie, but it is the TV industry's way to ignore the Nielsen error disclaimer and take the rating numbers at face value.

NBC continued to insist that it won the season and could substantiate the claim by averaging the ratings as of its own September 14 premiere, when the other two networks were not competitive. Klein continued to harass Dann through the mails, while Rukeyser and his key operatives Gene Walsh and Josh Kane aggressively pushed the story that the CBS arithmetic was faulty and its claim to victory unfounded.

And then Dann did an astonishing thing. He telephoned the corporate president of NBC, Julian Goodman, to complain of his treatment by the NBC network staff. In effect, he was asking Goodman to instruct his subordinates to concede the loss and to show the proper appreciation of the CBS achievement. Goodman was enraged.

I am told that in the wine country of California, the vintners all strive for an extraordinary grape, and when one of them produces the triumphant fruit the others recognize it and celebrate his artistry and good fortune. Dann asked nothing less from Goodman. In his philosophy, a winner is a celebrity among his rivals, deserving to be honored for his artistry. The sadness was that Dann was the only one left who thought that way.

Whether Dann actually won or not, his hundred-day drive for the numbers was an incredible piece of work, even though its worth—considering the millions of dollars it entailed—was open to question. Beyond enabling him to preserve his and CBS's reputation as winners, was there any real benefit to the network in the stretch run to overtake NBC? In fact, there was. Advertisers do not so much buy the present or future network as the past one. When they make their purchases for the coming fall, they base them on the network's rating performance the previous year. Whether they invest heavily in the CBS movies for 1970–71 will depend on the season's averages for the movies in the 1969–70 term. For one instance of its value, Dann's maneuvers brought those ratings up to a more attractive level.

Some advertisers relish the prestige of being associated with the leading network, others bank on the security of it. If an advertising agency should disappoint its client, it can argue that it did the least reckless thing, buying the network that had the greatest popularity and circulation. In days before demographics became a factor in what an advertiser paid for network time, each 0.1 in the average ratings for the season was considered to be worth $1.8 million in additional billings. So Dann's Operation 100 was not only good for the network morale but also, presumably, for its sales.

Further, it would be good for the affiliated stations' business. During February and March, Nielsen and ARB both make *sweeps* of the 112 local markets (*i.e.*, cities and surrounding areas) in which all three networks have affiliated stations, and it is on the basis of those sweep ratings that national advertisers who buy local schedules of commercials determine what stations they will use and what would be the fair amount to pay. Again, they use past performance as the indicator. The two rating companies also make sweeps in October and November. During the fall, the NBC-affiliated stations tended to dominate their local markets during prime time, but during the spring the CBS stations overtook them. That was clearly the result of Dann's mad run for the numbers.

Operation 100 made money for the local stations, and because of it CBS continued to have the confidence of its member stations with regard to its programing—all very important, to be sure, but probably not precisely what had motivated Dann. The flamboyance of his rating push and the controversy it generated actually embarrassed his superiors, particularly Bob Wood, who did not enjoy seeing the business turned into a circus in public. His embarrassment, however, did not prevent him from going before the CBS affiliates in May to boast of the network's rating supremacy in prime time, and also daytime, Saturday mornings, and the early evening news competition.

On the sidelines, I could only admire Dann's courage, imagination, and drive without really caring about what he was trying to achieve. At the same time, it did seem to me that his victory was, paradoxically, a victory for NBC. All of Paul Klein's theories about specials and "event" programs worked for Dann, but not the old CBS theories that Mike himself espoused. CBS envisioned the viewer as a creature of habit who did not want his weekly routines disrupted, NBC as one who was always in search of something new to examine.

Operation 100 was testimony to Dann's shrewdness and to the soundness of NBC's philosophy.

On the occasion of the final rating book, Dann phoned, his voice almost soprano with ecstasy.

"This is the happiest day of my life," he said.

He had told me that on other occasions. I wondered whether I would ever hear it again.

5

Fail-Safe

"Len, you caused such excitement over here today . . . I knew you'd want to hear it. Did I tell you it was going to go over? You rocked them . . . I was so proud of you . . . They raved about it, they knew we really had something . . . It was such fine work, such fine—the whole concept of the—the casting, the way you cut the film—you should really be proud. I—let me tell you—I was happy for you, for both of us . . . It looks good, Len—there's a good chance . . . I can't say how good, but it looks good . . . Don't worry . . . I'll get back to you when we know something."

The speaker was Mike Dann, the telephone conversation at the New York end practically verbatim. I took it down as fast as I could, just for flavor. At the other end was Hollywood producer Leonard Freeman. The date was February 6.

That same day I ran into Bob Wood in the corridors of CBS. Regarding the same show, with almost uncontrolled excitement, he let fly one of his famous malapropisms: "Just screened one of our new pilots. Boy, have we got something" —gesturing for emphasis—"a real potboiler!" He went on about how the show was relevant to the social upheaval in America, how this was the kind of show that was representative of the new direction he wanted the network to take, how the program was dramatically powerful. Summarizing his view, it was a blockbuster.

Now a quiz. Does the show make the schedule or doesn't it?

In the movies, never. Merle Miller devoted a book, *Only You, Dick Daring*, to chronicling how a program concept everyone at the network loved and gushed over came to nothing. I might be writing an acid account of the insincerity of network muckamucks, but this time the show made it.

It was in fact the odds-on favorite among the new pilot prospects for CBS, what the professionals call the right show at the right time, for all the reasons Wood expressed, and more. The show was *Storefront Lawyers*, produced not by a major studio but by Freeman, an independent, who was also responsible for an adventure series that was a hit on the network, *Hawaii Five-O*. In the television business, the producer of a hit has magic in him. Aside from that, Freeman was clearly proficient at producing action melodrama, giving it somewhat the production quality of a movie, much desired by the networks. *Storefront Lawyers* was to be an urban show for a network bent on urbanizing, a youth show for a network anxious to increase its youth audience, a program about contemporary life for a network troubled by its reputation for favoring escapism.

Moreover, having paid for the production of the pilot, CBS in return would become a partner in the ownership of the property and would have the foreign and domestic distribution rights. And the film would be shot at CBS Cinema Center, the old Republic Studios lot which CBS bought in 1966. But while all that was certainly in its favor, CBS would not have accepted the series unless the officials who made the program decisions genuinely liked it.

There was one other important recommendation for Freeman's series: the idea for it was not novel. It did not have the taint of originality, the riskiness of something untried. There was precedent on the networks for a series about young idealists working *outside* the established social framework but *for* the law-and-order orthodoxy. That was *Mod Squad*, a successful ABC series about hip-generation plainclothes cops, with typical integrated casting in the leads, two white (male and female) and one black. It would be going into its third year on ABC but it was only a freshman when CBS took note of its virtues and began the development of *Storefront Lawyers*.

Not surprisingly, there were to be six *Mod Squad*s in the new season, the original and five imitations: *The Young Lawyers, Matt Lincoln* (originally titled *Dial: Hotline*), and *The Young Rebels* on ABC, and *The Interns* and *Storefront Lawyers* on CBS. Not only would the thematic components and character relationships be similar, all six would be scheduled to open the evenings for their networks, *Young Rebels* at 7:00 P.M. because prime time starts half an hour earlier on Sundays, the others at 7:30 week nights. The evening's lead-off hour had become difficult to program effectively, in the sense of delivering an audience that was not too old or too young for Madison Avenue's aims. *Mod Squad* had demonstrated one avenue to good ratings and desirable demographics in that time period, a chief reason for the rash of imitations.

The Young Lawyers and *The Interns* were the predictable variations on the *Mod Squad* premise, courtroom and medical melodramas having had a long history of appeal in television. *The Young Rebels* (originally titled *Yankee Doodle*) was a more adventurous version concerning a mod-like group of guerrillas working behind the British lines during the Revolutionary War, with some obvious parallels to modern times. The basic departure of *Matt Lincoln* was that it developed its stories around psychiatric social workers dealing with disturbed persons, and *Storefront Lawyers* held close to the prototype as the story of three young law graduates with a large established firm, who spend part of their time representing clients unable to afford legal counsel.

Whatever might happen with *Storefront Lawyers* after it faced the rating test in September, the CBS program committee would not have to answer for selecting the show. They had done it right. The series had a model that was popular, a time period that was proven, and a producer who had the winning touch, at least with his other show. Everything added up favorably; it was the perfect new entry. If Wood and Dann failed with it, they would fail safely.

"We've got only one chance to get on in September," Ed Bleier said. "Otherwise, Warners is out of it until 1971–72."

Bleier, sales vice-president for Warner Brothers TV, was breakfasting at the Trattoria with Paul Roth, head of media for Kenyon and Eckhardt Advertising. They were among the Magi attending the three miraculous births at the networks.

Warner Brothers had been out of the business of producing series for television for several years, having suffered sizable financial losses in speculating for the medium after an initial success, but under the new Ted Ashley administration following the studio's acquisition by Kinney National Service it was re-entering the field—too late, however, to have developed any projects for the 1970–71 season. The schedules were being drawn up, and Warners had no pilots under consideration. But there was a chance that it might stir network interest in a revival of one of its old shows.

"What would you think," Bleier said, "of *Maverick* in its old Sunday time period on ABC?"

"Not bad," Roth answered.

"I mean a new version, of course, and here's the thing, we have Paul Monash to produce it. He did *Butch Cassidy and the Sundance Kid*. Brilliant job, if you haven't seen it. If you have, then you know."

Until the *Butch Cassidy* film, Monash was primarily known in television circles as producer of the prime-time serial *Peyton Place*.

"How does it sit with the network?" Roth asked.

"They've got two pilots for the hour, and one is supposed to be a little like *Maverick*. They're high on both of them, but I think we're still in the running."

"I think the *Maverick* idea sounds good. I'd buy it."

"Do me a favor, Paul. Tell that to Starger," Bleier said. "If he felt there was advertiser interest it might sway him."

Whether or not Paul Roth carried out the favor, Marty Starger was not to be swayed. Although all the networks were eager for Warners to become a program supplier again, there would be no charity. The argument against *Maverick* was that it was one of ABC's old successes, and to revive it would not only seem to betray a bankruptcy of new ideas but would look like a step backward for a network that wanted to convey a progressive impression.

As for advertiser support, unless it involves a large order, it counts for little. In this case, when an agency customer like Roth said he would buy the show, he meant he would buy not a whole or partial sponsorship but rather one minute of commercial time in it each week. It would be one of several shows over which he would scatter his clients' commercials. Like most agency media men, Roth bought participation campaigns—sometimes called scatter plans—with the networks, those being flights of one-minute and thirty-second commercials within several different shows in order to spread the risk and to reach a broader cumulative audience.

Maverick did not get on. Warner Brothers was out of it for 1970–71, its only hope for returning to TV production resting with its ability to get a number of program projects into the development mill during March and April. Bleier and his boss, Gerry Leider, might submit as many as forty or fifty concepts for program series, most of which would wash out in the early stages of development, either in the initial presentation, after submission of an outline, or with the first script. The projects which get beyond that stage, to the one at which additional scripts are requested, stand a good chance of graduating to the production of pilots.

That would give Warner Brothers candidates for the 1971–72 season, but even at that there would be no guarantee that it would make a sale.

Jennings Lang of Universal Pictures and Sid Sheinberg of its subsidiary, Universal Television, arrived in New York feeling reasonably sure they had what it took to save *The Virginian*. The ninety-minute Western series had weathered seven seasons on NBC and now was in danger of being jettisoned like *Daniel Boone* for demographics that were hard to sell.

In its prosperous days, before the refinements of audience analysis complicated the simple formula of selling programs on their total circulation, *The Virginian* had been the envy of CBS. Occupying ninety minutes and delivering substantial numbers of viewers, it solved programing needs for nearly half an evening. CBS once tried to spirit it away (NBC had to sign a new contract at an increase in price per episode to keep it) and once had tried, unsuccessfully, to imitate it. A second CBS attempt to create a ninety-minute Western was aborted during the development stage when it became known that NBC was having trouble selling *The Virginian* at rates commensurate with its rating level.

The seasoned Western was on NBC's eviction list in January, but Lang and Sheinberg had come from Hollywood with the makings of a deal that would save it. Mike Dann was agitated. He knew what they would be offering NBC, wanted it for CBS, and had no way of getting it. What they had was Don Knotts.

The comedian had advised his agents that he wanted to star in a one-hour variety series on television. Having left the medium for motion pictures, he was retreating back to the source of his popularity on discovering that the transfer from home entertainment to theatrical was not as natural as it seemed. Knotts's films were tepid at the box office. Mary Tyler Moore and Andy Griffith, both of whom would be back on the networks in the fall, had had similar experiences as movie stars. So had Dick Van Dyke, who signed contracts to return to CBS in the fall of 1971.

To the experts in the business the instant reaction to the idea of Knotts in an hour series was in Nielsen terms: a 34 share at least and probably top ten in the standings.

Under normal circumstances, Knotts would have gone to CBS. He had done all his TV specials on that network and had developed into a name through his featured role in the old *Andy Griffith Show* on CBS. Furthermore, he had grass-roots appeal, and CBS had the appropriate penetration into the rural communities—the C and D counties, as they are called in the marketing field, those of less than 50,000 population.

But, as it happened, Universal Pictures, having had the comedian under firm contract for a number of movies, also had him signed for a proposed television series to be produced by Universal Television. In order to do the variety series, Knotts needed a release from his TV obligation to Universal. This the studio was prepared to grant, but on one condition—that it had the right to select the network for the show. The value to the studio of that right was simply bargaining leverage, sometimes called *muscle*.

CBS was out of the running. Dann had not bought a

show from Universal in several years and had not developed a pilot with that studio for the new season. There was nothing to bargain with.

ABC had *Paris 7000* and *It Takes a Thief* from Universal, both in line for cancellation, and possibly would have renewed the two of them to get the Don Knotts show. But Universal does most of its business with NBC, and so on two counts it began its negotiations there: one to secure the relationship, two to secure *The Virginian.*

The more years a series runs the more it benefits a studio, both in lowering the administrative and production overhead and in raising the value of the repeat episodes when they are offered in syndication.

There was nothing strenuous about the negotiations. NBC renewed the Western with the promise from Sheinberg that the studio would make sweeping changes to revitalize the series in ways that would make it more attractive to younger audiences, and the network agreed also to buy a new hour of Universal programing to replace the canceled *Then Came Bronson.*

The judgment within NBC was that it was stronger for having Knotts, if only because CBS did not have him.

Don Knotts, coming into the picture at the eleventh hour without a pilot, was a blow to the studios with program prospects that had been a year in development. Knotts was the eighth firm and irrevocable precommitment for the 1970–71 season at the three networks. The others were Mary Tyler Moore, Flip Wilson, Andy Griffith, Danny Thomas, *Barefoot in the Park, The Odd Couple,* and the National Football League games. With eight program periods accounted for, that left fifty pilots or program proposals to vie for the remaining fifteen prime-time vacancies that would occur.

And when Red Skelton was signed by NBC for a half-hour series upon his cancellation by CBS, there were fifty candidates for fourteen spots.

But weep not for the series that would be shut out of the schedules. Nothing artful or thoughtful was lost to the world.

Television, contentedly, has supplanted the old neighborhood Bijou as the outlet for Hollywood's mass-produced B pictures. The new harvest of program pilots contained little if anything that would not have been developed for television ten years earlier.

In the hour formats there were five proposed variety shows, nine lawyer or courtroom dramas, six detective or crime shows, four medical melodramas, three Westerns, one science fiction, one international intrigue, one imitation of *Hee Haw,* one variation on *The Fugitive,* and other adventure programs concerned with a circus, an airport, and a globe-hopping archaeological team. The latter two were original at least in an occupational sense.

For the half hours, there were two comedy revues and twenty-one situation comedies, four in the Western idiom, four dealing with family involvements, four with girls working in the city, three with rural folk, two with singing groups, and others with a minister, a school, ill-matched roommates, and runaways to Tahiti. One way or another, all had antecedents on networks and so were safe.

The only unique prime-time series in the new group would be the Monday night football games.

Some that failed to make the schedules would carry over into the program development for the next season, but the majority would be finished as series candidates. The rejects were bound to have their only exhibition as summer timefillers in those dreary warm-weather anthologies for busted pilots which would have "Festival" in the title.

Mort Werner's schedule was the healthiest survivor of the 1969–70 season. With but five holes in it and three commitments already made there would be no problem getting it on the street by the February 20 deadline. Still, the NBC program committee met at least twice a week for four weeks to decide how to put the pieces together.

The pieces are, literally, magnetic plates on which are imprinted the names of all the current and prospective program series bidding for a place on a large metal board depicting the fifty half-hour periods of prime time. The board and magnetized titles are standard equipment at all three networks, a visual aid, like a combat map. With the help of rumor and reliable intelligence, but largely through speculation, the program strategy boards first lay out the likely schedules of their rivals and then proceed with their own most cunning designs. The problem is not just to arrive at a felicitous sequence of variegated entertainment for the television millions; it is to place the shows where they will have the best chance of succeeding against the programs in opposition and, where possible, to wreak damage upon the opponent.

Television is probably the only one of the show biz media that works at killing its own species. Having two or three hits on Broadway helps business at all the theaters; similarly a few important films are a tonic for the whole motion picture industry, and in the world of recordings there is nothing like a couple of thumping song hits to enliven record sales for all popular music. But in the TV system, success almost necessarily comes at the expense of a competitor, in the scramble for the advertiser's dollar.

Debates were few, and most civil, in the NBC strategy sessions. Don Durgin opened them with a tactical plan of his own, but few of his proposals remained in the final design. Typically, each member of the committee—general manager Bob Stone, program vice-president Mort Werner, sales vice-president Jack Otter, Hollywood director of programs Herb Schlosser, and audience research expert Paul Klein—had formulated a schedule plan of his own before entering the meetings, and over the four weeks a consensus would be forged from the six separate visions.

There was sentiment to retain *Dragnet* and *My World and Welcome to It* and to dispose of *Bracken's World*, but not so strong in any case as to bruise anyone's psyche or threaten his prestige when the majority decided otherwise. *Dragnet* would yield to *Nancy*, a new Screen Gems series about the daughter of a United States President who falls in love with a young veterinarian in Iowa. The logic was that NBC was short-suited in programs with distinct appeal to women, especially since the cancellation of Debbie Reynolds and *I Dream of Jeannie*, and needed one among the new shows to maintain a semblance of balance. *Dragnet* was male-appeal surviving in the ratings through its positioning between two high-rated shows, *Ironside* and *Dean Martin*. With the same rating inheritance, *Nancy* would not have to generate numbers entirely on its own and would have time to build. NBC historically had little success with situation comedy compared with the other networks and was determined, as it was every year, to try again at least once.

Parenthetically, although the lead for the comedy series, Renne Jarrett, suggested a Nixon daughter, the idea for the program originated during Lyndon Johnson's term of office and was rejected, after some feelers were put out to the White House, in the belief that the President might take some offense at the rural character of the show or feel the presidential office was being demeaned and exploited by a commercial enterprise. Producer Sidney Sheldon revived the project after Nixon's election when indications were that the new President would not object.

Red Skelton would get the *My World and Welcome to It* spot to bolster the ratings for *Laugh-In*. Moreover, Skelton would be opposite CBS's high-rated *Gunsmoke* and, having attraction to a similar audience, might serve to deflate it in the standings and lessen CBS's strength Monday nights. Skelton vowed to make drastic changes in the format he had presented on the TV networks for nineteen years (seventeen of them with CBS and the previous two with NBC) in the interest of making it more palatable to the young adults who were becoming the key to survival at the networks. At CBS, where at times he played to nearly 30 million viewers a week, 42 per cent of his audience was over fifty years of age and a preponderance of the remainder were juvenile.

As for *Bracken's World*, it stayed in the schedule because

of its basic female appeal and the belief that it would improve with age, and also as a concession to 20th Century-Fox TV, whose four pilots for NBC had all washed out.

The studio agreed to certain alterations in *Bracken's World*, the notable one being to abandon the mystery of the title character and make him visible. In the first year's episodes, Bracken, as head of a fictive Hollywood motion picture studio, was never seen, a story device inspired by the legendary reclusion of Howard Hughes. As testing indicated, the gimmick netted nothing in ratings. Leslie Nielsen, a perennial TV series lead, won the role. He would be leaving *The Bold Ones*, NBC's Sunday night dramatic trilogy, and his skein of the three alternating melodramas would be replaced by one in which Hal Holbrook portrayed a young activist Senator, a role he essayed in a Universal *World Premiere* film titled *A Clear and Present Danger*.

One other series would be remodeled for the new season, so extensively in fact that it seemed pointless to keep the old title. *The Virginian* would become *The Men From Shiloh*. In revising the program, again with a particular eye to the young audience, Universal patterned it after its own *Name of the Game* and *Bold Ones* as three alternating Westerns unified by several new motifs, one of which was the role of a wealthy ranch owner, played by Stewart Granger, who would take part in all three rotating stories.

NBC was left then with three hours open in the line-up and two other commitments, to Don Knotts and Flip Wilson. Knotts was assigned 7:30 on Tuesdays and Wilson the same hour on Thursdays, interesting strategy, since variety shows were a rarity so early in the evening. But it was fairly certain, from what was known of their development projects, that the other two networks would open the evenings with either situation comedies or the *Mod Squad* adventure imitations, so NBC would be counterprograming with a third program form.

Knotts would compete with *Mod Squad* and lead in to *Julia*, Wilson would go against *Family Affair* and half *The*

Jim Nabors Hour on CBS. The rationale in both cases was that the new variety programs appealed to totally different audience elements than the established programs in opposition, which in a way insured their safety. But it might have been more logical for Flip Wilson to be scheduled Tuesdays and Don Knotts Thursdays, where they would be competitive for essentially the same viewers as the opposition programs and force a showdown for rating superiority. The trouble with that strategy was that Wilson would then have preceded *Julia* in the line-up, for a ninety-minute parlay of shows with black leads, and that would have suggested segregation, there being only one other black-centered show on the network, *Bill Cosby*, on Sunday nights. Too long guilty of racial omissions, the networks had become painfully conscious of delicate feelings on the other side of the tube. The grouping of Flip Wilson and Diahann Carroll might have prompted charges of racism. Occasionally in programing there are considerations other than rating expediency.

One hour remained open on NBC, Wednesday nights at ten o'clock, for which six or seven drama pilots were in contention and each with the endorsement of one or more members of Durgin's program council. Partly from the riches of NBC's action-adventure development and partly from the Paul Klein philosophy that television must create its own events to stimulate the growth of audience and to keep the mature audience engaged in the medium, the concept for *Four in One* evolved.

Universal would provide four different series, each playing a limited engagement of six consecutive weeks. This would test Klein's theory that the introduction of a new show is a major event in television, and to introduce shows four times in a season would be preferable to just once. Meanwhile, as the ratings might dictate, any of the four could be resumed the following season as a standard endlessly running series.

Durgin and his lieutenants agreed to the format because it kept alive four pilots they had faith in, *San Francisco*

International, a series on airport adventure; *McCloud,* about
a contemporary Western lawman assigned to the police force
of a large Eastern city; *The Psychiatrist,* which describes
itself; and *Night Gallery,* a new Rod Serling omnibus of the
occult. All four had piloted as pseudo-movies.

NBC's schedule would be different from its rivals' in at
least two ways. While the others continued in the conventional framework of fixed program series on a steady weekly
course, it would have four periods a week in which several
series shared a time period or rotated in it. The other difference was at 7:30, the opening of the evening, and perhaps the
most difficult period to program. With Wilson, Knotts, and
Skelton, and Andy Williams on Saturday nights, NBC's answer to the 7:30 problem was the variety show, which three
or four years earlier had been the answer to the ten o'clock
problem. If it worked, there would not fail to be a proliferation of musical or comedy variety programs to start the evening on all three networks in September 1971.

The turbulence was at CBS. Wood versus Dann, with
Wood having all the allies in the executive circle.

As a veteran strategist outranked by a novice, Dann argued for the preservation of the CBS star system at all cost,
because it was vital to being first. Longer on the firing line
than Wood, he had been raised on the three commandments
of the network: (1) Be first, (2) Look first-class, (3) Seek
prestige.

You look first-class by maintaining a high standard for
the visuals and by spending whatever is necessary for appearances, economizing in less conspicuous areas than on the
screen; you get prestige easily enough, by tranquilizing the
profit motive periodically to buy Vladimir Horowitz for a
recital, Hal Holbrook for *Mark Twain Tonight,* Lee J. Cobb
and Mildred Dunnock for *Death of a Salesman,* or Sol Hurok
for an annual classical music special; but you run first in
the numbers by strict devotion to a set of rules, namely:

Cancel as few shows as possible, because the average

returning series will do better in the ratings than the average new series;

Build and nurture a roster of stars, because they will keep a loyal audience and deliver dependable numbers;

Play the sure thing and resist the long shot, remembering that two of every three new shows will fail and that new ideas most of the time will be rejected by the viewer.

Strict adherence to the rules had kept CBS pre-eminent in the ratings during the fifties and sixties, but the times and business criteria were changing.

It is the younger people, for the most part, who will look for the new things in television and the older who will not; thus had demography made two of the rules obsolete.

Like Gleason and Skelton, shows such as *Lucy, Beverly Hillbillies, Green Acres, Hogan's Heroes, Ed Sullivan,* and *Petticoat Junction* were all becoming so expensive, with their annual 8 per cent increases in costs, that, except as lossleaders, they were no longer good business despite the mass numbers they generated. Believing that CBS was courting an economic crisis, Wood pressed his advocacy of rebuilding the network with shows more inviting to youth.

While he agreed in principle that the network ought to urbanize and find a younger audience, Dann was distressed over the decision to cancel two of the network's mainstays, particularly Red Skelton, who was the keystone in the Tuesday night line-up. Letting Skelton go could wreck the night for CBS, and Dann knew that rebuilding an evening to competitive superiority could take years.

Wood prevailed, of course, and the big metal board sat with a vacancy at 8:30 Tuesdays where Skelton used to be, taking and rejecting suggestions. Since it was pivotal for the whole evening, it was not a spot for a new show. Too chancy. One thought was to move Glen Campbell into the period and replace his show on Sunday nights with *Hee Haw.* But Campbell had just been moved in January, and it is dangerous to move a show too often (*The Man From U.N.C.L.E.* was the classic case in point); eventually the audience deserts it.

Besides, Campbell was succeeding in neutralizing NBC's *Bonanza* on Sundays, which was an important function in itself. Were *Hee Haw* to fail in that assignment under the proposed shift all of Sunday could collapse for CBS in its attempt to shore up Tuesday, and Sunday is the costliest night to lose. So the plan was abandoned.

Then, during a final screening for Paley of the pilot *Crisis Clinic*, to establish whether he agreed with the decision to reject it for the schedule, Wood rose from his seat, crept under the projector's beam and moved some pieces on the program board. When the lights went on, *Hee Haw* was in the Skelton spot. Maybe it is hard to believe that such a simple and almost absurd act had a lot of meaning, but the fact is it did. It was, under the circumstances, probably the best of the possible tactical moves. Fine. But it does not take a network president to figure that one out. Wood, however, was the president without programing credentials, and this was his first triumph of scheduling. To his superiors it bespoke intuition.

Outside the network, the real surprise in the CBS schedule was the retention of Tim Conway in a new variety show installed at ten o'clock on Sundays, displacing *Mission: Impossible*, which was moved to Gleason's time on Saturdays. Conway's half-hour comedy series was a mid-season flop, and his recent variety special for the network had also done poorly in the ratings. Although the man was undeniably talented, those were strong hints that the mass audience was not interested. With such a poor track record, the advertisers were sure to resist—and they did.

Why was Conway retained? Asked separately, members of the program council stated there was confidence he would catch on. Conway was good at sketch comedy, and there was some feeling that he might appeal to the young. But one member of the committee confided that the Conway show went in because there was simply nothing else. The program development for 1970–71 did not anticipate the change in philosophy. Wood's wish for a new urbanized and youth-oriented network was to a degree frustrated by a lack of parts to assemble for it.

In some ways, that lack was just as well. CBS would not do too many radical things at once. Ridding itself of three old dray horses and making a start at building a new stable was enough for one season.

For Mike Dann it was too much.

"We can't win," he groaned. "We threw it away. We knock off Gleason and Skelton, 70 share points between them, and keep *Hee Haw* and Tim Conway—55 shares if they're lucky, and the same quality of audience that supposedly no one wants to buy. Meanwhile, Tuesday night is in the shithouse, and maybe Sunday, too. Where is that good business?"

Rushing into the market place with a program schedule by the last week in February is a network custom that has its reason in the eagerness of the medium's largest advertisers to lay out their fall-winter campaigns early and to secure the choicest time periods and shows for their peculiar commercial purposes. Automobile companies, for instance, have found Sunday night, with its family-together audience characteristics, the opportune time for television advertising; and products for women are usually best sold by TV on Mondays or after 8:30 when the wife/mother is free to give her time to the Bijou in the living room. An advertiser who waits too long to buy could lose the advantageous positions to a competitor.

The early-to-market network schedule not only has first access to the money but has a positive psychological effect on the advertisers, suggesting an orderliness and stability on the part of the broadcast organization—even a clarity of vision.

Elton Rule would forgo those benefits with his schedule and withhold the final draft until the rival webs had published theirs. That would give him and his program planners the opportunity to counterprogram, to place programs against

CBS and NBC where they would present an alternative choice to the viewer: for example, a musical where two dramatic shows were in opposition.

For ABC, there was far too much at stake, too much progress to achieve, to leap into the market with a hasty schedule. Better to risk losing some business in the first advertising splurge than to suffer through another season as the weak competitor. Johnny Cash and the January maneuvers had helped to narrow the audience deficit to 3.6 million viewers per average minute, and Rule would have to make the quantum leap in September to close the gap which made ABC the only network operating at a loss in prime time.

There was, for once, a supply of programing to build a schedule upon, at least one proven success to anchor every evening except Monday, and that night would be built around ABC's huge gamble on professional football. In addition, there were commitments for three series that seemed highly promising, video adaptations of two smash stage comedies by Neil Simon, *The Odd Couple* and *Barefoot in the Park*, the latter with a predominantly black cast, and the revival of Danny Thomas' old series, *Make Room for Daddy*, with the new title *Make Room for Granddaddy*. It was purchased as a series after it had played as a special on CBS in January and topped Johnny Cash's rating.

Marty Starger's program development unit had come through with several other series prospects which had tested favorably. Having the materials, then, Rule, Starger, sales vice-president Jim Duffy, general manager Marty Pompadur, vice-president of planning Fred Pierce, and vice-president of research Marvin Antonowsky closeted themselves in strategy sessions on the counterprograming of CBS and NBC.

An evening of television is not a chance arrangement of programs one after another. The planning must take into account the peculiar audience characteristics of each night of the week and of each half hour on the clock. It cannot be assumed that all people are available at all times of the evening and on all nights of the week. Furthermore, a successful network evening has cohesiveness as a system of companionable shows whose audiences tend to blend into one another. When programs are juxtaposed that have appeal to the same audience elements, they are said to have *audience flow.*

ABC's Tuesday night was one of the "perfect" evenings: *Mod Squad, Movie of the Week, Marcus Welby, M.D.,* all compatible and each feeding audience to the program behind it. Another was the CBS Monday night schedule: *Gunsmoke, Here's Lucy, Mayberry R.F.D., Doris Day,* and *Carol Burnett.* Evenings schemed so well are rarely tampered with, and the quest for such a chemistry is primary in the planning of any sequence of programs in television.

Any TV viewer will switch channels over the course of an evening, but nearly all prefer not to if one network provides the night-long anesthetic. Two established hit shows placed in sequence do not necessarily make a strong viewing argument if one is slanted to women and the other distinctly to men. Over a period of time the effect will be for both to lose their standing. Thus, when there is a strong show and a lesser one in contention for the schedule, occasionally the lesser will be chosen because, in its inherent appeal, it is more compatible with the adjacent programs on the network.

The unwillingness of public TV stations to block out programs for audience flow is one reason for their being a minor factor in the national television habit. For a time, the New York station, WNET, offered the preschool hit, *Sesame Street,* just after an instructional program on conversational German. Obviously, the two shows did not feed each other. But when the same station programed another children's series, *Misterogers' Neighborhood,* immediately following *Sesame Street,* both were stronger as a result. Children who had never heard of *Misterogers* when it played in isolation in New York the several years before *Sesame* was created became devotees.

ABC's effort at counterprograming its rivals would have

been a simple enough task except for the audience-flow considerations. A program slotted as an alternative to an entrenched CBS and NBC series would have to support and be supported by the contiguous shows. Bearing on the program committee's decisions as well would be the knowledge that certain programs play better on some nights of the week than on others and that not every show could successfully play in any time period.

Sunday, as the family day, naturally has the highest rate of tune-in and the most viewing by all elements of the audience—juveniles, teen-agers, young adults, and older people. It is television's best night for business and very costly to a network that trails in the ratings because the revenue potential is so lush. Viewing levels also tend to be high on Mondays, which perhaps is explained by the American habit of staying home and recharging after the weekend. It is, for some reason, an exceptionally good night for reaching women.

Tuesdays, Wednesdays, and Thursdays are the median nights, slightly lower than Mondays in Homes Using Television—the Nielsen term—but delivering the full spectrum of audience, male and female, young and old, moneyed and poor. The problem night is Friday, because of the sharp decline in the desirable mature viewers and the increase in the number of children and older people before the set during the later hours. It is, of course, a going-out night for young adults and teen-agers, and a baby-sitter night for television. Saturdays are much the same, but with greater sets-in-use.

The juvenile and geriatric audiences have strikingly similar viewing patterns, and they seem to be attracted to the same programs. As the most television-prone members of society, they tend to concentrate their viewing early in the evening, quitting for bed at nine o'clock, except Fridays and Saturdays, when they may stay up later (their sleeping habits are similar, too). Both ends of the age scale are best reached with simple and familiar programs, the game and panel shows, Westerns, situation comedies, animated cartoons, and light variety.

Fridays and Saturdays are difficult nights for experimentation with anything new in programing because the great bimodal nucleus of the TV audience on those nights resists newness. Lawrence Welk had hung in year after year as proof. Fridays and Saturdays almost repeat the 7:30 problem all evening long. The quest is for a rating that is sizable, with enough of the choice viewers in the composition to be marketable.

The clock creates more demographic undulations than the calendar. Prime time is prime because it is the period of the day in which television viewing is greatest, but within those three and a half hours, audience levels rise, peak, and decline, and there are parallel fluctuations by age groupings. Viewing crests between 8:30 and 9:00 P.M. and begins to trail off when Granny and the kids go to bed, but what is left in the middle of the evening is the slice of audience the advertiser most desires.

Illustrating the anatomy of a television evening are these week-long averages from the Nielsen demographic report for October-November 1969:

P.M.	*viewers per average minute*
7:30	75,380,000
8:00	80,380,000
8:30	81,230,000
9:00	75,890,000
9:30	71,840,000
10:00	63,450,000
10:30	57,750,000

Eleven o'clock (which is ten o'clock in the Central and Mountain Zones) is local time, and the viewing drops to nearly 40 million nationally; and by the next half hour, when the networks begin their late-night shows, it falls to about 28 million. However, that much pursued 18–49 age group grows from 36 per cent of the audience at 7:30 to 42 per cent at nine o'clock, and as the evening wears on it reaches close to 50 per cent.

Young children (under twelve) are 25 per cent of the audience at 7:30 but only 9 per cent at 10:30. Accordingly, programs have tended to be "family" entertainment until nine o'clock and somewhat more mature—viz., the movies—the last two hours of the prime-time evening.

It is the teen-agers who are constant, remaining 10-11 per cent of the total audience throughout the evening. Adult female viewing tends to be heavier than male in all prime-time periods; even eleven o'clock, when 34 per cent of the audience is adult male, 45 per cent adult female. That fact, too, affects the programing design.

In general, programs of interest to the very young and very old have the best chance of succeeding at 7:30; those of all-family appeal are best suited for the next hour; and the more sophisticated entertainment is indicated for later in the evening, the later the time slot the more sophisticated the show. Programs designed for women are likely to draw larger audiences than those for men.

Monday night was one of the reasons ABC was the third network. Year after year the network threw millions of dollars' worth of new programing against the sturdy CBS line-up and NBC's strong parlay of *Laugh-In* and a movie. With each ABC failure, the competing networks grew stronger. Desperate to get a secure claim on a healthy share of the Monday night audience, ABC signed a three-year contract with the National Football League for a schedule of thirteen Monday night games. The games would cost more than half a million dollars each, and they would only cover the network's program needs for one-fourth of the year. There was no assurance, however, that football could deliver a prime-time audience as effectively on Monday nights as it did on Sunday afternoons. It would not be easy to make money with the NFL games, but their purpose was to enable ABC to establish itself on Monday nights.

It was a night on which the CBS schedule strongly fa-

vored women and the NBC schedule had no particular definition with the sexes. Football was male, of course, and the
ABC strategy team sought to carry that demographic motif
through the rest of the evening. Mondays would open with a
new show, *The Young Lawyers,* and follow with a first-year
crime series reminiscent of *The Untouchables,* titled *The
Silent Force.* If *Laugh-In* was fading (and there were signs
it might be during the 1969–70 season, which was still in
progress), ABC might score a breakthrough.

Tuesdays would stand unchanged, and Wednesdays
would add the Danny Thomas show at eight o'clock and
Dan August at ten. The latter might not have made the schedule but for a contractual agreement with producer Quinn
Martin, which had been entered into during Tom Moore's
administration at the network as a cost-saving measure in
program development. Martin had produced *The Fugitive,
The FBI* and *12 O'Clock High,* and since he was a hit-maker
Moore felt he could be relied on to supply a new series every
season without putting the network to the expense of producing pilots. Under the contract, Martin was guaranteed
one new series for three successive seasons and in addition
was to provide the network with several movies made for
television.

After Moore's departure, ABC tried to get out of the
contract but could not. Martin was owed two series, one for
1970–71 and one for the season following. *Dan August* was
part of that obligation and was a series spinoff from the detective feature *The House on Green Apple Road,* which had
run as a Sunday night movie.

Pseudo-movies were also the source of two new Thursday night melodramas, *Matt Lincoln* and *The Immortal.
Lincoln* was vaguely in the *Mod Squad* mold and was bringing back to television Vince Edwards, who had once been a
big star in the title role of *Ben Casey.* The program had gone
into the schedule as *Dial: Hotline,* but Edwards wanted the
title to point him up as the central character, and at his in-
sistence it was changed. As for *The Immortal,* it was a new

variation on an old hit, *The Fugitive,* a nutty story about a
man on the lam from greedy people who want his blood because it has unique healing and rejuvenating powers.

There were to be four new ABC shows on Thursday night
pivoting on the redoubtable *Bewitched,* a surprising decision
in light of the odds. The odds against a single new show
establishing itself are high enough, but they multiply tenfold
for getting two off the ground in the same night. And for four,
they are almost incalculable. ABC had tried four new ones
on Monday night the previous season with these results: three
outright failures and one that won a renewal but only after
being moved to another night—and even then it was a marginal performer.

The fact was that the ABC planners had such faith in
The Odd Couple and *Barefoot in the Park,* especially after
the results of testing the pilots before sample audiences,
that they scarcely considered them new shows. And as for
Matt Lincoln and *The Immortal,* they were not so much new
shows as new *old* shows.

Since no network knew yet what to do with Friday in the
demographic era—it being rich in all the "wrong" components of audience—ABC strung together five situation comedies and capped the evening with the hour-long music-vari-
ety show *This Is Tom Jones.* The one new entry was *The
Partridge Family,* which starred Shirley Jones as the leader
of a professional rock group made up of her young children,
a situation inspired by the real-life musical act The Cowsills
(whose own TV pilot had failed the season before). ABC
purposely positioned it against the Andy Griffith show,
Headmaster, figuring the CBS program would attract older
elements of the audience, enabling it to draw off the younger.

Why Tom Jones was salvaged for the schedule was something of a mystery. The program had fallen short of a properly competitive showing all season, attracting on the average
25 per cent of the audience. In development was an hour
variety series with Robert Goulet, which seemed to have good
possibilities for Friday night and which received a strong

vote from several members of the program committee. Starger argued for the retention of Jones on the basis that it was embarrassing to cancel a show whose star had just been named Man of the Year by the Friars Club, the show business fraternity, especially when ABC officials would be seated at the dais for the occasion. In truth, the networks had weathered worse embarrassments, and the receipt of such an honor had nothing whatever to do with the exigencies of business. It was my own suspicion that *This Is Tom Jones* won a renewal because it was a British show. That meant, first, slightly lower program costs and, second, necessary trips to England, both for network executives and advertisers. Ten years before, virtually all the filmed TV shows moved from New York to Hollywood because agency men enjoyed making periodic trips to Southern California.

With an hour melodrama titled *The Most Deadly Game* installed on Saturday nights after Lawrence Welk, and *The Young Rebels* positioned on Sundays ahead of *The FBI*, Elton Rule had a new schedule.

Sixth Avenue experiences a beautiful metamorphosis after seven o'clock. The working force having disappeared, Sixth Avenue turns into a boulevard, with most of the automobile activity centering on the hotels, and the pedestrian traffic made up of evening celebrants bound for the elite restaurants and bars that line the midtown cross streets. All commerce by day, the avenue is romantic at night, and it must have seemed particularly so on February 20 to a man in a large office of an otherwise emptied Black Rock, who had a long night ahead of him.

Bob Wood sat at his desk studying a short note while he waited for the buzz that would indicate another call put through to Hollywood. The note, which had been slipped under his door, read: "Command is a lonely vigil. Jack."

It was from Schneider, and it pleased Wood greatly.

Schneider and Wood had come up through the station ranks and attended many a sales meeting together over the years. They had made it to the top tiers of the company, and it was reassuring to Wood in the lowlier job that Jack, who would someday probably have Paley's or Stanton's title, knew the nature of his ordeal and had thought of him that night. As much as anything, the note was an acknowledgment of an old bond.

Down the hall on the thirty-fourth floor, Jack Cowden and Charles Steinberg were standing by in case needed, especially if there were any calls from the press on the new schedule. Wood's two secretaries were trading a Friday night for overtime pay, putting through the calls to the West Coast. Otherwise, there was just the clean-up brigade in the CBS Building.

Cowden, who as vice-president of information services under four previous presidents was doubling without portfolio as an adviser and adjutant to Wood, had drawn up an agenda for him on the requisite courtesies in announcing the new schedule. The first item:

"Tell the losers: *Lancer, Get Smart, Tim Conway Show* [the half hour], *Petticoat Junction, Red Skelton,* and *Jackie Gleason.*"

These would be the hardest calls to make, but it goes with the presidency to be the one to inform the producer and/or star personally that his program has, with regret, been canceled.

The second was to notify by telephone those whose programs had been shifted to new time periods; the third, to congratulate the newcomers to the schedule and to inform them where their programs had been slotted; and the fourth, to call all those whose shows were being continued as before.

Fifth was to wire a copy of the press release announcing the new schedule to all affiliated stations; and sixth, to make personal calls to certain key members of the press who cover television. Finally, as Cowden's memo advised, "Fly to the Coast and return with producers of the new programs plus three or four West Coast news people for a press conference in New York at 21."

Wood's phone buzzed, and Don Fedderson was on the line. Three shows on the priority list would be handled at once, *My Three Sons, Family Affair,* and *To Rome With Love,* all renewed, but the last, as Fedderson already knew, had barely made the new line-up and probably would not have made it but for the producer's fine record with "heart" comedies. He had a piece of news for Wood: Walter Brennan, an established television name, had agreed to join the regular cast of the ailing show. True, this represented a step back from the network's new pursuits to a courtship of the older viewer in the smaller towns, but on the other hand Brennan was rating insurance for a series that needed help. The catch was that Brennan would commit himself for only one year.

"Don't let him do that to us, Don," Wood said. "His agents will have us over a barrel the second year and they'll kill us, because if we've got a hot show he'll be one of the reasons why. Get the standard deal, or tell him to forget it."

Hanging up, he buzzed Barbara to put through the next call.

He picked up Schneider's note again. Jack had been through this two or three times himself when he was president, and he knew how long a night it was. It was thoughtful of him to drop off the message. Command, ah, command, *was* lonely.

6

The Million-Dollar Muse

After all the standard requirements, there is a special ingredient that goes into the mix when programs are selected for television. It is fear.

On one level it is personal, the fear of failure, of making an unfortunate decision that would affect upward mobility in the company or, given a real clinker, job security. Knowing the penalties, few in the high-salary brackets (with their personal fortunes tied up in stock options) dared to run outsize or unfamiliar risks with the millions that were involved in the programing function.

One executive in a position of command received every new idea with the statement, "Let's examine it awhile and see what horrors it contains."

A vice-president of one of the networks confided to me, "We don't pick the shows we think will have the best chance of becoming popular. To be honest, we're attracted to those that seem to have the least chance of failing."

On another level, the fear is corporate. In the business world it is called discretion. Since television is a highly conspicuous business, and always under the watch of politicians, it does not benefit a broadcast company to look for controversy. Though it may be unavoidable in news coverage sometimes, all the more reason to avoid it in the entertainment sphere. Companies that at any moment may be caught in a swirl of public fury leading to government sanctions lose their attractiveness on Wall Street. In matters of programing, therefore, blandness is prescribed.

Since the business mission of broadcasting is to attract audiences and keep them happily tranquil, and since the viewership has demonstrated that it will abide mindless entertainment night after night, there is simply nothing of practical value to be gained from indulgences in programs that might be provocative or true to life.

A good program engaged the viewer but did not excite him.

A good program executive always played it safe.

Every year one or another network president, in a public forum, makes the clarion call for originality and promises to lead a new wave of creativity in the medium. It never materializes. Never, because it cannot.

A television agent testifies that every original idea sooner or later is reduced to a comfortably predictable, hackneyed format as it becomes amended by the network program staffs, and progresses to the front offices.

"Even if you start with prime beef it still comes out sausage," he says. "We had a proposal for a free-form variety series—but as different from *Laugh-In* as the *Lucy* show—and took it to one of the networks. The whole point of it was the kaleidoscopic form. It was to be nobody's vehicle. And when I took it to the network, the guy sat there smugly and said, 'Who's gonna be the host?' You bring something to them, and they start with the plastic surgery, and what you wind up with is something very reminiscent of one or two shows that have been seen before. Everything on television becomes a composition of stale ideas that once worked."

Christopher Knopf, a veteran television script writer and a past president of the Writers' Guild, expressed his own bitterness and that of some of his colleagues in an interview with Dave Kaufman in Hollywood, published in *Daily Variety* on January 20, 1970: "In documentaries and in news, certain truths can be told, but you can't tell them in commercial drama. You can't take up real problems seriously. . . . The main problem of TV writers as I see it is that they are very anxious to have meaning for their lives, and they are not finding it through their writing, which I think is tragic.

"We're being blunted in TV. Our enthusiasm, our sense of experimentation, of making a terrible mistake one week and working it out the next. Our whole process of growth has been blunted. In TV, the whole committee approach has done more to injure the individual writer than anything else, because he has come to accept it as a way of life.

"We're feeding middle America all the pap we know as lies and nonsense; we are feeding things we personally resent, which have no resemblance to real life."

Knopf stated that the salvation of the writer was in being rescued from television by motion picture assignments. One who had been "rescued" in that fashion, Tom Gries, told of making the change not for money but for a sense of achievement, for the relief from the "punishment" of meaningless work. In a speech to the Phoenix, Arizona, chapter of the National Academy of Television Arts and Sciences on September 23, the former television writer who became a director and writer of theatrical films stated: "Movies are the relevant medium. They speak to the people. For a lot of us, the gut satisfaction has gone out of TV, and that's why writers and directors who are given a chance to say their piece in motion pictures just don't want to go back. Why? Turn on any dramatic show tonight in any series—and I promise you that from the first three minutes' viewing you'll know all the character relationships, all the plot convolutions to come, and about half the lines of dialogue. And whatever the conflicts, there will be no catharsis, no dramatic release, because network fears and government pressures have smeared the tube with chicken fat."

Television tamed some writers by inventing a new creature, the producer-writer, who was both author of the product and the executive concerned with its business values. With his stature elevated and his ability to earn money vastly increased, he came to conform to the ways of the system and became enveloped by the fear syndrome.

One who deplored the system's conversion of writer into businessman, in the early stages of the trend in 1959, was Hollywood writer Stirling Silliphant. In the *Variety* anniversary edition that year, he wrote, "How a man can willingly surrender his freedom baffles and torments me. For the act of writing, even writing for television, is a rare and delightful witchery few are privileged to practice. A creative thought is something a majority of human beings never experience through long gray lifetimes.

"Thus, to permit insight to be curtailed, sensitivity to be blunted by deliberately plunging into the miasma of memos and meetings, office politics and disputatious executives, to scan the rating cards with mounting overconcern, to blow hot and cold with daily hearsay and gossip, to feel morning fear and cocktail-time bravado with all the other frightened people, to trade surface dialogue with weather-vane agents, to be torn and confused by hundreds of points of view, all prejudiced and self-serving, to suffer through the endless monotony of preparing a film for telecast, with hours wasted in projection rooms and over hot movieolas—*why?*"

Probably because a hit television show—with its over-seas sale, its off-network residuals, and the products licensed from it—is worth a fortune. Silliphant later was to join the ranks of the hyphenates.

A proposed comedy series which failed to make the CBS schedule but one that intrigued Bob Wood for its aptness to the times was *Man in the Middle,* produced by the inde-pendent producer-writer team of Harvey Bullock and Ray Allen. The comedy was built around the bewildered neutral-ity of a middle-class citizen, portrayed by Van Johnson, caught in a crossfire of the political and social extremism of the persons closest to him. His mother-in-law was of the Minute Man mentality and his daughter inclined to New Left radicalism; his wife was rigidly *petit bourgeois* and his business partner leaned to the hippie values.

Wood liked it because it dealt humorously with the real divisions in American society. He felt that if people could laugh at their own hardened attitudes, it might serve to ease some of the ideological stress in the country. There were some casting flaws in the pilot, however, and some uncer-tainty in the CBS program council about the treatment of the theme. In addition, there was debate over whether the dia-logue adhered to the network standards for continuity ac-ceptance. Although rejected for this schedule, *Man in the Middle* was put back into development for possible mid-season replacement service in January 1971.

Conceptually the Bullock and Allen project owed a debt to a famous British series, *Till Death Us Do Part*, which first went on BBC-TV July 22, 1965, as a one-shot in a comedy

anthology series. The following year it became a series unto
itself. It was instantly controversial, and its frank language
and blasphemies produced an explosive public reaction, but
it was one of the highest-rated television shows in the United
Kingdom, and despite the furor it continually created in
Parliament and with the citizenry it ran for three years. This
was a program about a middle-aged bigot, Alf Garnett, living
in the same household with a son-in-law who was an assertive
liberal.

What caused the commotion was not their philosophies but
the realistic language ("kike," "coon," etc.), the father-in-
law rarely resorting to the polite forms of hate. Because of
the ratings it intrigued network people on this side of the
Atlantic, and because it was the kind of material they rel-
ished, the TV and motion picture writing-directing-producing
team of Bud Yorkin and Norman Lear bought the rights for
the development of an American version. Lear, as writer and
director, would give it an entirely new story line but above
all other elements would preserve the central bigoted character.

For three years and through two separate pilots it incu-
bated at ABC, and with the February schedule-making that
network finally gave up on it. Officially it was discarded
for testing poorly.

Creative Management Associates, agents for Yorkin and
Lear, took the pilot to CBS in March and found the network
receptive to it. CBS put it through careful testing in its own
theater-laboratory at Black Rock, a room in which members
of the public responding to tickets randomly handed out on
Sixth Avenue screen-test programs from plush theater seats,
pressing buttons situated under the armrests to indicate
pleasure or displeasure at whatever times they may experience either. After this screening, they are asked to fill out
forms seeking demographic data and answers to simple
questions pertinent to their evaluation of the show.

Curiously the pilot tested extremely well for CBS. Possibly this was because CBS tested its shows in New York and

ABC its shows in Hollywood, but more likely the time interval between one network's tests and the other's accounted for the discrepancy. Public consciousness of the ideological polarity in the country increased between the fall of 1969 and the spring of 1970, as it had with the sensitivities between the races, the classes, the generations, and the sexes. ABC tested the pilot when there was still some disbelief in the national rift; CBS when the national anxiety over it had become serious.

Wood decided to buy the show to highlight the second stage in his drive for relevancy. In all probability, it would start in January. And since there would be no need for two shows of the same kind, *Man in the Middle* was dropped from development.

In the spring, all in a rush, a number of motion picture stars became available for television series. The changing market for movies had created a new generation of box-office names for the film houses—Dustin Hoffman, Jon Voigt, Robert Redford, Jack Nicholson—and the older stars were no longer in perpetual demand by the studios. Their following still existed, but it was not going to the movies as often as before.

Dick Van Dyke had signed to return to CBS for a weekly series in September of 1971, and Henry Fonda agreed to star in a situation comedy that would tool up for ABC as early as January 1971. When ABC committed itself to a series from Lew Grade's ATV in England on the strength of the co-stars, Tony Curtis and Roger Moore, the networks became caught up in a panic to sign names. Within a few weeks ABC had also signed Shirley MacLaine for a series, NBC James Garner and James Stewart, and CBS Glenn Ford.

But as suddenly as it started, the spree ended. What were the networks buying? Marquee names without program formats, a short cut to program development whose precedents in television were most unencouraging. Debbie Reynolds had not fulfilled the promise of star power at NBC, nor had Jerry

Lewis, and the rating history for Doris Day at CBS was spotty, a slow start that picked up only after her series was transferred to Monday night, where it inherited ratings from some of the network's strongest shows. In their feverish contracting of stars, the networks were also committing themselves to great sums of money, and so were escalating program costs at a time when they were desperately trying to reduce them.

But the most sobering thought of all was that the networks had veered from their intended course. The new mission of television was to recapture the young audience desired by Madison Avenue, and to achieve that they should have been trying to sign Dustin Hoffman, Jon Voigt, Robert Redford, and Jack Nicholson.

Program development is distantly related to what large industries call research and development, the continuing investment of money and manpower in exploration of new products for the future.

Between March and May, production companies and program packagers present hundreds of proposals in prospectus form for new program series. After they are sifted through, perhaps fifty of them at each network will be selected for what is called a *step deal*. The projects are brought along in steps, or stages, to the point at which commitments are made for the production of pilots. By then the field will have narrowed to fifteen, or fewer, at each network.

A story outline, the first stage, will cost the network $1,500. If rejected, the project may then be offered elsewhere. But if the network continues to be interested, it will order a script, paying $3,500 to $5,000 for it. A pilot script (or shooting script) is the next stage, finished and refined: price, $10,000 to $15,000 for one of an hour's length, depending on the credentials and fame of the author.

At the next step scripts or treatments for subsequent episodes are requested, and if those appear promising the network will order the pilot episode. Total cost to the network for a single project which has progressed to that stage is likely to be $600,000 for an hour-long show, about half that for a half hour. If the pilot is rejected when the schedules are devised, there is no recovery of the expense.

In trying to cope with inflation, the networks have been in perpetual search for ways to reduce the financial burden of program development, but most of the economy techniques have produced poor results. Attempts were made to buy programs from short demonstration films supported by a number of scripts ready for shooting, but that was soon abandoned. As with trailers for movies, snips of the more dramatic scenes can be deceptive, making a program seem more tense and action-packed, or more amusing and prepossessing, than it really is.

Another approach was to secure the exclusive services of a successful producer and trust him to put together a winning show. Some half-dozen series came to the networks that way, and none of them succeeded. Without a complete pilot there was no way to visualize how elements of the project meshed.

There were, however, three successful techniques for the conservation of program development costs, although each had limitations. The summer tryout had been productive of several successful series, but the economics of summer necessarily confined the experimentation to taped programs or imported shows. The TV special which doubled as a pilot was also a source of new series fare (*Laugh-In* came to NBC that way), but for the most part yielded only variety shows. And the video movies, the *World Premiere* features, proved a resourceful way to turn up new shows in the adventure-melodrama form.

Costing the networks about as much as a theatrical feature, around $800,000 for an original exposure and a repeat, the made-for-TV movie is not much more expensive than a pilot and has the particular value of testing the program concept on the air, although the danger here is that some program proposals will work well enough for a single performance but will not sustain interest as a series.

Specials typically are produced at between $200,000 and $350,000 in the hour length. But those made as pilots carry added costs which may amount to as much as $250,000, and this applies as well to the video movies. Part of the expense of a pilot project is in keeping the unit together—the actors, producers, writers, and the standing sets—until the network decides whether to do the series or give up on it. For that duration, since they are prohibited from making other professional commitments which might conflict with going into full-scale television production, the creative and performing talent must be compensated.

The first rule in program development at the networks is never to deal with amateurs. There are two reasons: one, the professional can be depended on to deliver the film merchandise in good order, on a comfortable timetable and with fairly consistent quality; two, the production professional is as attuned to the economic verities of the system as the network officials. No idealist, he understands the mission and is bound by the same cautions. The amateur, on the other hand, may have notions of the reformer.

The professionals are a small and relatively closed society of program suppliers who have either come up through the ranks of the production companies or moved into that end of the business from the networks, ad agencies, or talent offices. Thus, in working with the professionals in Hollywood and New York, the networks restrict themselves to a single set of attitudes and values and perpetuate a narrow programing mentality.

Year after year the same minds are picked for ideas, the same creative spirits milked for inspiration. New writing and producing talent filters into the system at a slow rate, usually through spot assignments in individual episodes for series, and in time they, too, fall victim to TV's assembly-line requirements for its enormous consumption of programs, and also to its fail-safe conditions.

Thousands of people are employed by the networks in a wide variety of jobs, but it is a cardinal sin for any to venture a program suggestion. One who made that fatal error was Don West, a former trade-magazine editor who became assistant to CBS corporate president Frank Stanton. West was struck with an idea for a radically new program form and, being close to the front office, thought he might be privileged to develop it within the company, without giving up his position. Stanton, who never associated himself with the company's light-entertainment shows (that was Paley's area; his was news) and who rarely took part in the brainstorming sessions for the prime-time schedules, agreed to let West pursue his project, but not from his corporate office.

Richard Doan, who writes a news column for *TV Guide*, came upon the information that Stanton's assistant was developing a show and reported it as if to imply Stanton's own involvement. On January 7, 1970, he received the following wire from CBS's chief administrative officer:

APPRECIATE YOUR EFFORTS TO UPGRADE MY ROLE AND CAST ME AS BEHIND SCENES PROGRAMER. BUT REGRET YOU DID NOT MAKE EFFORT TO CHECK YOUR STORY WITH ME. HAD YOU DONE SO WOULD HAVE MADE CLEAR THAT DON WEST WAS GIVEN LEAVE FROM HIS DAY-TO-DAY DUTIES AS MY ASSISTANT MIDYEAR SO THAT HE COULD CARRY FORWARD FULL TIME HIS IDEA AS A DEVELOPMENT PROJECT FOR MIKE DANN. HAVE ASSIDUOUSLY AVOIDED INVOLVEMENT IN WEST'S EFFORTS NOT FOR LACK OF INTEREST BUT TO GIVE HIM MAXIMUM FREEDOM FROM FRONT OFFICE IDENTIFICATION. AS RESULT HAVE NOT SEEN A SINGLE FRAME OF HIS PILOT AND WILL NOT UNTIL IT HAS BEEN PASSED UPON BY DANN AND HIS ASSOCIATES. IN FACE OF THESE FACTS HOPE YOU CAN UNDERSTAND MY EMBARRASSMENT IF NOT OUTRAGE AT THE FABRICATION IN YOUR STORY. MOREOVER AM INFORMED BY DON WEST THAT IN HIS CONVERSATION WITH YOU HE DID NOT IDENTIFY ME IN ANY WAY WITH HIS PROJECT. FRANK STANTON.

West's film was made not as a pretentious pilot but on home-movie equipment, merely to illustrate his concept. I called Dann to ask whether he had seen it yet and what he thought of it.

"Piece of shit," he answered wearily.

Within a week, West was gone from CBS. At the pay window he discovered there was some confusion as to whose payroll he was on. Corporate had sent down word that since he was involved in programing activities he was no longer on its payroll and should be on Mike Dann's. Dann was not interested in having him on *his* payroll. West emptied his desk and departed.

Corollary to the networks' aversion to amateurs is the requirement for a slick professionalism in the visual aspects of production, as if to compensate for shortcomings in content with a high standard in appearance. If a show is to play in prime time, it must look like the big time.

There are six other rules for the development of new programing:

The series concept must be in the nature of a formula, so that an endless stream of new episodes suggest themselves, facilitating rapid production of scripts;

It must have continuing elements which appeal to viewers week after week and with which they identify;

It must be fashioned to win 30 per cent or more of the audience, ideally the young adult audience;

It must win its audience early, since a show passed over the first week or two may never catch on, and therefore should have names in the cast or special exploitation values to ensure tune-in the first week;

It should be easy to like, with heroes and villains readily indicated and no complex exposition, so that the viewer will not be driven away to simpler entertainment;

Whatever else, it must have a suggestion of newness without being so new that its pattern will be alien to what the viewer has liked in the past, making him feel insecure.

But the viewer's security is less an issue than that of television's practitioners. An advertising agency that makes a sizable investment in a program series would not normally choose to risk the client's money on a long shot that has never been around the track. Nor would a network executive risk his company's money, nor a studio production chief his company's on a show that might have limited prospects of selling.

When a show is packaged—the idea combined with the people who are to execute it—the first question from the network or advertiser is: Who are the *weenies?* A weenie (derived from "winner") is an important name in the credits, and the right combination of weenies will get almost any kind of bad show on the air. Cases in point: Debbie Reynolds and producer Jess Oppenheimer in the 1969–70 season; or *The Ugliest Girl in Town* the season before, produced by the veteran situation comedy hit-maker, Harry Ackerman; or *The Survivors*, which almost had more weenies than viewers.

A weenie is not so much a name you can trust as one you can use to defend yourself. ("Don't blame me, boss. It was a Persky and Denoff show, and they're the guys who did *Dick Van Dyke*.") Frequently it takes but a single hit to establish a name that will sell for years as a weenie. Leonard Stern, whose big credit was Jackie's Gleason's *The Honeymooners* in the original version and who had another winner in *Get Smart*, will continue to be a name that sells a package even though he's had a succession of misfires in *Run, Buddy, Run, The Good Guys, He and She*, and *The Governor and J.J.*

The networks draw from a small pool of program sources—a half-dozen major studios in Hollywood and perhaps a score of independents—continually relying on the same creative and production talent. An inbred group, they succeed each other in the same jobs.

Although they may have come from the heartland, they live on the fashionable East Side of Manhattan or in the plush suburbs of New York and Beverly Hills, Santa Monica, Westwood, or Bel Air in Southern California. They travel the country by jet, seeing clouds from the windows, to do business with each other. Their principal contact with the great television audience is with the household domestics they employ.

Theirs is a small world, and it is their window on the world that is television's vision.

Bud Yorkin and Norman Lear had made their initial mark in television by producing a number of excellent TV variety shows, including the much-honored Fred Astaire dance specials, and had graduated to motion pictures. After the films *Come Blow Your Horn*, *Never Too Late*, and *Divorce: American Style*, they wrote, directed, or produced (separately or as a team) such features as *Inspector Clouseau*, *The Night They Raided Minsky's*, *Start the Revolution Without Me*, and *Cold Turkey*. They were hot, and they really didn't need an absorption in television with a regular weekly series.

But they liked the project of the British bigot series—whose title for the American version became *All in the Family*—and when Bob Wood agreed to buy it for CBS, making a firm commitment to begin the series either in January or September of 1971, they had visions of establishing a new kind of freedom at the networks. Once the contracts were signed and the deal irrevocable, they determined that they would not budge from the conditions agreed to even if CBS were to have second thoughts about the nature of the language or the level of sophistication of the series. They were not looking for new credits; they were not planning to be back year after year with television projects. They could afford to hold their ground.

That Wood was one of the few men in television not ruled by the common fears was evident from his interest in the series in the first place. There were other ways to get a 30 share, but he liked this way and felt it would be good for CBS. Besides, Yorkin and Lear's films were successful with the young people.

Others in the company began to worry about *All in the*

Family, however. While they were no less sure than Wood that it would make an impact, they were also sure it would create needless trouble for CBS. NBC had discovered with *Laugh-In* that ethnic jokes were dangerous, and that network's censor, Herminio Traviesas, normally permissive, had to rule them out-of-bounds. CBS's censor, William Tankersley (known affectionately as Mr. Prohibition), disapproved of avant-garde subjects in entertainment programs. Through his years of experience in the medium, the grave Texan who ruled over CBS program practices believed in a universal television that played to everyone and offended no one.

As time grew closer for the series to go into production, there was pressure for changes to tone down aspects of the show which might disturb segments of the viewership. The word "Goddam" was used several times in the pilot, and there was probably no more inflammatory word that could be spoken on American television. Affiliates in the Bible Belt were going to scream.

Then there was the matter of the opening scene. The bigot and his wife go off to church, while the young people stay at home to practice their religion. When the old man returns, he's greeted by the young man zipping up his trousers as he comes down the stairs. Somewhere in television land that was not going to sit well.

Wood met several times with Yorkin and Lear to discuss CBS thinking about the program. Grudgingly they conceded on "Goddam." The use of the word was not vital to what the series would be trying to express, and it would be too bad if the public became aroused and angry for the wrong reason. They also agreed to eliminate the zipping of the pants. Maybe it was realistic, but sex was really irrelevant to the program's theme.

But that was it for concessions, they insisted. They would not compromise this into another bland show. CBS bought the series, and now the network would have to live with the Yorkin and Lear standards for it.

During the meetings with Wood, Lear frequently drew

out a pad and scribbled notes. His agent noticed and later asked him what he had been writing.

"I love the way that guy talks," said Lear. "All clichés. I wanted to take them down so I don't forget when I do the dialogue. It's perfect for the bigot."

7

The Men from Sales

A handsome man who seemed born to executive-suite life, Elton H. Rule communicated a sense of manifest destiny at ABC. It was as though he were fated to lead the network, not only to lead it but to raise its standing in the caste system of broadcasting. Cool and genteel, and bearing a striking resemblance to Franklin D. Roosevelt, Jr., when he was in his early fifties, Rule suggested a man who had lived his life as though his surname were a prophecy.

Some executives look back in amazement at how far they have come in the world, while some never have a moment's doubt, from their earliest years, that they will go all the way. Rule was of the latter sort.

Under his administration ABC was shaking its old loser's complex. Although the rating improvement had been undramatic during his two years at the helm, Rule had been careful from the first to promise a gradual closing of the rating gap, and there had been palpable gains made. His leadership suffused the ranks with a new spirit, which was fanned into excitement by the new program schedule for September.

It had a good *feel*, and it was regarded with respect by the opposition. The new line-up seemed another in the succession of astute and confident moves by Rule, who had come in as president of the network at perhaps the lowest point in its history. He was growing stronger in the ABC hierarchy and moving closer to the post everyone knew would some-day be created by the heads of the corporation, Leonard Goldenson and Simon B. Siegel, that of overlord to the com-pany's multifold broadcast operations—the TV and radio networks, the TV and radio stations owned by ABC, the na-tional sales division for the stations, news, sports, engineer-ing, program syndication, and the international division—as distinct from ABC's theater, motion picture, amusement parks, and recording interests.

But the closer Rule moved to that new tier of manage-ment, the greater his jeopardy and the more uncertain his future with the company; for the other executive who had long seemed in line for that promotion was his arch foe, Ted Shaker, and it was known to their intimates that each would sooner leave the company than be forced to report to the other. Goldenson and Siegel knew it, too, and faced with the dilemma they held off establishing the post, trusting that time would aid in the decision. Time or a showdown.

The stage was set for a classic executive-suite war, which became a source of some tension to lesser executives who stood to either advance in rank or be swept out as partisans, depending on whether Rule or Shaker prevailed. Since nei-ther principal was known for infighting or for the tactics of piecemeal assassination, it had to be assumed that circum-stances would eventually produce a confrontation between the antagonists and that in a single explosion the manage-ment decision would be resolved.

In the organizational scheme the two were co-equal, each holding the title of group president and both on the corpora-tion's board of directors. ABC's executive order took this form:

CORPORATE

Leonard Goldenson, *President*
Simon B. Siegel, *Executive Vice-President*

GROUP

Elton H. Rule   Theodore Shaker   Sam Clark   Everett Erlick

DIVISIONAL

ABC-TV	Owned TV Stations	Theaters	Legal
Network	ABC Spot Sales	Motion Pictures	
	ABC Films	Recordings	
	ABC International	Music Publishing	

The division presidents reported to the group presidents vertically above them, and they in turn reported to Siegel, along with the executive in charge of engineering and the presidents of ABC News, the four ABC radio networks and the owned radio stations.

A shy, humorless man who looked like an aging clerk, with pale straight hair that was not as blond as it was underpigmented, Siegel was the unlikely person in whom the economic control over all facets of the American Broadcasting Companies, Inc. was concentrated. His uneasy conversation and social diffidence were traced by some of his men to a lack of college education and to the general knowledge that he had spent most of his professional life in the accounting department of the Paramount Theatres system (which merged with ABC in 1953), with little expectation of rising higher. In 1950 his salary was under $20,000 a year; in 1970 he ruled over men making five times that amount.

Always in the background, letting the flamboyant Goldenson appear to be running things, Si Siegel had the power over careers at ABC. He was also the author of the corporation's fiscal policies, the keeper of its checkbook, as it were, and the one person on whose wisdom Goldenson totally relied.

They were an odd pair in the world of big broadcasting, two theater men who through the quirks of business had become publishers of the air waves, heads of a communications empire that had been valued at $400 million by International Telephone and Telegraph chairman Harold Geneen when he set out to acquire it. But at heart they remained motion-picture exhibitors, and after a day of multimillion-dollar television transactions it was not unusual for them to stay overtime to check the individual receipts of the theaters they controlled, a thrill carried over from the old days.

Not long after CBS called in management consultants Booz, Allen, and Hamilton to study its organizational structure, ABC engaged McKinsey and Company for similar purposes. The heads of both broadcast corporations had reached the age at which they had to think about retirement and a new order of management. Both were advised to create a subcorporate second line of authority for the supervision and co-ordination of the main profit centers, which would free the corporate chieftains to work at the final merger with a larger company.

At ABC, in particular, the recommendation was to decentralize the power and to redesign the financial procedures so that the television network had a degree of economic autonomy, at least to the extent that it would not have to impose on the exchequer of the parent corporation for every program purchase.

The McKinsey recommendation did not sit well with Siegel, who took offense that the dilution of his power should be the main conclusion of the survey. In a display of hurt feelings he gave Goldenson his resignation, but his old friend salved the wounds, and eventually Siegel concurred that there would have to be a younger man in supreme charge of all radio and television activities—ABC's "Mr. Broadcasting" —who would orchestrate the divisions so that they worked in concert toward common corporate objectives.

Shaker was closer to the job than Rule by reason of tenure in an important administrative capacity at headquarters, and he was also four years younger than his adversary; but his main advertisement for the promotion was a sparkling record of profit improvement from all the divisions in his purview every year since he joined the company from CBS in 1962. Shaker's five divisions were, together, the biggest money-makers in ABC, Inc., and the redemption of the TV network, which had been a losing operation. If the broadcast side of the corporation was showing a profit in the annual report to stockholders, it was because Shaker's area was producing more than enough to offset what the network was dissipating.

But Rule, because he had rescued a near shambles, was not overshadowed. In a peculiar way, lack of tenure in the hierarchy was working in his favor. Having within two years projected himself as a forceful and popular leader, he came to represent to management a kind of miracle worker who might infuse the company with a new vitality. Rule's edge over his rival was that he now had experience in both the network and station spheres of operation and had proven himself effective in both, while Shaker's expertise in broadcasting over a period of twenty years (half of them with CBS) was almost exclusively in station administration and spot sales. The network was, and would always be, the showcase for the corporation, and in ABC's case it represented a new frontier for profits.

When Rule came into the presidency of the network early in 1968 the entire company was in shock over the collapse of its proposed merger with ITT and desperately trying to recover from two years of partial paralysis while the merger was pending. The network had fallen so far behind CBS and NBC in the rating competition that *Variety* once described it as running fourth in a three-network race. Organizationally it seemed to be coming apart. Morale was low, and bright young executives were leaving steadily. Throughout the affiliate body (those 180 TV stations which represent the network's local outlets) there was a loss of faith in ABC's ability to compete and an indifference to the network's appeals for a supportive effort.

To the advertiser, ABC's desperation invited a buyer's anarchy. Ed Scherick had resigned as program vice-president in 1967 when the schedule he devised was, in effect, overruled by the company's largest advertiser, Bristol-Myers, whose advertising chief, Marvin Koslow, was permitted to rearrange the shows to his own convenience. A somewhat similar privilege had also been given to Bill Hylan of J. Walter Thompson Advertising, and because ABC needed the revenues it allowed sponsors such as Clairol the freedom to put on specials that were barely more than half-hour advertisements for their products.

When the merger failed, Goldenson and Siegel promptly took steps to reorganize, for psychological as well as tangible reasons; it was necessary to present the impression of a rebirth and to show some forward movement prior to the shareholders' meeting in May. Tom Moore would be moved up to a new administrative position, and Elton H. Rule, the veteran general manager of their Los Angeles station, KABC-TV, would be the new president of the network.

Rule was personable, mature, good-looking, bright enough, and Anglo-Saxon Protestant (a big point with a Jewish management fearful that ABC might become known as a Jewish company). Moreover, Rule had established a record of progress at KABC-TV, which had been moving up both in revenues and in ratings. One thing more in his favor: as a station man aware of station problems Rule would probably go over well with the affiliates, as Jack Schneider had when CBS picked him for the presidency.

On a Friday afternoon, January 5, 1968, Rule boarded a plane in Los Angeles on a summons from Goldenson, and was offered the job as network president. That he did not seize it impressed his bosses. He would have to think about it, he told them; his family loved California, and he was happy with his situation there. He spent an evening that weekend at Moore's home in Darien, Connecticut, and the only other guest was one of Moore's neighbors, Ted Shaker. They discussed how it would be with the new team, Moore as general, Shaker as colonel, Rule as a captain.

On Sunday, Goldenson had his answer from Rule. He would accept the presidency but only under certain conditions. He would take no direct orders from Moore or Shaker but would report directly to Si Siegel, just as they did. If Goldenson and Siegel wanted him on that basis, as president with full authority, he would be pleased to have the job. It was decided that Moore would have the network under him in the table of organization but—as he would find out later —would only serve as an adviser.

On Monday morning, Jack Gould in the *New York Times* carried a story of Tom Moore's promotion at ABC to chief over most of the broadcast divisions. That afternoon the ABC board of directors held their regular meeting. That evening, Moore found himself with less power in the company than he had had as network president. To release information before it is disclosed to the board and made official is a large sin, and from the details in Gould's story it seemed apparent to Goldenson that Moore had been, if not the source of it, excessively co-operative. Angry, Goldenson did not defend Moore when certain directors were critical of the network's failure to fulfill its profit projections. When the meeting concluded, it was Shaker who emerged with expanded duties, and Moore who wound up with three of the less glamorous divisions reporting to him, none of them a major profit center, and nominally the television network.

Furious at having his promotion revoked and at having been left to take the blame for the network's economic failings, Moore stormed in on Goldenson and Siegel in a rage. There was little communication between them after that. By summer, he had left the company.

Moore's mishaps had a natural way of increasing Rule's power in a brief period of time, but the new network president also made his own contribution to his growing stature. He quickly established a new executive cadre at the network and gave his men the freedom to operate without intensive supervision from the top. His appointments were good ones. A brainy young attorney for the network, I. Martin Pompadur, became its general manager, second in command to Rule. Frederick Pierce, who had given a good account of himself both in audience research and in the sales department, was named vice-president of planning, responsible for charting the new course for the network toward its recovery. Ellis Moore, a neat Ivy League type who had once headed NBC's public relations, was picked by Rule to head the network's publicity department, and he lent the appropriate low-key tone to the administration. And James Duffy, who had been sales vice-president under Moore, stayed on in that capacity and seemed if anything more compatible with Rule's regime than with the preceding one.

Rule also seemed to bring something new to Hard Rock: luck.

Although far behind the other networks in circulation, ABC suddenly found itself a beneficiary of CBS's shortcomings in the young adult demographics. The changing market place served Rule's cause, for while there was a large rating gap in total homes ABC was competitive in the average number of preferred viewers delivered. In general, old programs tend to appeal to older people and new programs to younger. Having more new programs than the other networks, ABC found an old disadvantage working in its favor.

Then Rule was to profit from an NBC lapse. If anything had been more competitively anemic than ABC's nighttime schedule it was its daytime schedule. When Monty Hall, packager and host of *Let's Make a Deal,* failed to get the new terms he was seeking from NBC at contract renewal time, he switched the show to ABC. Not only did the game program carry over its hit rating when it moved, the effect on the two networks was amazing. NBC's daytime ratings went into a swift dive and ABC's improved all around the new program. *Let's Make a Deal* was one of those keystone shows in daytime that supported the hours before and after it, and NBC had failed to realize it. Prime time held the glamour, but the big network profits were in daytime.

Tom Moore, who seemed luckless in all his ploys, yielded to a man who, it appeared, could not fail. Elton Rule was moving up faster than the network.

Since Rule was one to maintain neutrality in office politics, his open conflict with Shaker seemed something more than a competition for a higher position. Although of similar professional background and social style—both veterans of the TV sales game dating to the infancy of the medium and both of neat suburban cut and clubby sophistication—their executive styles were vastly different, Rule insouciant and Shaker driving and intense. Rule chose to delegate authority and to trust the people under him; Shaker could not let the merest facet of his responsibility escape his personal inquiry. He demanded strict adherence to his standards from those reporting to him. It followed that Rule was the popular executive and Shaker in continual discord with those who worked for him.

As head of the stations division, Shaker had been Rule's immediate superior in the company while he was general manager of KABC-TV, and Rule carried to New York with him the sore memory of Shaker's overbearing supervision. Whatever came between them after Rule's arrival in New York as head of the network, his bitter feelings toward Shaker dated to the six years he had served under him.

On a February day in 1970, Shaker phoned Ellis Moore with a request. He seldom made use of the public relations department, preferring to keep his profitable divisions out of the news.

"Ellis, on Monday I'm going to be making two important announcements which are very delicate, and I wish you'd handle them for me personally."

"Sure," said Ellis, "what about?"

"Personnel," Shaker said. "I'm going to announce new presidents of two of my divisions."

"Who's leaving?"

"I'll let you know in a day or so."

A few days later he called Moore again.

"Say, about the press release I asked you to do for me. I'd still like you to do it, but there's been a change. There won't be two men leaving, only one."

"Who's that?" Ellis asked.

"Me."

Shaker, the best-entrenched and most powerful executive below the corporate tier at ABC, was suddenly out of the picture. It happened this way:

John Campbell, whom Shaker had appointed president of the owned stations division eight months earlier, resigned after a series of clashes with his boss. Although it was a prestigious and high-paying job, Campbell gave it up from a feeling of being smothered. Before him, Jim Conley had left for similar reasons. The executive erosion troubled Siegel.

Within days of Campbell's departure, Don Coyle, the president of ABC International, tangled with Shaker and was fired. Coyle had been with ABC for twenty years and headed the international division five years before Shaker came to the company. He would not be dismissed as a hireling, and he called for a showdown in Siegel's office. In Shaker's presence, Coyle won the corporate officer's backing.

Shaker complained to Siegel that as head of a group of divisions he had the right to fire men reporting to him.

"Are you saying you have more rights in this company than I?" Siegel shot back.

"No, of course not, Si, but I don't want this man any longer."

"You seem to be putting it on the basis of either you go or I go," Siegel said.

That was, of course, the end.

One of his colleagues met Shaker at the elevator and could not restrain the question, "What happened, Ted? Was it Elton?"

"No, it was my smallest division that finished me," he answered; "the least of my worries."

Without firing a shot, Rule prevailed. There was no High Noon with Shaker. He remained clean and unpolitical.

On March 23, Goldenson and Siegel created the job of supreme broadcast president over all the divisional presidents. The new title was president of the American Broadcasting Company, not to be confused with Goldenson's title, president of the American Broadcasting *Companies*, Inc., although to some it did not seem too far removed.

Siegel fired Don Coyle in July.

When Shaker left there was no doubt that Rule would get the big job; the suspense at ABC was over who would succeed him as network president and Campbell as head of the owned stations.

Julius Barnathan wanted the stations division and made no secret of it. The job had once been his, but he had been asked by Siegel to relinquish it temporarily to help in the administration of the network. A few years later he was made head of engineering, and there he remained, a noncombatant with no chance of moving up in the company, his talents wasting. When Shaker and Campbell were gone, Barnathan went to Rule and to Siegel to ask for his old job. The responses were noncommittal.

He phoned me at home one night to ask what I thought his chances were. I told him I had no idea but I was about to do some checking on who might be in line for the two vacancies and would try out his name in my questioning. Then I dialed Rule at his home in Scarsdale.

Rule was the kind of executive newspapermen like—cordial, discreet, unequivocating, apparently honest. His willingness to answer a reasonable question not only bespoke a respect for the other man's profession but conveyed the impression that he had nothing to hide. Never a publicity seeker, Rule nevertheless did not shrink from encounters with the press, understanding that it went with the job.

He had a way of answering delicate questions that told you whether you were hot or cold, without volunteering what he was not privileged to talk about. I reeled off a series of names to him, asking where they stood with regard to the two vacancies, and when the interview was over I felt reasonably sure that Jim Duffy would be president of the network and Dick O'Leary president of the owned television stations.

Duffy ran the best sales outfit at the networks. As was often said in jest, you *had* to be good to sell ABC. If he were Rule's choice, Siegel would approve it. From his corporate position he had spotted Duffy many years before, when the young man made the change from publicity in Chicago to sales for the radio network. Later it had been Siegel's idea to move him into television sales and then to advance him to vice-president in charge of that department.

As for O'Leary, he had caught top management's eye as a general manager of the Chicago station, WLS-TV, because it had spurted in the ratings during his stewardship, becoming a full-fledged competitor with the NBC and CBS stations there for the first time ever. Whether O'Leary really was to be credited for the accomplishment or whether he was the lucky beneficiary of a series of management blunders at the CBS station, WBBM-TV, was moot; but the record did show dramatic improvement by the station during his term, and when the appointment went before the board of directors that record would be all that mattered.

He was also one of Rule's favorites, having served under him as general sales manager of the Los Angeles station prior to his promotion to the Chicago station. Rule was proud of him for his success as a station manager.

After speaking with Rule, I phoned Barnathan. It was not pleasant to tell him what he hoped not to hear.

"I mentioned your name, and he said you burned your bridges."

"Meaning what?"

"Meaning, I suppose, that you said something to offend Siegel, and he can't see his way to forgiving you."

"The bastard. I'm the unloved son and can't do anything to please him."

"Look, that was only Elton's appraisal."

"No, he's right. He levels. Since I'm not in the running, I'll have to go with Plan B."

"Which is what?"

"Make a move. I've had some offers."

The most fascinating species of broadcasting executive is the one who fails his way to the top, and it is interesting that the species is not rare. Some careers have been freaks of lucky timing, some have been built on personality, some on an exceptional golf game, and some on good connections. They refute everything American children learn at school about the virtue of diligence, education, and dedication.

In the business world, ineptitude is often rewarded. I have watched men move to ever higher positions of authority, always leaving disaster in their wake.

Julie Barnathan was of the opposite species; he succeeded at everything and was bound for oblivion. There was no job in his entire professional career that he did not perform with distinction, and yet he was an annoyance to his management. Top officers of the other networks recognized that he was prize personnel, one of the best minds in all of television, but neither NBC nor CBS ever tried to hire him away.

Barnathan's problem was partly that he did not look the executive and partly that he lacked the managerial refinements for network television; he spoke his mind too readily, and often coarsely. Squat of build and looking ten years older than early forties, having let his Seaman First Class physique decline to a pot belly, he was out of the mold. His clothes were too flashy, and his total style betrayed his tenement Bronx beginnings. But he was a walking actuary table who worked complicated mathematical problems in his head, could learn anything new with amazing rapidity, and knew the television business as well as any man.

Ollie Treyz, when he was president of the ABC network, discovered Barnathan in the research department and used him for a time as a human computer and general problem-solver. In a display of courage and imagination, Treyz gave Barnathan the critical assignment of heading station relations, which involved persuading the affiliated stations to carry more of the network's shows. If anyone did not answer to the accepted type in affiliate relations it was Barnathan. The job involved contact with Southern, Midwestern, and other hinterland businessmen who distrusted New Yorkers and were accustomed to back-scratching and flattery, techniques that were alien to Barnathan. He looked Mafioso, and his personality seemed to corroborate the image. Yet, in a short time he became popular with the station operators and had the respect and indebtedness of many whose problems he helped to solve. He was able to trade that in on what the network needed from them.

Sometime later, when he told Siegel he had received an offer to go with Capital Cities Broadcasting, a prosperous station group, he was promoted to executive in charge of the ABC-owned TV stations. He ran the division well, but when Shaker joined the company Barnathan was asked to surrender the post, since Shaker would need authority over the stations to hire away the CBS spot sales force (which he succeeded in doing). Those men joined Shaker on the promise of moving into key positions at the ABC stations.

Barnathan then became general manager of the television network under Tom Moore, the day-to-day steward of its operation, and it was probably no coincidence that when he held that position and took part in the program decisions and strategy ABC caught up with the other networks in the ratings. Possibly it was also no coincidence that when he lost that job, at Moore's request, the network took a downturn from which, in 1970, it still had not recovered. Moore and Barnathan had been an effective meshing of opposites, the smooth Mississippi politician and the Bronx street fighter. But Barnathan was too assertive for Moore, too lacking in the gentlemanly arts. Siegel granted Moore his wish and moved Barnathan to another problem area, engineering.

He had had no experience in the technical side of television, but it became his responsibility to convert the company's facilities to color in the year, 1965, that CBS decided, finally, to go to color. It would be a costly undertaking—involving a capital outlay of nearly $50 million—which ABC could ill afford; but for competitive reasons it could not remain the only black-and-white (therefore backward, out-of-date) network. As a novice in engineering, greener than any of the 1,750 technical personnel under his direction, Barnathan would be responsible for keeping ABC on a technological par with the other networks and in the vanguard of covering special events by remote pick-up.

It was a surprise to everyone but Barnathan that he was equal to it all. Less than a year after he was in the job, I overheard engineers discussing him with incredulity. He had not only already mastered the fundamentals of a highly advanced technology and kept up with the rapid changes but was also imaginatively putting to use new electronic devices and showing skill in designing plans for coverage. The techniques of covering the Olympics, golf, and other sporting events advanced noticeably under Barnathan's engineering administration, but for all his achievements in the field, he was not happy being on the technical side and hoped to return to the more competitive arena of business and programing.

Only Siegel could make that possible, and Barnathan had somehow fallen from grace.

His lack of polish was sometimes mistaken for surliness, and it is possible that his way of shouting in a discussion was taken by Siegel as a show of disrespect.

Goldenson and Siegel did not like a man who could not check his emotions. Barnathan was loyal, experienced, and immensely able, but he had one serious flaw.

He was not bland enough for television.

The television industry grew out of radio, a straight carry-over. In the United States, television was conceived as radio with a picture.

During the early fifties there were two vital functions in the new industry: to put programing on the air that would make families want to purchase TV sets, and to send out

salesmen who could convince advertisers that television
would sell their products. The first function was assumed by
the radio men, the second produced a new breed.

Network and station managements were then deeply
concerned with programs because the medium's selling problem at the time was its lack of circulation. When television's
penetration in households approached that of other media,
there would be no difficulty in getting sales. It was the only
time in the history of the medium that program priorities
superseded all others. If there was an abundance of original
and quality drama at the time (*Studio One, Philco Playhouse, Goodyear Playhouse,* and later *Playhouse 90*), it was
in large part because those shows tended to appeal to a
wealthier and better-educated part of the public, the part
best able to afford a television set in those years when the
price of receivers was high.

Until television had circulation numbers to sell, it had
to rely for advertising upon its glamour, the face-to-face effectiveness of the medium's pitchmen, and the stylishness and
éclat of its salesmen. Lacking a strong argument for an advertiser's billings, the new industry found that its welcome at
ad agencies depended on the kind of man it sent out to call
on them.

Those were the gray-flannel-suit days, when advertising
people were particularly caste-conscious and absorbed with
good taste and the trappings of status. They would be re-
pelled by aggressive, ill-shaped, or flashy-dressed representatives of the new medium but would not be averse to lunch-
ing, having a drink or playing golf with clean-cut, modish
Anglo-Saxon types who surpassed advertising men in the
paraphernalia of the good life.

In the principal advertising centers—New York, Chicago, Los Angeles, Detroit, St. Louis, and Minneapolis—a
new representative of broadcasting emerged: the smooth,
hail-fellow, brand-conscious, sports-minded, trim, alert
young-military-officer-in-mufti, who was skilled in the small
talk and up-to-date language of marketing and advertising.

He would spend the better part of twenty years selling the minutes between and within the television shows, and that would be the practical extent of his involvement in the art of broadcasting. He would, to make the sale, convince the advertiser that by going on television he would become a *communicator*, and so every ad became not a sales pitch but a "message," and in time the salesman was himself convinced that communications and selling products were the same thing.

As the conduit to the money for the broadcast companies, the salesman would climb the executive ladder in an industry that would grow ever more dominated by profits, and by his training his first response would be to the advertiser's needs.

In the seventies, when the old order of broadcaster—the founders of the industry—went into retirement, he would inherit the television system.

The salesmen of the fifties had come of age. Elton Rule had risen to president of the American Broadcasting Company, Jim Duffy to president of its television network, Dick O'Leary to president of the owned stations, Dick Beesemyer to vice-president of station relations, and Jim Shaw was the new vice-president of sales at ABC. At CBS, Jack Schneider had gone beyond the network and group rule to the corporate level as understudy to Frank Stanton, and he was clearly in line to succeed Paley someday as chief executive officer. Bob Wood was president of the TV network, Ralph Daniels of the owned stations (later to be succeeded by another salesman of the fifties, Tom Miller), and Clark George of CBS Radio. At NBC, Walter Scott had made it through sales to chairman of the board, Don Durgin to president of the network, and Jack Otter to sales vice-president. With but a few exceptions throughout the three network organizations, the general managers of the local stations were men who had graduated from sales.

The advancement of the salesman was even more pervasive than that, extending to a majority of the individual stations in the important broadcast groups, those multistation baronies which comprise the second greatest power bloc in American broadcasting—Group W (Westinghouse), Metromedia, Taft, Storer, Capital Cities, Corinthian, Triangle, Cox, Scripps-Howard, Golden West, Hearst, General Electric, RKO General, Time-Life, Cowles, Post-Newsweek, Kaiser, U.S. Communications, among others—and it was clear that there, too, they were in line for succession to the highest levels.

The cycles of administration in broadcasting over its first half century had to a great extent been determined by the priorities of the system. In the early days of radio, the leaders of the medium had been engineers. Later, as radio flourished, they were showmen and businessmen who infiltrated through their association with the industry as advertisers (William S. Paley, for example, and Edward J. Noble of the Life Savers Company, who bought the NBC Blue Network, which became ABC). And when television became so prosperous that Wall Street was intrigued by it, the accountant and finance specialist came into executive prominence.

In 1970, two things mattered: keeping the companies in the money and getting them out of legislative or regulatory trouble. That called for a new set of heroes—the salesman and the lawyer.

As the broadcasting industry's problems multiplied in Washington during the sales executives' climb to the management posts, the company chief counsel gained importance. The order of succession was beginning to be formed at both CBS and ABC, and indications were that the new corporate leadership would in both cases involve such a pairing.

NBC had already arrived at the new mix. In the ruling triumvirate were chairman Scott, whose background was sales, and executive vice-president David Adams, whose field had been law. But the third member, president and chief operating officer of corporate NBC, was Julian Goodman, who had neither legal nor sales experience, coming up through the news division, where he had been an administrator. But although he was the glaring exception, Goodman sought to make his mark not in exceeding his predecessor, Robert Kintner, as a champion of news, but in bettering him as a practical businessman.

Paley indicated the pattern for the future at CBS when, in 1969, he promoted Schneider to the corporate level and named general counsel Richard Jencks new president of the CBS Broadcast Group. Jencks had no experience on the line in television or radio, but he had been deeply involved in the legal tribulations of the company, was expert in communications law, and versed in the implications of various Federal Communications Commission regulatory proposals. Moreover, unlike the executive on the line, he had been exposed to congressional and other political pressures. Barring some fatal error on their part, Schneider and Jencks were positioned to become chairman and president, respectively, of CBS, Inc.

Goldenson appeared to be making similar preparations for succession at ABC. With Rule's appointment, a new subcorporate level of management had been created consisting of four men, all of whom reported to Siegel. They were Rule, who governed all of broadcasting; Sam Clark, his counterpart over all nonbroadcast activities of the corporation; Everett Erlick, chief counsel; and Roland Tremble, head of finance.

Within a few years, perhaps even months, two of the four would probably advance to the top positions in the corporation. Since broadcasting was its largest producer of revenues, and since Rule, at fifty-two, had age in his favor, he appeared to be in line for the next step up.

But that advancement would be dependent on whether he continued to improve the broadcast fortunes of the company.

8

Babbitt at Fifty

On April 4, delegates began to arrive in Chicago for the annual convention of the National Association of Broadcasters, an organization dedicated to combating change, with, everything considered, a fine record in that endeavor. The same day, a small militantly critical newspaper known as the *Chicago Journalism Review* was beginning a Conference on Broadcast Communications, which in its way was a counterconvention.

Purposely, the little conference was held at the Sheraton-Blackstone Hotel, directly across the street from the Conrad Hilton, where the broadcasters were in conclave, so that symbolically it would re-enact a historic confrontation. For the hotels were situated at the intersection of Chicago streets—Michigan Avenue and Balbo Drive—where the Yippies and other dissenters to the Democratic National Convention in August of 1968 had had their violent encounter with Mayor Richard Daley's police.

It was out of that fiasco that the *Chicago Journalism Review* came into being. A well-written sheet staffed by professionals from newspapers and broadcasting, it purported to expose the big business news media when they lacked the courage or freedom, or just the integrity, to be truthful.

There were the obvious contrasts in the two meetings. The National Association of Broadcasters, with its attendance of 5,000, was a swarm of white, middle-aged, prosperous-looking businessmen wearing identification badges. Across the street, only 200 were at the CJR sessions the first day, the number dwindling to around fifty the second, but the group was not exclusive as to race, gender, or professional standing. It did, however, predominate in young people and reflected their styles of haberdashery and hair, as well as their passionate idealism. On that single weekend, the CJR conference concentrated on such matters as the jeopardy of the free press in the United States and the importance of greater access to the media for all groups in society. The NAB convention and its related events spanned a period of six days, April 3 to 8, with the chief issue the customary one of threats to the American broadcasters' economic well-being.

The young idealists assailed the broadcasters for their insensitivity to the total public they served, their personnel policies discriminating against racial minorities, their greed, and their inadequacies in news and public affairs. Among the several resolutions passed at the conference was one to organize citizens' groups which would appeal to the federal and municipal governments to treat cable television (CATV) as a public utility and to keep it out of the abusive hands of the licensed broadcasters.

If it was a confrontation at all, it was a mild one. There were no demonstrations or manifestations of anger toward the broadcast establishment outside the meeting room. As for the broadcasters, they scarcely paid attention to the smaller convention across Balbo Drive. It was just a minor nuisance, and criticism was nothing new to them.

"Fifty Golden Years, and the best is yet to come . . ."
There was profound irony in the theme line of the broadcasters' convention in Chicago. The first fifty had indeed been golden years, golden in a literal sense. Radio and television had created a lot of millionaires among those who were awarded licenses by the federal government to broadcast in the public interest. But if the best were really yet to come, it would probably be in wholly different terms. The old broadcasting system, of 1920 to 1970, appeared to be in its closing phase.

The year of American broadcasting's fiftieth anniversary

was filled with forebodings of convulsive change. Most of the owners and managers of stations who attended the annual industry meeting knew that the grand old business faced drastic upheavals in the seventies and would probably never be the same again. Far from a buoyant golden anniversary celebration, the convention was a call to arms against the forces working to destroy the old order.

Massive change in any of the forms of show business usually can be traced to any of four factors, singly or in combination: (1) new technology, (2) new legislation, (3) new economics, and (4) new standards on the part of the audience. Vaudeville was killed by the technology of radio, motion pictures, and recordings; the theater also suffered the effects and had to adapt itself to new times and a smaller potential audience. Television turned radio into an electronic jukebox and, in taking over the function of the Hollywood B movie, drastically changed the shape and standards of the motion picture industry.

Now television was threatened, not by one but by all four factors of change.

Cable television and the video cassette were the main technological menaces to the existing system, with pay television still an object of concern. Although it had long been suppressed by the broadcast and motion picture lobbies, pay TV remained on the horizon and its advent now appeared inevitable through new FCC rules permitting stations to engage in over-the-air subscription service and through the cable systems, whose operators were promising varied and highly sophisticated utilization of the direct connection to the television receiver. So serious was the cable threat, and so imminent its spread over the country through the FCC's determination to establish operating rules, that the National Association of Broadcasters retained the New York public relations firm of Phil Dean Associates to augment its own campaign of alarums to the citizenry that cable was endangering the American system of free television. Dean himself would travel about the country spreading the word that cable would never fulfill the promises of its promoters.

The system that delivered a television picture by wire rather than over the air (and which had come into being modestly as a means of improving TV reception in areas where it was poor) was a real and present danger to the broadcaster. Refinements in cable technology gave the systems the capability of a forty-channel service, a prospect that would enable the medium to serve selective audiences usually shut out of free television because of its profitable addiction to mass-appeal programing. That aspect of CATV was what suddenly made it the darling of intellectuals, ethnic minorities, and local politicians, for in addition to carrying the local stations and relaying signals from other cities, the cable franchises would originate programing of their own, which might include such highly localized remotes as school board meetings, public hearings from City Hall, and neighborhood ball games.

Futuristically, since houses could be wired to send out data as well as to receive pictures, cable could supplant the program rating services that project their numbers from probability samples and perform such functions of two-way communications that would allow the housewife to order her groceries over the line. Linked to computers, cable systems could retrieve programs that had already been broadcast on the air for viewers who wanted to save them for the next day or the next month.

But it was not the manifold future miracles of cable that worried the broadcasters in 1970; rather, it was the simple matter of CATV on a national scale fractionalizing the television audience and upsetting the economics under which many station operators had grown accustomed to making a profit of from thirty to forty cents on the dollar. Instead of three or four program choices for the viewer at any given hour, there would be a several-fold increase, and never again would the average commercial station have the same day-long

hold on the mass audience. Furthermore, the cable franchises would, with their own programs, be in competition with
the broadcasters for the advertising dollar.

Less predictable were the possible effects of the video
cassette, the cartridge form of television which, throughout
Europe as well as in the United States and Japan, was bidding to develop into a visual counterpart of the phonograph.
Programing of every conceivable type—educational, cultural, popular, technical—was, by the middle of the year,
being recorded on film or tape cartridges in anticipation of
a world-wide boom in a new audio-visual medium. When
the cassette units that played through the television sets at
home were mass-produced at prices the middle-class consumer could afford, how would he behave as a viewer?
Would he give up commercial television to program his own
receiver with movies, plays, or other entertainments? Or
would he be unable to resist the programs fed out over the
air, feeling out of touch with the outside world if he cut himself off from conventional television? Would broadcasting
be forced out of its petty puritanism (born of its intention
to be offensive to the least number of people) through competition with a new medium whose programs were not bound
by the same moral inhibitions and artistic limitations?

At the very least, the cassette threatened to vie for the
viewer's time and to diminish the average number of viewing
hours per day in the more affluent households. Together with
cable and pay TV, the new development augured a smaller
and harder-to-please audience for the commercial broadcaster; in short, less circulation to sell to the advertiser. Furthermore, a wired nation—*i.e.*, one in which cable had become dominant—would alter the character of the television
audience, probably in much the same way that the radio
audience became redefined as several different audiences—
those partial to news, telephone talk, rock 'n' roll, classical
music, country music, jazz, acid rock, old-fashioned pop
music, or a combination of sports and breezy personalities.
Television had always had a horizontal audience, playing

to what was considered to be the mass taste. Cable's deed
might well be to turn the stations into vertical entities, each
addressing itself to a specific audience, whether white-collar,
blue-collar, ethnic, suburban, teen-age, geriatric, or whatever.

It would take several years for the new technology to
subvert the present system, and there was always the possibility that the new developments would never catch on. Even
so, there was for the broadcaster the immediate jeopardy of
new regulatory proposals from the Federal Communications
Commission in the wake of the serious economic blow to
radio and television resulting from congressional action to
halt the sale of cigarette advertising after January 1, 1971.

The loss of cigarette billings alone had the television industry in a panic. Tobacco business annually came to nearly
$220 million in an industry that grossed just over $3 billion
a year. Collectively one of the largest and most reliable customers of the networks, the cigarette companies usually
bought early to stake out the most desirable advertising positions, and rarely haggled over price. The networks had been
unable to develop new business sufficiently to replace the
cigarette advertiser in 1971, and they were prepared for a
chaotic market in January. Since the economics of television answer to the laws of supply and demand, and since
there would be less demand and a greater supply of available
minutes for sale in 1971, the other advertisers were in position to beat the networks down to substantially lower rates,
and that would resonate at the local stations which were in
competition for the national advertiser's dollar. It followed
that if buying the networks became much cheaper, more buying would be done in the national medium and less in the
local.

The cigarette issue was, from the beginning, the measure
of the station operator's dedication to profits and unwillingness to meet the terms of his license. Clearly, since the Sur-
geon General's report, which linked smoking to cancer, and
heart and respiratory illnesses, it was not in the public interest to promote the use of cigarettes. A broadcast license

is granted under the law to those who vow to serve the "pub-lic interest, convenience, and necessity," but only a handful of stations gave up cigarette advertising voluntarily, and then only when it became evident that they would lose it anyway.

The majority, through the National Association of Broad-casters, waged an unsuccessful fight to kill the legislation, arguing that it was discriminatory toward the broadcast media since cigarette advertising would not be forbidden in the prints. But, of course, the validity of the bill was that newpapers and magazines are not licensed in the public in-terest, while the electronic media are. Having lost the fight, the American broadcaster was faced with an economic crisis and would have to practice a strict austerity to preserve his standing with his stockholders.

On top of the cigarette crisis were two devastating pro-posals for rule-making at the FCC which the broadcasters felt were calculated to break up the industry. One would curtail the networks' dominance over prime time, the other would break up the concentration of media in cities where a single owner may have radio, television, and newspaper properties. Both proposals had hung in the balance for years, but the FCC now seemed anxious to push them through.

Concern over the cross-ownership of newspapers and broadcast stations in a single city had predated Nicholas Johnson's appointment to the Commission in 1967, but it was he who turned the concern into alarm. Johnson focused on such media baronies as Walter Annenberg's complex in Pennsylvania. In addition to owning two of the major news-papers in Philadelphia, one of three VHF television stations, a powerful AM radio station, and an FM station there, An-nenberg also owned AM-FM-TV combinations in Altoona, Pennsylvania, and Binghamton, New York (at the Pennsyl-vania border), and a TV station in Lancaster, Pennsylvania. Potentially, these properties gave him extraordinary power to shape opinion in the eastern part of the state, and if he did not take advantage of it the possibility existed for his successors.

In a practical case, the question of multimedia ownership came to the fore in Chicago with the purchase by WGN Continental Broadcasting of the fine-arts FM station, WFMT. It was a profitable station and perhaps the most prestigious FM property in the country, but what prompted the issue of media monopoly was that the station had long been identified as politically liberal, while WGN, a sister corporation to the *Chicago Tribune* and *New York Daily News,* was associated with the conservative viewpoint. Reacting to the possible silencing of one of the few liberal electronic voices in the city, a Chicago citizens' group was formed to fight the acquisition, to keep the parent Tribune Company from enlarging its media empire in the city, which already included two newspapers, the *Chicago Tribune* and *Chicago Today,* and two stations, WGN-TV and the 50,000-watt clear-channel WGN Radio.

Although vigorous, the fight was technically unsuccessful, for the sale was approved by the FCC. But the attacks continued, and fearful of being hurt by the publicity over a property of limited profit potential, WGN donated the FM station to the nonprofit group which operated the local educational TV station, WTTW. Its slight income would help to support the noncommercial station.

By the time of the National Association of Broadcasters' convention in April, the sentiment was strong in Washington to limit media ownership in any market to one newspaper, or one TV station, or an AM-FM radio combination. Such a rule was almost a certainty and would bear on future station purchases, but the dreadful question was whether its enactment would be retroactive, forcing the existing multimedia owners to divest themselves of radio, TV, or newspaper operations in the same city.

Coupled with the one-to-a-market rule was a long-pending FCC proposal to reduce the networks' dominion over prime time. The original proposal, made to the Commission by Westinghouse Broadcasting, was known as the "50-50 rule" because it advocated a 50 per cent division of programing of the evening hours from seven to eleven o'clock between the networks and the local stations. By way of compromise, after considering arguments against the proposal by stations, networks, and program suppliers, the FCC drafted a plan to restrict the networks to three hours of prime time each night. In a practical sense, 7:00 to 7:30 P.M. was not normally considered prime time, since the network or local news was usually carried at that time, and the new rule meant simply that the networks would have to give up thirty minutes a night for the affiliated stations to program in their own way, either with programs they produced themselves or with those purchased from syndication. If the latter, the single restriction was that they be first-run programs and not shows that had previously had exposure on the networks.

The theory behind the proposal was that it would help to make the local stations stronger, giving them premium time in which to develop identities of their own, hopefully to deal with issues pertinent to the communities they served. But the industry view was that the rule would make both the stations and the networks weaker.

The vast majority of stations had no desire to invest in the expensive production of local shows for which they probably would not be able to sell sufficient advertising, or to risk the expense of another half hour of syndicated programing. Besides, if they had ever really wanted to do either they were always free to deny the networks program clearance for those choice hours. But most stations preferred to press the electronic button that would bring on the network show. For giving their time to the network they collected station compensation—a small portion of the revenues the network received from its sponsors—and in addition there were station breaks to sell, for which the stations received premium rates. That had been paradise.

At a closed seminar of broadcasters in 1967, the question put to one station operator was, What is your biggest expense?

He answered: taxes.

A TV station that had been built on a capital outlay of less than a million dollars twenty years before was now worth $12 million or upward, depending on the size of the advertising market it was licensed to serve. In markets of a million or more people, the license for a network-affiliated VHF station could be worth $50 million. Assuming they could be purchased, the network flagships in New York City were considered to be worth as much as $150 million, and even more, depending on the rating situation.

All this meddling by the FCC and Congress was hurting the broadcaster's ability to increase his profits.

Worse than that, far worse, was that the specter of change was tending to reduce the market value of his stations.

Nick Johnson, the FCC commissioner with long hair, had invitations to both conventions and predictably chose the little CJR conference, where he was guest of honor and featured speaker. If nothing else told the NAB delegates that the group across the street was an assembly of radicals conspiring to overthrow the system, it was the young commissioner's presence there.

At thirty-four, after three years on the Commission, he had done more than anyone in at least two decades—including the overrated Newton Minow—to look after the public's share of the air waves. Even while he held the lowest seniority on the Commission, he succeeded in reminding the broadcaster of the impermanence of his license and in frightening him into serving the minority as well as the majority of his community. He was a critic, a reformer, an activist, a zealot, and—worst of all, from the broadcasters' standpoint—an achiever.

He led the fight to break up the media baronies, he spoke before citizens' groups telling them of their right to challenge broadcast licenses (and thus was held responsible by the industry for the raft of licenses that had been filed against), and he campaigned against discriminatory censorship which tended to shut off the air waves to new ideas and to dissent against the existing order in the country. From his voting record on the FCC, it was apparent that he desired a sweeping revision of station ownership, retiring those who had profited so handsomely from radio and television and transferring the broadcast privilege to others, who might treat it with more reverence.

That he had success as a reformer was due in no small measure to his ability to express himself well and to his intelligent use of the print media and public forums to promulgate his arguments. But mostly he succeeded for the best of reasons: his criticisms were hard to deny and his positions often devastatingly valid.

The industry used to have a way of silencing commissioners who took their jobs too seriously. The technique was to vilify them as censors, charging them with overstepping their authority in acting as dictators rather than regulators. Such charges usually reflected on the administration responsible for the appointment, and none wanted to be held guilty of telling a publisher what to publish or a broadcaster what to broadcast. It did not work with Nick Johnson, who simply ignored the charges, published an article in *The Atlantic Monthly* on the media barons, befriended the Smothers Brothers when CBS evicted them for their outspokenness, wrote a book critical of television while on the Commission, and continued to address citizens' groups on their right to apply for the existing broadcasting licenses.

He was, of course, despised by the industry and portrayed as an enemy of the people. The logic there was that the American people loved television (as they demonstrated in the ratings), and Johnson wanted to destroy the system that provided what they loved. *Broadcasting*, the trade journal that profited on flattering the industry, huffed and puffed in trying to expose Johnson as a show-off, an office seeker, a nihilist, and at last as a subversive. It reached a low point in

trying to hold him up to ridicule as the only commissioner
to close his office in observance of the first anniversary of
Martin Luther King's assassination.

Johnson's speech at the CJR counterconvention mainly
reprised his dissent in the FCC's decision the previous week
to fine an educational Philadelphia FM station, WUHY, for
broadcasting an interview with Jerry Garcia, leader of a
rock group, The Grateful Dead, without censoring the four-
letter words that were native to his idiom. The interview had
been taped for a cultural program series dedicated to the
avant-garde and underground culture, but while such words
as fuck and shit might be acceptable language to that select
audience, they had *always* been taboo on the air.

It was a case that troubled the FCC because it was difficult for the seven commissioners to establish whether the
words were obscene or merely indecent, and what the limits
of indecency were in broadcasting. In the end, the entire
Commission determined that the issue had better be left to
the courts. Still, the majority voted to punish the station with
a token fine of $100.

Johnson, in his dissent, had stated, "What this Commission condemns are not words but a culture—a life style
it fears because it does not understand."

Nothing is ever really accomplished at the formal NAB
sessions. The organization is too large and unwieldy for
practical business meetings with the full membership, and
its agenda always more ritualistic than utilitarian.

The real convention takes place on Monday night of the
convention week at the annual banquet hosted by Broadcast
Music, Inc., for the elite of the industry who operate stations.
The standing guest list, augmented every year by a few
names, consists of all past and present board members of
the host music licensing firm, BMI (most of whom are broadcasters), and all who have ever been officers of the National
Association of Broadcasters. Also invited are members of
the FCC and a handful of intimate press. Ostensibly a so-

cial evening, with a sumptuous spread of comestibles and no speeches, it provides the meeting place for the powerful station men with strong political connections to discuss their mutual problems and, over a dinner wine, to join in a consensus on a course of action to be recommended to the board of NAB.

On entering, guests are given a carefully laundered and pressed butcher's apron, their names gloriously embroidered across the front in longhand. The only other ornament is a tag at the waist, replaced every year, with a Roman numeral designating the number of consecutive years BMI has asked the guest to attend. Mine read IV, but there were many indicating XXII. If the apron was supposed to be an equalizer, the tag signified that some were equal longer than others.

Feeling conspicuous in my apron, although the only ones not wearing them were the waiters, I stood off to the side with a bourbon trying to make myself believe that this was really a gathering of broadcasting's mightiest station operators and not a Kiwanis stag in Nebraska. The oxymoron of the apron —rich men decked out as working class—seemed to me a dull joke and somehow irrelevant to broadcasting. Surely unintended by BMI, the crowd in its white uniform eerily suggested the Ku Klux Klan.

It was, to me, significant that no network executives of high rank were in attendance and that, of the commissioners, Nick Johnson was conspicuously absent (although Russ Sanjek of BMI later assured me he had been invited). This was a scene from *Babbitt*, and there are some who just cannot handle it.

I spotted Ollie Treyz, a former network president and the sort of person who could play this kind of thing either way, and walked over to him. He was taking it seriously, the apron foolishness and all, which meant it was not playtime for him but business. Treyz had become a consultant to television advertisers and was working on the syndication placement of a game show called *He Said, She Said.* He knew this group well.

"What do you make of the convention?" he asked.

"I hear there's a lot of trading going on."

"You better believe it," he said. "It's not a convention this year, it's a giant game of Monopoly. You know what it is—it's a lawyer's convention. I've never known these guys to carry their general counsels around like this before. At this very moment, while they are all standing here having cocktails, their lawyers are bending heads in suites at the Hilton working out station trades in case the Commission should make the one-to-a-market rule retroactive."

Clair McCullough, chairman of the Steinman stations and a long-time part of the NAB power structure, approached us.

"We were just talking about the mood of this convention," Treyz said to him. "What really is the mood, Clair?"

"Militant."

"How do you mean, militant?" I asked.

"We're bitter about this rule, and we're going to fight this thing. All the broadcasters are together on this one, and if you ask how do we feel right now as an industry I'd have to say militant."

McCullough went on to circulate among the others.

Militant, the broadcaster would back the NAB in its fight to keep the FCC from breaking up the media monopolies. But he would not be so foolish as to count on a victory. In the meantime, it was valuable to be among his fellow broadcasters to explore the trading of stations, if that should one day be necessary.

Shortly the waiters passed the word, and the "militants" quit the oyster bar and hors d'oeuvres spread, carried their cocktails to the tables set up for ten and, over the continental dinner with three wines, discussed whether a station in a top-fifty market was equal to two in the next fifty.

The day before the CJR conference opened, Willard Walbridge, a Houston operator who was chairman of the NAB, spoke at a seminar of the Chicago Broadcast Advertising Club, one of several satellite events to the big convention itself. What Walbridge said became ammunition for the young rebels. It was this:

"Somewhere and sometime someone first wrote or uttered the phrase 'the public's air waves.' May *his* soul rest in peace; he has left us none.

"For there is no phrase so apt for the glib detractor, so useful for the demagogue, so sly for the covetous competitor, so relevant for the cynical military revolutionary."

Walbridge had fired the opening shot of another bungling campaign by the industry to answer critics of the medium. His device was to defend the medium by suggesting that something was wrong with its detractors, down to a hint that the critics might not be true-blue Americans.

The concept of "public air waves," he said, was a "lazy oversimplification of the extremely complex relationship among the three limited partners involved—the public, the government, and the broadcaster." Later in the speech he was to make the admission that "in broadcasting—nothing happens until we make a sale."

Walbridge, in his argument, usurped two-thirds of the public's ownership of the air on which broadcast signals travel, suggesting perhaps that the government and the broadcaster, in their "complex relationship," each owns one-third of the air people breathe.

It is a poetic idea, maybe, but the air *does* belong to everyone and is not like land which can be homesteaded. What Walbridge betrayed was a notion on the part of entrenched broadcasters that they had squatters' rights to their frequencies because they had occupied them so long. It was precisely this attitude that made Nick Johnson and others want to break up the industry. And in confessing that nothing happens in broadcasting until there is a sale, Walbridge established that the broadcaster yields his own one-third claim of the air waves regularly to mammon.

In reaction, the rebel convention passed the following resolution:

"We vigorously object to the effort of Willard E. Walbridge . . . to redefine the 'ownership' of the airways. His statement of April 3 to the Broadcast Advertising Club of Chicago was self-serving nonsense.

"We affirm the basic legal and ethical principle that the air waves belong to the people. They are leased to broadcasters to serve the public interest, convenience, and necessity. But the broadcasters have turned the air waves into lucrative commercial enterprises serving private interests rather than public needs, befouling the air waves in the process of selling products that pollute the air and land and water.

"We urge the FCC to reassert the public interest, rather than simply creating artificial scarcity of channels and distributing the loot.

"As an immediate step, we urge that the FCC require that one-third of prime-time broadcasting be of a sustaining or public service character, in line with the proposal developed by Commissioner Nicholas Johnson."

Years of contact with station operators, documenting their crises and deeds in both small and large cities, have taught me that most of the men who control the country's electronic media bend to two things: money and political power. They will carry programs against their principles if they are profitable, and they will sell out their last vestige of First Amendment freedom to any politician who would give them a sense of permanence as licensees. They are pushovers for a government that would seek absolute rule.

The Nixon Administration had only to charge the networks with unfair treatment to persuade a majority of affiliated stations that their sources of national news were biased; and the effectiveness of the White House campaign to collar the networks, beginning with Vice President Spiro Agnew's attack in his televised Des Moines address on November 13, 1969, was his immediate intimidation of the stations. When the government criticizes broadcasting, it effectively dictates its requirements to the industry.

The American television system is not built upon networks but upon local stations. If that comes as a surprise to a single reader, it proves the failure of a good idea. The British system is based on a national service that allows for regional contributions; the American, democratically, was conceived as multiple independent and autonomous local services whose primary obligations were to their immediate communities. A multiplicity of stations would guarantee competition between them to better serve the areas within their coverage span, and if it suited any of them to affiliate with an unlicensed national program service that was their privilege, *so long as they assumed the responsibility, as licensees, for what was broadcast through their facilities.*

Undeniably the theory has merit, but it has never worked properly in the United States, because the stations have allowed the networks to dominate the system. Why? A single reason. Because it is economic to do so.

A station may produce a program of its own, sell it to a local used-car dealer at break-even or a loss, and nurse it along for months until its rating is sufficient to attract advertisers with large budgets who make it profitable. Or the station may push a button in the master control room that would bring up the network with a glamorous, nationally promoted show—and receive in return a small percentage of the network's advertising revenues for the program (called *station compensation*) and about two minutes per hour within and adjacent to the show, which it is privileged to sell locally.

The costs of local production vary from market to market, depending on whether unions are involved. In the largest cities, a fairly pretentious local show playing five days a week might cost $25,000 a week to produce, a more modest one $10,000 a week. The rule of thumb in cities the size of New York, Los Angeles, Chicago, and Philadelphia is that each rating point is worth approximately $200 a minute. In local programs, it is permissible to sell five minutes per half hour. It may take weeks, or even months, for a local program to build up a 10 rating; in that event, the program theoretically would gross $10,000 a day. Out of that amount, the station would pay commissions of 15 per cent to the advertising agency and 11 per cent to the station representative. Given discounts, in addition, and a certain number of unsold minutes, the net revenues would realistically average approximately $6,000 a day. For a program that cost $25,000 a week, the profit would be $5,000. Not bad—but what of the early months when the program played at ratings of 2 and 3 and was sold to local merchants at half price? And what if it never catches on and runs at a 5 rating for six months or a year?

In the medium-sized markets, a single rating point is generally worth $50 to $60 a minute to national advertisers, and in the smaller ones perhaps $25 and $30. Since the small markets receive ratings only twice a year, there may be no proof of a local program's success for six months.

The national advertiser, working through a New York or Chicago advertising agency, might buy minute participations in a movie or an off-network rerun like *Gilligan's Island* in Wichita, Kansas, but he would eschew the locally produced program unless it had a satisfactory rating history. As one understanding broadcaster put it: "The buyer has to worry about his own ass. He can't afford to take chances. The movies and *Gilligan's Island* he knows about; the local show he doesn't."

Obviously, when the station operator is faced with the choice of creating a local program or taking a network show, he is far better off punching up the network. Not only does it simplify the pursuit of income, it also reduces the need for studio space and staff. Hit the network, make a buck. Guaranteed. The compensation for carrying a network show is a negotiated amount that usually ranges between 8 and 12 per cent of a station's own time rates. Over the course of a year, it can amount to quite a bit of money. To the New

York stations they own, the networks each pay upward of $4 million a year in compensation; in cities like Chicago and Los Angeles, more than $2 million; in markets the size of Detroit, St. Louis, Cleveland, or San Francisco, around $1.5 million. Even in the smallest markets, network payments may come to $250,000 a year.

All the stations need offer is their air time.

The networks, however, are not free to program all day long, to the despair of some station operators. So that the stations might fulfill their obligation to perform vital services to their communities, the FCC requires that there be some local time. That viewers can seldom tell the difference between network and local time is not because the level of local programing is so high but because local programs are so rare.

Having the opportunity to be a communications force in his locale, the station operator spurns it for immediately lucrative "canned" programing—movies or nationally syndicated shows which have no relevance to the service he is licensed to perform. Often they are reruns of film shows that have previously played the networks or cheap revivals of old game shows which had had a network vogue (*Truth or Consequences, Beat the Clock, To Tell the Truth*). Of more substance are the talk shows such as *The David Frost Show* and *The Mike Douglas Show*—television's "desk jockeys"— but they are risky items for syndicators and have had a high rate of failure (Donald O'Connor, Steve Allen, Woody Woodbury, Dennis Wholey, and Regis Philbin, among numerous others).

An old practice that had been considered disreputable in earlier television times was revived in 1969 with new-found respectability that can only be attributed to the higher quality of programs involved and the greater eminence of the advertiser. When it was associated with bowling shows and was circulated by bowling-equipment manufacturers who received a plug every time the pins were set, it was called *barter*. In its new form, it is called *advertiser syndication*. The program series are created by one or two national advertisers who assume all production costs, and they are given free to stations in exchange for two advertising positions. The station may then sell the remaining spots as pure profit. Typical of the shows are *The Galloping Gourmet*, *This Is Your Life*, *The Pet Set*, and *The Real Tom Kennedy Show*.

Since it costs the station manager nothing and allows him to make money, and since it is a bargain for the advertiser, who does not have to buy the commercial time and who amortizes the price of the show by placing it in as many cities as he needs for his marketing purposes, advertiser syndication has become a booming new field, with new companies formed to specialize in it.

By 1970 it appeared to be growing into a kind of secondary network, one that was ruled over by the advertiser, who determined the shape and substance of the program. The individual station willingly gave up local time in this way.

Again it is a generalization and there are some conspicuous exceptions, but for the most part any programing outside of news that is designed to contribute to the spiritual, intellectual, social, or cultural enrichment of the community is usually confined to the hours of the broadcast week that are least desirable to advertisers—weekdays after midnight or before dawn, and Sunday mornings and early afternoons—because the viewing potential is so hopelessly low.

In most large cities it is possible to receive a choice of educational programs on commercial stations at six o'clock in the morning. Religious shows are generally aired on Sunday mornings when religious people are in church. Discussion programs on local issues most often are cast into TV's Sunday ghetto, those hours when the Nielsen surveys show the least inclination for viewing in the majority of television homes.

But add it all up, and over the period of a year it comes

to a numerically impressive account of local service. It is in these fringe-time periods, with low-budget programs, that the typical station fulfills the promises under which it was awarded its license and by which it wins its renewal every three years.

A station may decline to carry any portion of network service at any time, but rarely are the peak viewing hours—7:30 to 11:00 P.M. (Eastern Time)—sacrificed to programs of local origin and local importance. When they are, the station managements are so overcome with their own magnanimity that they expect nothing less for their contributions of public service than the Nobel Prize.

The typical station is not physically prepared to produce more than a few routine newscasts a day, a few unpretentious public affairs shows for the weekends, and perhaps a daily children's show interlaced with stock cartoons (*Captain Andy, Fireman Fred,* and the like), or an interview show for women. There is no such thing any more as a staff writer, except in the news department; the resident directors are usually involved with cuing up commercials within the local movies; the production staff busies itself with commercials for local automobile dealers or department stores; and the director of programing is little more than a film buyer. Having toured numerous stations throughout the country in markets of all sizes, I have been impressed only with the size of their sales and clerical staffs. The outstanding exceptions are the television stations of Cincinnati, particularly WLWT and WCPO-TV, which still produce daily programs in the grand manner before studio audiences, utilizing local musicians and performing talent.

Few stations have any real identity with the viewership beyond their channel position, their network source, and the faces of their newscasters. It is probable that the television consumer would have no awareness of them as station entities except for the two-second billboards, mandatory under FCC regulations, which identify their call letters once an hour. And some resourceful stations have even figured ways to turn the station identification slide into revenue by carrying an advertiser's message alongside it.

It was a noble theory to make the station the basic component of the system and hold it responsible for what it broadcasts, but in practice it has been about as effective as holding the newsstand dealer responsible for what appears in the papers. Like the newsstand operator, all the average station owners really want to do is sell.

The American broadcaster is one part conscience and nine parts profit-motive. The better ones may be three parts conscience. Even so, it is a sorry ratio for media with such power and penetration in a society.

In his defense is the fact that the broadcaster did not begin with the intention of plundering the air waves. He was simply allowed to indulge in bad habits by an inattentive government; a historically apathetic, sometimes even sympathetic, regulatory agency, the Federal Communications Commission; and an abstruse Communications Law dating to 1934, written before anyone could foresee television as the dominant medium of, much less foretell its implications on, American life.

Admittedly, it took some courage to invest large sums of money in the new medium during the forties and early fifties, and mindful of that the FCC exempted the television operator not only from a high level of performance but also from many of his basic responsibilities as a licensee in order to help him build television into a sturdy business. It became a good business soon enough, but the early permissiveness established precedents for practices which put profits before service and for the FCC's passivity. Moreover, after two decades, the Commission continued to accept the broadcaster's argument that he was entitled to make princely profits because he had risked so much to pioneer the new medium.

Why—the broadcaster asked when his license was challenged by another applicant—turn over such a fantastic money machine to a Johnny-come-lately who never risked a dollar in those dark early days, taking it away from one who helped to build television into a great business? The rest of the question was, Why me?

The patterns of performance were fairly general, as over the years one broadcaster learned from another how to pull the maximum profit from the medium.

How much was the broadcaster to be blamed? He had been spoiled not by the intended system but by the one that had carelessly evolved. Confederate to the indolent FCC in keeping the original theory from realization was the specialist at law, the communications attorney. His first trick was to scare off the FCC from any attempt at considering the quality and effectiveness of a broadcaster's service to his public by charging government censorship. The lawyers have said over the years that the Commission is supposed to regulate, not evaluate, and any expression of dissatisfaction with the level of television programing by a commissioner was called an intrusion by the government into the content of the medium.

Secondly, the attorneys succeeded in reducing to gibberish the key phrase in the Communications Act, "the public interest, convenience, and necessity," calling it too abstruse for the FCC to use as a criterion of performance and a station's right to a renewal of its license. The terms are not defined, they argued, and who is to say what the public interest is?

Robert Sarnoff, in a speech while he was still chairman of corporate NBC (he has since become chairman of the parent RCA Corporation), once ventured a definition. He said the public interest was what the public was interested in. It was patently a definition to justify broadcasting's excesses in commercial entertainment. A young child may be *interested* in lighting matches and an older one in experimenting with drugs, but any parent knows that neither is in their best interest.

The term *public interest* may be hard to define, but it is not without meaning. Nevertheless, for many years the FCC accepted the possible validity of such a definition as Sarnoff's, which then made ratings the arbiter of the public interest and made a social virtue of the broadcaster's devotion to the numbers. The net effect was that an individual could be awarded a radio or television license for promising to serve the public interest, convenience, and necessity, but would not lose it for really failing to do so.

Now the typical operator of a station is a great advocate of free enterprise. He wants to be free to do business in his own way, without government curbs or interference. But he wants the government to protect his exclusivity to broadcast. He does not want an expansion of the spectrum so that more broadcasters may get in to compete with him, and he does not advocate free enterprise for the cable operator or the pay television entrepreneur. And he probably would have fought public television, too, if it were not for the fact that a public channel meant one less commercial competitor on the dial.

Basically, that summarizes the broadcast industry's ambivalent relationship with the FCC. It is wicked when it attempts regulation that interferes with the pursuit of maximum profits, requires the broadcaster to program for the poorer classes who are unattractive to advertisers, makes it a condition of licensing that he prove his attempt to ascertain community needs through meetings with civic groups, and insists that he present both sides of any issue according to the fairness doctrine. But on the other hand, the Commission is the parent to whom the broadcaster runs to protect him from new competition and from the new technology that could make him obsolete.

Appointments to the FCC are made by the President subject to Senate approval, and whether or not the choices are favorable to the industry's status quo frequently depends on the Administration's mood. Because the big favors to broadcasting come from Washington, station operators tend to be highly responsive to the values and desires of the governing powers.

Swaying with the powers in Washington is built into the fabric of American television, and therefore it was ironic that an industry that is natively reactionary and pro-Establishment should suddenly be on the make for the youth audience with which it has nothing in common. Dissidents and persons with off-center views were continually being cast out of the industry, and yet it was with people like them that television wanted to identify in 1970. For strictly business reasons, rating demographics.

The program schedules offered such syndicated series as *The Now Explosion* and *The Music Scene,* along with the network series *Mod Squad, Storefront Lawyers, The Young Lawyers, The Interns,* and *The Young Rebels,* all designed to prove that television was "with it," in tune with the new generation, paying tribute to their idealism.

But the real-life young rebels were across the street from the NAB convention, at the *Chicago Journalism Review* conference, and they aroused a single emotion in the broadcasters: loathing.

9

Specials: Beauty and Truth

Raquel Welch is sculpture. Not through movies did she become the American goddess of sex but through exploitation campaigns with still photographs. Frozen pictures are her medium. Movement, in her case, is best left to the imagination; a careless motion picture camera could at any time explode the myth of her sensual appeal. As for her performing talents—singing, dancing, acting—they are, to put it politely, limited.

Yet her first television special, which aired on CBS

April 26, not only drew one of the season's highest ratings but also a stream of favorable reviews.

Why?

How? is the better question.

On Sunset Strip, just off Doheny in an unimposing building constructed as residential, were the offices of Winters/Rosen Productions, one of the many young independent firms in Hollywood that were flourishing as the major studios declined. David Winters, looking like affluent local color on the Strip, his hair bushy, his costume culled from the exotic boutiques of Los Angeles, and his fingers warted with jeweled rings, worked in an office that seemed furnished for a séance. Down the hall, his partner, Burt Rosen, dressed in a neat business suit, suggested an up-and-coming studio executive. The few arty touches around his otherwise conventional desk, an art-glass shade and some antique-shop bronzes, advertised a taste for the offbeat in a man who regularly would deal with the dead-center business types who bought shows, represented actors, or negotiated contracts.

They were a good complement for the times, one member free to be creative, the other looking after the tawdry business particulars, and together in mild rebellion against the pat formulas of television presentations.

Both had proper show business credentials. Winters had been an actor since the age of five, earning his chief credit on the stage in a dance role, Baby John, in *West Side Story*. The film version had brought him to Hollywood, where he remained. As a choreographer, he was but one step removed from directing and so made the transition. In the course of things he learned cinema photography and camera techniques. Rosen had been a production assistant at 20th Century-Fox before becoming, at twenty-five, vice-president of programing for Four Star Productions, involved chiefly with a series of specials, each built around a star, which Celanese was sponsoring in syndication. Winters directed some of them.

As a team they were innovative and capable of unusual

production effects without violating the commercial purposes of television shows. They went into business together in 1968.

Winters/Rosen had been through three difficult specials, two of them with Ann-Margret, the other with Nancy Sinatra, difficult because the performers lacked the stature, the iridescence, and the range of talent to carry an hour-long program confined to a television stage. It was necessary to invent for them novel sequences, so that the camera's infinite variety would seem to be theirs.

The programs came off well as television fare, flashy and diverting, and they aggrandized the participants. Winters/Rosen, for a new company, had a good name.

In the spring of 1969 Rosen was in New York trying to develop new projects for the company. Over drinks at the Regency bar with John Allen of the McCann-Erickson agency he learned that Coca-Cola would need a powerhouse special the following April to draw attention to its packaging changes and modernized graphics, and into which the Coke bottlers' seasonal campaign could be tied. To change the design on all its trucks, dispensing machines, bottles, posters, and six-pack cartons was a vast operation for Coca-Cola that would cost millions. Allen, as senior vice-president for radio and television at the advertising agency, had recommended heralding the new look with a superspecial on TV that would be glamorous, innovative, and of interest to the largest possible number of people, including the young, who are the prime consumers of soft drinks.

The problem came down to a name to build the program around that was certain to produce an audience—someone like Raquel Welch, Allen said, although he was sure she would not want to do television.

"If I can get Raquel, do we have a show?" Rosen asked.

Allen gave him a handshake, symbolic of a deal.

Back in the hotel room, Rosen telephoned his partner. He recalled Winters mentioning that he had once coached Raquel in dancing for a few weeks. Also, Winters/Rosen and Raquel Welch were represented by the same talent agency, Creative Management Associates, so that reaching her would probably not be a problem.

Winters had no luck getting Raquel's home number from the agency, but he did get a lead from an out-of-work actor who was employed as a bartender. Raquel was, that very evening, filming scenes for the picture *Flare-Up* on location in Los Angeles, outside the night club The Losers, on La Cienega Boulevard. Driving there, Winters confronted her with the proposal.

The answer was no. She had been asked to do television before by better-known producers and turned them all down. She was not Mitzi Gaynor, who could stand on a sound stage and entertain, and she had no desire to give her name to a show in which she would do little more than introduce a succession of variety acts. Besides, television had too many taboos, and Coca-Cola was too conservative a company. There would be no way to realize her talents. Winters asked if she had seen the Ann-Margret specials. They were for a young, sexy performer whose career had stopped making progress, and the two TV shows revived interest in her as a beauty and as a possible rival to Raquel. She had indeed seen the shows, and she confessed to being impressed with a poetic filmed sequence of Ann-Margret in Sweden, photographed in soft focus and portraying her as a daughter of the land, sensual but sensitive to nature and moved by literature.

That, said Winters, is the way we want to present you— a creature of nature, a child of the sun. You and the sun. That's the premise—he was making it up as he spoke—we follow the sun across the world as you pursue it as your source of life, your wellspring of inspiration and joy. Trust the cameras, the costumes, and the scenery. We'll build a beautiful show, and we'll build it around you.

I like that, Raquel said. Now I'm interested.

After the night's shooting for *Flare-Up* they drove to the restaurant she chose, Dolores', a cheap hamburger joint. Winters liked her for that. The others in Hollywood always

have to go to Chasen's or The Bistro. He also had favorable
vibrations about her husband, Patrick Curtis, who would
come with the package as his and Burt's co-producer. It
would be a groove, Winters decided.

Excited that he had their agreement, he phoned Rosen
at once, waking him at three in the morning in New York.
He was still laying out the format: *following the sun to
Mexico, Big Sur, Sun Valley, and England and Paris for
the great props.* . . .

Rosen was on the phone with John Allen that morning.
Within forty-eight hours of their conversation at the Regency
all the necessary papers were in motion. Raquel Welch would
carry Coke's message in April 1970 in a program budgeted
at around $400,000. That kind of money carried a mandate:
ratings.

A month later, Coke sold off half the sponsorship to Motorola, another company seeking a showcase for a spring
campaign. Both sponsors would help build an audience for
it by promoting it on their trucks, in ads, and with posters
at the point of purchase.

Meanwhile, Rosen, figuring up the probable costs of so
ambitious a special, without knowing in advance how much
co-operation there would be from foreign governments and
airlines, estimated that it would probably exceed by some
$50,000 what the sponsors had agreed to pay. That could
be recovered or even turned into profit through sales over-
seas and repeat showings in the United States, but even if
the company broke even with it, the *Raquel* special would
be a major credit and a chance to do more business with
Allen, one of advertising's most astute impresarios of the
television special. He and Winters would defer 25 per cent
of their fees as producers, and they convinced CMA, representing both the packagers and the star of the show, to accept
a smaller commission. With those concessions, Rosen reck-
oned, the show would come in just about on budget.

One hour of television, and a year's deadline—seemingly
favorable conditions. But there was this complication: Raquel

would be spending virtually the rest of 1969 filming *Myra Breckenridge* and would not be available for the TV project until she completed the motion picture. That meant the special would have to be shot during the winter months.

Out went the concept of chasing the sun.

It would have been warm enough in Mexico, Yucatan, and on tropical islands, but that would severely limit the scenery and background possibilities. Besides, Rosen was smitten with his own idea to pair off Raquel with the Welsh rock singer Tom Jones as the meeting of the English-speaking world's female and male sex symbols. That left no choice but to go to London, since Jones, whose own TV series would be in production there, was unable to travel.

After the signing of contracts the war began, the entire production experience a clash of hostile camps, Raquel/Curtis versus Winters/Rosen. The New Wave producers had their encounter with old-fashioned star temperament.

It began with Rosen's triumph in securing guest stars. In addition to Tom Jones, the biggest popular name in Britain for the American TV audience, he had also signed Bob Hope, highest-rated performer in American television, and John Wayne, the most sure-fire name in the American heartlands. Pure rating insurance.

Raquel was displeased. She had hoped he would try for Arlo Guthrie.

A *Playboy* interview with Raquel—one of those verbatim transcripts from a tape recording—brought John Allen to Los Angeles on a note of crisis. She had been unsparing of four-letter words in the interview, and, as Allen reminded Rosen, Coke is a very conservative company. It is all right to sponsor the nation's Number One sex symbol, the *sight* of whom is supposed to make every man think of rape, as long as she keeps it clean. Rosen, of course, was not Raquel's keeper or party to the interview, and there were no clauses in the contract prohibiting the star from using salty language off camera. There was nothing to be done. Coke's morally rigorous customers would not, in all probability, have read the *Playboy* interview, and anyone who had—if perchance he were to identify Raquel with Coke—might think better of the product for it. Coke would brave it, and the project proceeded.

Summer was given to the script, while Raquel was shooting her movie. Three young writers were assigned to it— Doug Tebbles, the head writer, in his thirties; Larry Alexander and Jonathan Axelrod, both in their twenties—on the theory that they would have fresh ideas, being not so experienced as to have become fixed in the ways of typical television vaudeville. By fall they had produced a first draft, then rewrote it extensively after meetings, and in December the shooting script was ready, at least for the London sequences. It was decided that the music director, Don Randi, would also go to London to record the music track there because it could be done more cheaply than in Hollywood.

In December, Rosen received a crisis call and flew to London. Raquel detested Randi's arrangements. "That's not *my* music," she said. "That's Roy Rogers' music." The producer was able to persuade her that it was her music.

In London she filmed her dramatic scene to compare with Ann-Margret's in Sweden, reading Tennyson's "The Lady of Shalott" in period costume. Caught up in an acting mood, when it came to the ultimate event of Male Sex meeting Female Sex—her song duet with Tom Jones—she soberly turned to her director, Winters, and asked, "What's my motivation?"

The best line, and it never got into the show.

Winters almost came around to liking her again in Paris, where, in subzero weather, she gamely went down the Seine on a barge for the cameras. But she was determined to keep it a hot war.

In Sun Valley she temperamentally decided to leave a day before the shooting wound up, taking with her the red parka used for her scenes. Refusing to lend it to Winters to complete the sequence, she boarded a plane and was gone. Eventually he found a similar parka and had it dyed red. The double who wore it, an Olympic skier who substituted for the star in all the beautiful skiing sequences shot from a helicopter, was a man.

At the pyramids of Teotihuacán in Mexico, she denied the newspaper photographers a picture session but was unable to get rid of them. They remained on the set, taking their shots like snipers, and one who advanced too close to Raquel was thrown to the ground by Curtis. Their fight set off a free-for-all, and although no one was seriously hurt, the incident served to create another delay in the shooting, added to the many which began when the crew was affected by the flu epidemic in London. There were more delays to come.

Just before the final scene, in which Raquel was simply to thank her guests and say good night, she closed a sketch with Bob Hope by accidentally falling off a table and breaking a bone in her hand. There was a hospital delay, and when she returned for the scene Winters camouflaged the cast on her arm with a bouquet of flowers.

Cutting the film was a mammoth job, since it entailed reducing 50,000 feet of exposed film to 2,000 feet for the program. A normal ratio of film shot to film used was 10 to 1. For *Raquel* it was 25 to 1.

It was now late February and the pressure was on. With delays and travel the shooting had consumed three months (although only forty actual filming days), and time was short for the finishing work so that a print could be delivered before April 1 in time for the Canadian telecast. (Canada frequently is accorded advance showings of specials produced for the United States networks). It would take three weeks of editing on top of ten months of planning and shooting to produce a stunning but insignificant hour of television which would evaporate from the viewer's mind within a day.

Bent over the Movieolas in their editing rooms one night, Winters and Rosen heard a voice behind them that had boomed at them too many times before. "Where are my fucking close-ups?" She and Curtis were off limits but there was no way to eject them so they closed down the facility for the night. Expectedly, Rosen heard from her lawyer, Barry Hirsch, the following morning. A reasonable man, he did not pursue the inquiry into her close-ups when reminded that the contract specified that Winters, as director, had final creative authority and control.

Raquel was an hour of illusion and artifice. There was a double for her horseback scenes, riding in a wig and an identical caftan, just as there was for the skiing. Tom Jones did most of the work in their song together, but judicious editing of the film made it appear that Raquel was making an equal contribution. All her singing was enhanced in the recording studio by a female quartet. And the dazzling dance number in Mexico, shot from a low-flying helicopter, gave Raquel the assistance of the Ballet Folklorico de Mexico. Her part in it was largely a fashion show; she had fifteen costume changes.

A single number, the opening song, "California Dreamin'," cost more than $25,000 to produce. Shot in two countries, France and Mexico, it involved more than twenty scenes, including glimpses of the Eiffel Tower, the Arc de Triomphe, Notre Dame, and other postcard backgrounds. With any reasonably accomplished singer who could carry off the number on her own talent, the song would have been performed in a TV studio and would have cost whatever five minutes represented pro rata of a video-taped hour.

But the real marvel of the program was a dance number before a fountain to the song "Raindrops Keep Falling on My Head." To shoot it took three days. Winters had Raquel perform a series of simple dance movements dozens of times each: skipping toward the fountain, turning around, kicking her right leg out, kicking her left leg out, going knock-kneed with an arm over her head, and others of the kind. All were painstakingly filmed from a variety of angles, and then, against the music, Winters spliced them together so that they formed the dance of a free spirit expressing the song. The sequence was danced in the editing room.

"This was Raquel Welch tripping the heavy fantastic,"

wrote Bill Greeley in his review for *Variety*. "This desperate mishmash was shot on 100 locations. It had 200 costume changes. It had 7,000 fast cuts. It had helicopter shots. It had telescopic lenses zooming in and out to the point of viewer nausea. It had three big name guest stars, war-dancing Indians, and Beatles music.

"None of the above could hide the outstanding lack of talent in this big woman with the smallest voice since the boop-boop-a-doop girl."

But other reviewers, including several of the important ones, received it with enthusiasm. Jack Gould's notice in the *New York Times*, while not effusive, was favorable. A particular favorite of mine among television critics, Rick Du-Brow of United Press International, was unrestrained in his praise.

"It is called *Raquel*," he wrote, "but it would not have been amiss to call it *Raquel and David* because of the staging and direction of David Winters. He has pulled off a visually gorgeous hour and Miss Welch profits mightily by it. In the end, in fact, what is fascinatingly triumphant—more than any of the stars in the show—is Winters' singularly uplifting sense of beauty, exuberance, and repose. His past shows have also exhibited this distinctively-styled view, but never with such exhilaration. Before the show is on very long, one realizes that the director has given it a motion picture, rather than a television; look."

There was, incidentally, one bit of censorship in the hour. Nothing to do with the overexposure of the star's plentitude, however. In a night-club scene with Tom Jones, there was a fast cut to the audience of no more than four or five seconds' length. I saw the original print and did not notice, but the fast scene did not escape a representative of Coca-Cola. Someone in the audience was holding a glass in which, among the ice cubes, was a slice of lime. Three frames of film, possibly, but it had to come out.

Coca-Cola is not served with a slice of lime.

The vital statistics for *Raquel* were a 36 rating and a 51

share. Translated: 51 per cent of all persons watching television in the hour were tuned to the special, representing 36 per cent of the TV homes in the United States.

The numbers, however, were unofficial, since their source was an overnight national survey by the American Research Bureau and not the regular national Nielsen report. As it happened, the special was televised during one of the Nielsen Company's four "dark weeks" * (it measures only forty-eight weeks of the year), planned hiatuses in which the rating company adjusts its survey apparatus. Given a choice CBS would have preferred scheduling the show during one of the regular Nielsen weeks so that its anticipated large rating could be counted in the network's circulation average for the season—indeed, Mike Dann repeatedly urged the ad agency to change the date so that *Raquel* could be part of his Operation 100 campaign to win the ratings in the final weeks of 1969–70—but, dark week or not, Coke held fast to the April 26 date because it conformed to the timetable of its own marketing plans.

For the discriminating television viewer, there are probably no better weeks of the year than the Nielsen dark weeks, for those are when the networks tend to play off the cultural and thoughtful programs which are presumed to have no rating punch but will serve a public relations argument that the networks are not totally preoccupied with serving mass interests and tastes. They are packed into the dark weeks so that their poor rating performances are not charged against the networks in the season's averages.

During the Christmas dark week of 1969, CBS offered a repeat of the children's drama that originally played on a Saturday morning, *J.T.*, in the *Gunsmoke* time period; a Sol Hurok presentation, *An Evening of Tchaikovsky*, featuring the Russian virtuosos Emil Gilels and Mistislav Rostropovich; the first of the Walter Cronkite conversations with former President Lyndon B. Johnson; and a Friday night news

---

* Also known in the trade as "black weeks." Every fifth year there are are five black, or dark, weeks.

special, *Correspondents' Report: End of a Decade.* NBC also scheduled a news special, *Election '69: What We Learned. Variety* called it "Television's Dark Week Festival."

Along with *Raquel,* the networks bunched into their spring dark week of 1970 both parts of CBS's two-part documentary *Health in America;* separate NBC documentaries on mental health and venereal disease, and a science special, *The Whale Hunters of Fayal;* and ABC's Jacques-Yves Cousteau special *Return of the Sea Elephants,* and an installment of the three-part ecology series *Mission Possible: They Care for This Land.* Also, the special coverage of Earth Day on all three networks.

Outside the dark weeks, from September 1969 to April 1970, the three networks had aired only thirty-seven programs among them in prime time which could be classified as nonentertainment specials, and eighteen of that number were sports specials. According to the Alfred I. Du Pont–Columbia University analysis of the specials in that period, only eighteen could be considered news documentaries—and, of those, eight concerned the Apollo flights. So the unrated week in the spring contained approximately 20 per cent of the special news documentaries the three networks offered all season.

One thing more about the dark weeks: since they are not counted in the ratings the networks generally choose not to waste first-run episodes and instead schedule reruns of their series. Thus, in addition to having staked out the best time period of the week for family viewing—Sunday night at nine —*Raquel* was advantaged in the ratings in that its competition, *Bonanza* and the ABC movie, would be in dark week repeats. Official or not, the numbers for *Raquel* exceeded the expectation of Coke and Motorola and lost John Allen none of his standing as one of advertising's canniest showmen.

He did not look the part. Peering through thick lenses which magnified his eyes, and having somehow resisted the cavalier style that seems to mark a big-time advertising executive, Allen suggests an electronics engineer who works with the innards of a TV set rather than with the software for it. As one of a vanishing breed of agency men who shop for and develop special programs for television—a breed supplanted by media experts who figure up the circulation per dollar and buy TV time at the most advantageous prices—he was in the forefront of the good providers.

Allen had been instrumental in breaking down the CBS resistance to two "series" of specials, the Charlie Brown animated shows and the National Geographic nonfiction anthology, both of which had become proud offerings of the network, playing four times a year with unfailing rating potency. The Charlie Browns (based on the *Peanuts* cartoon strip of Charles Schulz) had become perennials, minor family classics with the unusual history of attracting larger audiences for the repeat shows than for the originals. *Charlie Brown's Christmas*, in its fifth annual showing, pulled a phenomenal 53 share of audience in December of 1969. As for the National Geographics, they were a revelation in an industry which had long held it a principle that nonfiction did not appeal to a mass audience. The success of these specials, and of the occasional Walt Disney nature shows on Sundays, opened the way to wildlife, travel, and anthropology documentaries both on the networks and in syndication.

Since both series were novel ideas when they were proposed to CBS by Allen—Charlie Brown for his client Coca-Cola, the National Geographic shows for another client, Encyclopaedia Britannica—they were stubbornly resisted by network executives. The verdict from the CBS program department when the first Charlie Brown cartoon was screened was negative: too thin a story, the animation too slight, better left as a comic strip. The exact opinion, expressed by one of Mike Dann's lieutenants, had a familiar ring: "Piece of shit."

Even fully sold to two sponsors, Aetna Life Insurance and Britannica, the National Geographic specials were rejected by CBS in 1965 basically because they smelled like losers, but there was also a policy justification for turning them down. The network did not and would not accept docu-

mentaries from outside sources. The basis for the policy was
that CBS would be held responsible for factual information
that it broadcast, and since that was so it would provide the
factual programing from its own shop. While that much of
the argument was reasonable, the assignment of all nonfiction projects to CBS News, whether or not it had anything
to do with journalism, was not. Nonfiction and news are not
necessarily related.

Allen pursued CBS for both series in the belief that their
chances of succeeding were better at that network than at the
others, and his unseen and perhaps unwitting ally in both
instances was the man who assiduously stood apart from all
decisions on popular programing, CBS corporate president
and chief administrative officer Frank Stanton.

Allen and the chairman of his agency, Paul Foley, had
argued with lesser CBS officials that the network's nonfiction
policy was too rigid and falsely predicated. Natural phenom-
ena could better be discussed and interpreted by naturalists
than by news reporters. The argument persuaded CBS elder
statesman John Karol, one of Stanton's mentors and a close
friend (Karol, in fact, hired Stanton for the CBS research
department in 1935, after he had taken his doctorate at Ohio
State) that the policy should be loosened. A few days later
he phoned the agency to inform Foley and Allen that it had
been.

The Charlie Brown placement on CBS was somewhat
subtler. In the wake of the program staff's coolness toward
it, intelligence was passed along that Stanton was fond of
the *Peanuts* strip and that he had a personal relationship
with the creator, Schulz, which had grown out of a phone call
Stanton once made to the cartoonist in San Francisco just to
express his admiration. In a more recent communication,
Schulz had told Stanton that a TV version of the cartoon
was being attempted, and he said that if it became a television show he hoped it would be on Stanton's network.

Stanton in no way intervened in the decision to accept
the Charlie Browns, nor did he have the knowledge of why

it was accepted. The story of his relationship with Schulz had come from an outside source, but it was enough to make advocates of the program staff.

John Allen's persuasion led CBS to accept a pair of properties it did not really want, and they turned out to be gifts. CBS has been taking credit for them ever since.

Coca-Cola figured in another TV special a few months later, but not as a sponsor. In fact, the company used all the pressure it could muster as well as direct appeals to NBC to be kept out of it. The program was *Migrant*, a news documentary produced by Martin Carr, which for intellectual content, human insight, and social value was worth two hundred *Raquels*, although its audience was less than half the size.

Carr's documentary was a ten-year follow-up to the original television exposé of the inhumanities against the migrant workers in the United States, the memorable *Harvest of Shame*, produced by the late Edward R. Murrow and David Lowe, telecast November 25, 1960, and probably never surpassed as poignant, muckraking journalism in television. Centering on the migrant fruit pickers of Florida, *Migrant* showed that little had changed in ten years and that they remained a miserably impoverished and still shockingly exploited working force at the lowest end of the social and economic scale. Cited by name as one of the perpetrators of the sins, paying slave wages and providing substandard shanties for housing, was Coca-Cola Food Company, which has vast interests in the $400 million Florida citrus industry for such product divisions as Minute Maid, Hi-C, Snowcrop, Tropicana, and Donald Duck. In one sequence a representative of the company was shown interrupting Carr's interview on camera with a poor black woman and attempting to drive him off the property.

NBC had been unable to sell a minute of sponsorship in the program. And while it was trying to find a customer, several special-interest groups were doing their utmost to suppress the broadcast, making it clear that if they could not do so the network would be punished with legal and political harassments. It was an old story. CBS had been made to suffer for *Harvest of Shame;* for Murrow's March 9, 1954, denunciation of the late Senator Joseph McCarthy on *See It Now;* for its 1967 exposé on *Hunger in America;* for *Biography of a Bookie Joint,* in 1961, and for a 1967 report on marijuana smoking on the Northwestern University campus by its Chicago station, WBBM-TV, among others. In 1970, its two-part *Health in America* drew acrimonious charges of distortion from organized medicine. ABC had years of grief for its *A Political Obituary of Richard Nixon* (1962), which had featured an interview with Alger Hiss by Howard K. Smith. And NBC had its own long record of congressional and pressure-group misery for such earnest investigative reports as *Who Killed Lake Erie?* (1969), *The Battle of Newburgh* (1962), *Whose Right To Bear Arms?* (1967), a profile of New Orleans District Attorney Jim Garrison, and an examination in 1970 of chemical-biological warfare.

Good documentaries were bad business for broadcast companies that had allowed themselves to become extensions of the advertising industry and had no insulation from the petty political purposes of legislators and governors, who could retaliate in a number of different ways. Not only was there the expense of producing and presenting the programs, but also the added costs of legal defense, flights to Washington for testimony, and occasional losses of business from advertisers. And added to the burden of paperwork and correspondence were the man-hours, particularly the absorption of top management officials diverted from gainful business activities.

Courage is a requisite for good journalism, and courage is not easy to ask from companies that must answer to stockholders, advertisers, affiliated stations, and the source of their own valuable licenses—the government—before they answer to the public.

It is perhaps not coincidental that the television docu-

mentary flourished, locally as well as on the networks, during
John F. Kennedy's time as President and went into swift decline afterward. The climate of enlightenment generated by
the Kennedy Administration was conducive to journalistic
searching into social ailments and blight; later, with the beginnings of polarization in the society, the searcher became
suspect, as though his purposes were sinister instead of salu-
tary.

For practical reasons, the TV networks let the documentary fade as a program form and, to keep up appearances,
adopted instead the magazine format done so well by Canadian television, compendia of short pieces mixing together
light and serious subjects with an occasional investigative
film. The few full-length documentaries televised by the networks in any year would in the majority confine themselves
to safe subjects, with an occasional bold examination of an
aspect of the war in Indochina, a national reality that could
not go ignored too long.

ABC went beyond the selection of "soft" subjects for its
documentaries to the extent of letting the principal sponsors
of its news specials—Minnesota Mining and Manufacture,
B. F. Goodrich, and North American Rockwell—make the
determination of subject matter from a list of documentary
topics submitted by ABC News. One of the projects that appealed to 3M during 1969 was a program on the railroads.
It was listed by ABC under the working title of *The Death of
the Iron Horse*, but at the sponsor's behest it went into production as *The Golden Age of the Railroad*, an alteration of
title that dictated also a change in the program's concept.
The advertiser wanted to do a program on railroads, but not
from a negative view. Thus, in a year when railroad service
was deteriorating and when a news organization might have
provided a public service by calling attention to the railroad
crisis that was to be severely felt in the country during 1970,
ABC offered an ode to the glories of railroading.

So cautious had the networks become in the production
of searching documentaries that three of CBS's finest investi-

gative reporters were left to sit for months without assignments. Jay McMullen, Gene DePoris, and Martin Carr were the forgotten men of CBS News, "the ghost unit," as they called themselves. Through the long arid period they occupied themselves writing memoranda to their bosses suggesting new documentary projects, some of which produced a response but little more. McMullen, who had been responsible for *Biography of a Bookie Joint* among other muckraking programs, proposed a documentary on corruption in Saigon. The project was considered for a time by his superiors and then abandoned. Later he was assigned to film a program on patent medicines, and then was ordered to fold the project. DePoris had started work on a program about the military-industrial complex, and that, too, was scuttled.

McMullen took a year's leave of absence, and Carr accepted an offer to join NBC News. There he proposed a follow-up program to *Harvest of Shame*, re-examining what the Murrow-Lowe documentary had found to be the lot of the migrant worker in 1960. Permitted to make a preliminary survey, he returned from Florida with a strong recommendation that the network go forward with it. NBC News president Reuven Frank gave his approval.

The miracle of *Migrant* was that it was televised at all. Television news had been under constant fire in Washington ever since the political conventions of 1968, and particularly as a result of the telecast of the Democratic nominating ceremonies in Chicago during which CBS and NBC gave coverage to the demonstrations and street violence, cutting away periodically from the convention rites at the International Amphitheatre. Most Democrats were convinced that their attention to the violence had cost Hubert Humphrey the election for the presidency. Meanwhile, the Nixon Administration and Republicans generally were sure that the networks were anticonservative. Both sides were vengeful and distrustful of television's power, and the conservatives in particular were enjoying a campaign, led by Vice President Agnew, to discredit television news as biased. It was not an auspicious time for a hard-hitting exposé that would make waves in the business world which might wash into the political sphere.

As if that were not reason enough for strategic silence, business conditions were poor in 1970 and the networks deeply involved in austerity programs to keep their profits up. President Nixon's penchant for scheduling his speeches and press conferences in prime time (the primest time, 9:00 P.M.), knocking out commercial programing, was costing them millions; and with *Migrant* NBC would be subtracting yet another revenue-producing hour from its evening schedule. Finally, the network would be presenting a program that would embarrass, possibly hurt, one of its regular advertisers. Coca-Cola had already spent more than $2 million with NBC for participation spots in the new fall line-up, scattered over a dozen shows, and while it probably would not cancel the purchases as a result of *Migrant*, the prospects could not be good for a renewal of its business.

The efforts to suppress *Migrant*, or at least to dilute it, began about a month before the telecast. Although, to that point, no one outside the network had seen the film, NBC's announcements to the press gave sufficient hint that Carr's film would show the wretchedness of the migrant worker's life and that, whatever else, it would not be sympathetic to the fruit growers. Too, Carr's movements among the migrants were known to growers, so was the trend of his questions.

The Florida Fruit and Vegetable Association sent out a series of letters, which might be described as warnings. One was to Chet Huntley, who narrated the film, suggesting that NBC might not be in possession of all the facts, and then purporting to document the ways in which living and working conditions for the agricultural migrants had improved since *Harvest of Shame*. On June 22, letters went to both Dean Burch, chairman of the FCC, and Julian Goodman, president of NBC, from the Washington law firm L. Alton Denslow and Joseph O. Parker, representing the Association. Burch was told that although NBC had been furnished with "documented, factual information" to the contrary from the Association, indications were that NBC would televise a film reporting that little or nothing had been done in Florida to to improve the lot of the migrant worker. Such a biased presentation, the letter stated, "could result in grave injustice to the people of the state of Florida, particularly the workers and their employers."

And then the key paragraph:

"If the film is shown by a licensee of the Commission and is in fact a slanted news presentation, Florida Fruit and Vegetable Association will request the Commission to specify and issue as to whether such licensee is adequately discharging its responsibility so as to warrant its continuing to be a licensee."

This was a threat—cutting through the legalese—that any station carrying the program was in danger of being challenged.

The letter to Goodman requested that "you bring the views which we express here to the responsible operators of each station to which this documentary will be offered."

About two weeks before the telecast, NBC's affiliated stations received a letter from the Florida Fruit and Vegetable Association:

"This Association is in receipt of news which has caused us great concern over the possibility of NBC News televising a completely slanted documentary on migrants and migrant conditions in Florida.

"Our Washington attorneys have registered our concern with the chairman of the Federal Communications Commission and to the president of NBC. We are attaching copies of this correspondence for your information and consideration. . . ."

The purpose of the enclosures, of course, was to alert them that notice had been served on their licenses.

On Wednesday, July 15, the day before the telecast, the documentary was screened over closed circuit to the NBC affiliates, a standard practice with almost every television special or series episode, especially if in any way controversial, so that the station managements might make their determination as responsible licensees to clear the time for the broadcast. Don Mercer, vice-president of affiliate relations for NBC, went on camera to preface the screening with word of the Association's objection to the program, but he said that those involved in the program had given assurances that it was an honest and accurate report.

In Houston, where Coca-Cola Foods is headquartered, the company learned of the screening and two representatives requested permission of KPRC, the Houston affiliate, to attend it. While normally the screenings are only for the immediate affiliate family and not for outsiders, the station consented, being unsure of its obligation in light of the controversy. Coca-Cola representatives then descended on NBC headquarters, and late into the afternoon of the air date they were demanding cuts in the program from Goodman and Frank. Hours before air time they were accommodated with a single excision in the film, not sufficient, however, to keep *Migrant* from implicating Coca-Cola Foods along with the other companies exploiting the pickers.

After the broadcast, the Florida Fruit and Vegetable Association dispatched another letter to NBC, calling the program "biased and inaccurate" and asking for equal time to answer it.

The statement, by the Association's manager of the labor division, George F. Sorn, read: "It does not appear that NBC made any substantial effort to balance the one-sided presentation in spite of the fact that they had in their possession massive factual documentation provided by this Association which clearly shows the many improvements made before the program was filmed. Based on the apparent inaccuracies and bias, and because of their damaging aspects not only to Florida agriculture and the state of Florida but also to the workers themselves, we will request equal time so that a proper balance may be offered to the nation's television viewers."

A week after the broadcast, the Senate Subcommittee on Migratory Labor, headed by Senator Walter F. Mondale of Minnesota, opened hearings on the treatment of migrant workers, and Carr, who produced the film, was among those called to testify. Another was J. Paul Austin, president of Coca-Cola, Inc., who had figured in the pressures brought upon NBC in a small way. He had put in a call to Goodman, as one corporation president to another, asking that he meet with the Coca-Cola representatives just before the telecast. For most of the week that followed, he conferred with various advisers, including McCann-Erickson, on what to do about the NBC program and how to proceed at the Mondale hearings.

When he appeared before the subcommittee, Austin testified that the NBC documentary had correctly presented the housing and working conditions of migrants as deplorable. He condemned the ill treatment of the migrant farm workers and vowed to transform the migratory work force into a stable, year-round group with the same fringe benefits as other Coca-Cola employees, including health insurance, job security, and vacations. The long-range plan to correct the conditions would begin in September, he said, and would be completed in seven years.

NBC did not grant the Florida Association equal time.

In January, Coca-Cola shifted all its network billings to CBS and ABC.

Raquel was good for Raquel Welch—the ratings indicating her dimensions as a star—and it was good for Winters/Rosen, for Coca-Cola and Motorola, for John Allen and McCann-Erickson, and for CBS. There would be many more shows of the kind. Raquel herself might elect to do another special some time, and although it was certain that Winters and Rosen would not be a party to it—of their own choice, if not hers—they would undoubtedly have many more shows in which to supply camera and editing razzle-dazzle where native talent was lacking in their subject.

Migrant was good for a lot of downtrodden and vastly neglected people, for the moral health of the country, for NBC's image as a news organization, and for the American television system—and it would not be stretching things to add for the human race. But it would probably not soon beget another of its kind. Among practical businessmen the so-called "bottom-line," after costs are subtracted from revenues, was decidedly against it. Whether it was good for Martin Carr was moot. It was certainly an estimable credit. Added to *Hunger in America* the documentary projected him into the forefront of investigative journalists in the medium. But the crises it created, and the financial losses it sustained, stood to condemn him and his kind to ghost status indefinitely.

10

Network Families in Conflict

A young sales representative of Westinghouse Broadcasting (which prefers to call itself Group W) encountered in his travels one of the old tribal chieftains of the industry, the head of a group of TV and radio stations making its headquarters in the South.

"How's your boss these days?" the older man asked.

"Busy and successful as ever."

"That's too bad. I wish him worse."

"I thought you were good friends," the younger man said.

"No longer. Tell him I call him a son of a bitch."

For years the networks had had their quarrels with Don McGannon and reason to dislike him, but his alienation of his own kind, the local TV station operators, was something new. As president of Westinghouse Broadcasting, the most powerful of the broadcast groups after the three networks by nature of the important licenses it held, McGannon was, among the broadcast gentry, the acknowledged statesman who frequently led the fight against the networks when they encroached on station incomes. His was the company nearest to a fourth commercial network, with stations in many of the major cities, and the most individualistic of the station groups. Group W produced two successful programs for syndication, *The Mike Douglas Show* and *The David Frost Show*, and made a practice of scheduling one special a week on all its own television stations, independent of the networks' specials, some of which were produced within the company and some purchased from foreign systems.

McGannon was Frank Stanton's only broadcast rival in the art of developing and projecting a corporate image. His company held periodic public service symposia for other broadcasters, including the networks, to attend; it often donated its own public service productions to other stations free for the asking; and although it made great amounts of money in the same rating-mad way as the other stations and groups, its lavish advertising campaigns year after year told only of Group W public service, as though that were its basic broadcast product.

"McGannon prays in public," an unloving network executive once said of him.

It was McGannon who rocked the radio networks and precipitated drastic changes in the nature of their service when he canceled all his radio affiliations and demonstrated to the rest of the industry that there was more to be gained, in ratings and profits, with independent radio stations. He created his own world-wide news organization to provide the news service he surrendered when he quit the radio networks, which later led him to establish the first of the all-news radio stations.

In television, Group W was affiliated with all three networks; unlike radio, this was where an independent station was seriously disadvantaged. Two of McGannon's stations were in the NBC family, two in the CBS and one in ABC, and because they were major market stations they were important affiliates of all three networks. This was McGannon's power, and it gave him the right to be intractable. Operators of lesser stations do not attempt insurgency against a network unless they are willing to risk the loss of their affiliation to the independent stations in their markets. A station that may be worth $50 million on the open market would be worth less than half that without a network affiliation.

McGannon led the fight against NBC when it tried to increase the number of commercials in its movies and then against ABC when it tried to ramrod a fourth commercial position in *Batman*. Recognizing the inevitable, he discontinued cigarette advertising at his stations eight months before the law was passed outlawing such commercials on TV and radio. McGannon had credibility in Washington and was an effective spokesman for the industry at congressional hearings. For his achievements on behalf of his fellow broadcasters he was honored in 1964 with the Distinguished Service Award of the National Association of Broadcasters.

But now he was out of favor with the peerage and reviled by his old friends because he had done the unforgivable. He had, in Washington, recommended and promoted a change in the system.

He was upsetting the old comfortable way of doing business with an idea that challenged the broadcasters to work harder for their money, even though there was potentially more to be made McGannon's way. What he was responsible for was a new FCC proposal that would restrict the networks to three hours of prime time, returning the rest to the local stations to program in their own way. Although the rule would only be made applicable to stations in the top fifty markets (*i.e.*, population centers), actually it would affect the rest of the stations as well since it would not behoove the networks to provide service on so limited a network.

Under the new plan the networks would be restricted to

three programing hours sometime between 7:00 and 11:00
P.M. (Eastern Time) and would be forbidden to sell shows
any longer on a syndicated basis. Assuming that the seven
o'clock half hour would continue to be used by stations for
newscasts in most situations, the station would need to program only an extra half hour each night. Furthermore, every
commercial minute in that time period would be theirs to
sell and to enjoy the revenue from, and since it was premium
time commanding high rates, ultimately it should be more
profitable than taking network programs off the line.

But few were enchanted with the opportunity to do something of their own in a period of peak viewing. The majority
of stations were distressed at having to invest more of their
own money in program matter, realizing that they might have
to gamble for months, or even years, before they struck the
formats that would compete adequately for ratings. They
shared a single worry: where is the new programing to come
from?

One of the FCC's intentions with the proposed rule was
to create new and diversified sources of supply for the television screen, since the networks had taken to dealing with
a limited and inbred number of Hollywood suppliers given
to turning out the same kinds of shows year after year. The
extra half hour promised to open up experimentation with
program forms both at the local level and in national syndication, and to insure that the stations would use it in a bold
new way, the FCC included a restriction against the use of
off-network reruns or movies in the reclaimed time period.

For years individual stations had used the tyranny of
the networks as an excuse for their unproductiveness but,
presented with the opportunity to produce for themselves,
virtually every station declined it and approached the problem with expectations of buying shows from outside sources.
The prospects were dreadful, especially for securing shows
with the production gloss of high-budgeted network programs. Because the syndication market answered to the laws
of supply and demand, the price for any syndicated property

with a proven ability to produce audience would be inflated by the time the new rule, if passed, would take effect. That was to be the fall of 1971.

Not only would each station need seven more half hours of programs a week from what was available in the syndication market, its two network-affiliated competitors would be looking for the same amount of new programing. For every station the weekly need would be equivalent to one full night of a network schedule. Bidding against one another for the most functional shows among those that would be offered, they would be creating a sellers' market in syndication, which by their lights was unhealthy.

The plan McGannon inspired increased the broadcasters' economic risk, forcing them to buy what for many years they had been receiving free, fodder for the viewing masses. The stations would join the networks in fighting the FCC's pending prime-time access rule. That would be a bond between the networks and their station families at the affiliates meetings in May.

The scene is a dusty Western street. A portly man sidles up to a tall figure leaning against the hitching post outside the jailhouse, collects him with a nod, and together they join the mob gathering at the corner outside the bank. The people are drinking. A Mexican band has stationed itself nearby.

Not the opening of a script but a recess during the CBS affiliates meeting on one of the permanent sets of the CBS Studio Center lot in Hollywood. After the presentations and speeches, conviviality. The band begins to play, network president Bob Wood circulates among the groups of station men, and in a fantastic anachronism the Old West becomes the set for a businessmen's cocktail party. This is that once-a-year time when the television station operator actually rubs against the celluloid glamour he electronically purveys.

But for the trappings and the presence of stars, a network affiliates meeting is fairly typical of a manufacturer's annual industrial show for his distributors. While it does provide a forum for a discussion of grievances and problems of mutual concern, its primary function is to kindle enthusiasm for the seasonal product so as to generate orders for the new line of merchandise and to inspire the localized selling of it.

To be sure, the television trade has in this regard some natural advantages over the rubber tire or computer software industries. The stars, for one thing, and for another some expertise in theatrical presentations. CBS, since it owns a film lot (the old Republic Studios), arranged for the screening of its new wares to take place in a reception area in among the sound stages and street sets where many of its series were filmed. The classic Western street, familiar through *Gunsmoke*, was but one cocktail party site. Another was staged in the standing set of a gracious post-Victorian American town. In both cases, the open air was all that was genuine. Amid the wonderful façades, the television operator with drink in hand may well have relived the multitudinous plots of thousands of video playlets, and then returned to his city or town, that link in the CBS chain, with the sophistication of having partaken firsthand of the make-believe.

At the banquet in the Century Plaza, there was one star or featured player for every table. CBS knew how to pour it on, and it was the rare affiliate who did not find the luxury and the glamour intoxicating.

Thus primed for the business sessions, the station operators accepted with enthusiasm Wood's plan to modernize the network with programs of contemporary social realism and to abandon the meaningless quest for rating supremacy. They supported his decision to slough off such old successes as Red Skelton, Jackie Gleason, and *Petticoat Junction*, and many concurred in the wisdom of it.

"Perhaps the most compelling reason of all for revising our program schedule was that we are starting down a new decade," Wood told them. "The winds of change are at gale force. Everything is being tested and challenged. . . . For television to stand still while all this is happening is to be

out of touch with the times. . . . The days are gone in programing when we can afford to be imitative rather than innovative. Indeed, if we are not only to lead but to survive,
we must be responsive to the forms and concepts of today.
We not only have to hold the audiences we have—we have
to broaden our base. We have to attract new viewers, viewers
who are part of every generation, viewers who reflect the
growing degree of education and sophistication that charac-
terizes American society, viewers who live in every part of
the country. . . .

"We are taking a young, fresh, new approach to programing. We're not going to be afraid to try the untried."

Hollywood with its stars and sound stages, and the Century Plaza with its glittering lobby and all-night room service, gave a special eloquence to his remarks.

The selling of a new program schedule is done in three
phases: first to the advertiser, then to the affiliate family,
and finally to the consumer. Sponsor solicitations begin the
day the program layout is formulated in February, and the
television viewer is "sold" through on-the-air promotions
and other forms of publicity all through the summer. But in
many ways the most important sale is to the affiliated stations, because the fate of any program depends on the number of stations that will carry it. Obviously a show that is
televised on 200 stations will reach more people, and therefore achieve a higher rating, than the same show carried on
160. The higher the rating, generally speaking, the more the
advertiser will pay for his one-minute position in the show.

Notwithstanding their opposition to the FCC three-hour
prime-time proposal, most stations preferred not to carry the
full network line-up of programs, but chose to carve up the
schedule in their own proportions and in their own way. Each
station operator surveyed his network's schedule for what
he assumed would be a weak spot, and there, in place of the
show transmitted from New York, he inserted a syndicated
program (usually an off-network rerun of recent vintage)

which, in the high-rated environment of network prime time, would be sold at the station's highest advertising rates. With its own program there, the station receives 100 per cent of the revenues; taking the network's program it is compensated at approximately 12 per cent of its prime advertising rate. Clearly a profitable practice, and one that has tended to spread from year to year as the station managements found the need to increase their net earnings.

Perhaps the most common procedure was to withhold half an evening of network shows for a locally scheduled movie. Of the displaced program series fed by the network, some were transferred by the station to other evenings to take the place of other shows, some were played on a delayed basis in fringe time such as four o'clock on Saturdays, and some simply dropped or yielded to an unaffiliated UHF station in the market.

A good network affiliate would accept 90 per cent or more of the schedule, a poor one less than 80 per cent, and the network with a preponderance of good affiliates was bound to prevail in the autumnal race for the ratings. Winning the national numbers does not so much testify to a superior program schedule as to superior distribution.

Success has a way of perpetuating itself in television. CBS and NBC, as historically the good providers, tend to achieve greater affiliate support than ABC in program clearances. Partly this comes from having kept their stations so prosperous over the years that they have had less need to withhold large chunks of the schedule for local sale, but there is another reason, and that is the stations' fear of reprisal. CBS and NBC can deal with a refractory affiliate by terminating the relationship and offering it to another station in town pledging better co-operation. In a majority of cases that would be the ABC station, happy to trade the hindrunning network for one of the leaders. Since an important factor in the market value of a station is its affiliation contract, it follows that in most circumstances the CBS outlet would be more valuable than the ABC.

Lacking an implicit threat as negotiating leverage with its own member stations, and lacking also their faith in the network's ability to provide them with hits, ABC has had to endure a kind of affiliate anarchy, a wholesale tampering with its program line-up and callous rejection of costly new programs. Such was the spiral: ABC ventured a new show, too few stations carried it, advertisers buying the circulation therefore paid too little for it, the show failed in the ratings, and ABC was forced to cancel it and offer a new program in its place, which in turn would be passed over by the stations. Thus failure perpetuated failure.

The most regrettable aspect of the stations' right to refuse network programs is that it is usually exercised for base economic reasons and not out of responsibility to the citizenry, and it has contributed to a television system which favors old programs to new ones. When the station operator selects the programs to delete from the schedule, his candidates are not usually the established shows but the first-year series; any of the carry-over shows would be assumed to have developed a following in his community, but the new are not yet anyone's favorites and so are the most expendable.

The ABC meeting in Hollywood spanned four days, May 11 to 15, one day longer than the CBS meeting and twice as long as the NBC, indicating the size of the mission, which was to convince the station managements that a strong network in full contention for the ratings would be in their best interest and that in the long run their full support of the network's program schedule would profit them more than the immediate gain of forgoing certain new series.

It was not a hard point to make, and in truth the ABC stations did want to help the network become stronger, but most had an immediate obligation to their own owners and stockholders to produce greater profits than the year before. And in a year in which business was lagging, it might even be necessary to drop an extra network show to bring the profits up.

Yet, for that, the ABC affiliates were at a loss to understand why their network should be the only one of the three to approve of the Westinghouse plan to reduce network prime-time to three hours a night. The ABC stations wanted to fight the proposed FCC rule and could not enlist their own network in the cause. Corporate president Leonard Goldenson, in a letter to affiliates, later explained why. The rule, if enacted, would cut the program inventory of all three networks by the equivalent of one full night of the week. ABC had been replacing its program failures at the rate of twelve per year and with the new rule could cut the waste substantially, concentrating its successful programs in the twenty-one hours a week that would be allotted by the FCC. In addition, ABC would probably be the beneficiary of the advertising spillover resulting from the truncated broadcast evenings of the rival networks. Ultimately a more limited prime time made up of established programing would serve to strengthen ABC in the three-network competition. Although the position made absolute sense from the network's standpoint, it created a rift in the family since the stations remained concerned about having to program the half hour themselves.

Although their fortunes are linked, there is no abiding love between network and affiliate. Their animosities are long-standing, centering typically on disputes over money. For one thing, they compete for the national advertiser's dollar. It is convenient for an advertiser to buy a campaign on a network that would spread his message instantly over 180 or more stations, but it is perhaps more scientific to buy the stations on an individual basis, spending as much as may be deemed necessary to accomplish marketing objectives in each city. Networks and stations sell against each other, and that makes them rivals within the same family.

When the stations fought ABC's attempt to put an extra commercial in *Batman* and NBC's bid to add commercial minutes in the movies, they acted not from concern for the viewer's sensibilities, not to spare him a surfeit of sales messages, but rather to fend off precedents by the networks that might encroach on the stations' share of the national advertisers' budget. If the networks had more time to sell, where would the new money come from? Out of spot television, their end of the business, they reasoned.

Networks and member stations was an arrangement of convenience and not a natural relationship. Five TV stations in each company were of the bloodline, the owned stations which the networks were created to serve in the first place; the rest, from a network view, were a venal, grasping, uncontributing, disloyal pack whose entree to the fortunes that were to be made in television involved nothing more than having air time at their disposal. The network assumed all the risk in the programing, sales, and promotion of a new schedule; the stations took of it what they wanted and were paid, to boot. Moreover, they never ceased asking for greater compensation for feeding off the network.

It could not sit well with the networks that station groups such as Storer, Taft, Capital Cities, and Corinthian were attractive to Wall Street because of their affiliations and their handsome earnings per share, while companies such as CBS and ABC which fed them were somewhat less attractive because of their huge annual risk in program inventories.

But money was not the entire basis for the hostility that had grown between the stations and the networks to which they belonged. There was, at the station end, an old distrust of the networks because they were based in New York and peopled with slick, sophisticated types who seemed to patronize the grass-roots operator. In many cases, the distrust ran deeper than that. The networks were Eastern businesses, with Eastern values and viewpoints, and in certain minds they were *Jewish* businesses, which to some hysterical fundamentalists of the hinterlands meant that their first allegiance was to some ancient Christ-killing secret order. Of course, the view was not peculiar to managers of stations. A television critic in the Midwest revealed, in his cups, his suspicion that the motion picture and television industries were captives of a Jewish conspiracy that was bent on subverting Christian morality.

Bigotry is unbecoming to a trustee of the American air waves, but applicants for station licenses are not screened by the FCC for their psychological qualifications or their essential humanity. One of the first criteria for a license award is money: Is the applicant financially qualified to build a station and keep it operating until it becomes profitable? Passing that test, a prospective station operator need only take the hollow pledge to serve the public interest, convenience, and necessity, as he interprets them, and to honor the regulation of the FCC regarding operational procedures. It is possible that the broadcaster's whole system of values descends from the fact that the FCC gave primary importance to his financial fitness to run a station.

As to the idea that the networks are Eastern, liberal, and Jewish, it is largely myth. While it is true that the heads of the three parent corporations are Jews, the fact is that William S. Paley's identification with his ethnic origins is slight and Robert Sarnoff's even slighter. Both move in the high social circles normally thought of as Anglo-Saxon Protestant. Leonard Goldenson and Si Siegel are not quite so assimilated, but neither do they hold the controlling stock in ABC, Inc., and with an exception or two the board of directors—whose approval is needed for practically every program deal made—is non-Jewish. Frank Stanton, Walter Scott, Julian Goodman, Jack Schneider, Dick Jencks, and Elton Rule—the other top officers of the broadcast companies, some of whom are heirs apparent to the highest offices—are Gentile, as were such leading figures of the recent past as Robert Kintner, James Aubrey, Oliver Treyz, Merle Jones, Ted Shaker, Tom Moore, John Reynolds, and Tom Dawson.

With the exception of Lou Cowan, who had a fairly brief tenure at CBS, there has never been a Jewish president at any of the three television networks, nor is there likely to be until there no longer is Jewish top management in the corporations. Hyperconscious of the suspicions surrounding the coincidence of three Jewish generalissimos in the three great broadcasting corporations in America, Paley, Sarnoff, and Goldenson appear to have taken such extreme caution against fueling the idea of "Jewish networks" that they have in fact discriminated against Jewish executives who might have qualified for leadership posts. (Cowan, when he was appointed president of the CBS network by Stanton, reportedly had said to him, "But, Frank, I thought you knew. I'm a Jew." Stanton's reply was, "Don't insult me. Do you want the job?" But that was the exception.)

If top management had ever handed down a Jewish point of view (whatever that might be) to the next tier of executives—some command or commandment subversive of Christian or basic Puritan American values—or put the interests of one ethnic group above that of the others, the scandal would certainly have broken out by now, considering how many executives have left the companies.

So much for "Jewish control," but there were network affiliates who still believed it and who felt uneasy at being instruments of a giant conspiracy (although not so uneasy that they declined to reap what profits they could from it). And as for Eastern rule, the lie to the myth there was that most of the highest officials of the three national broadcast companies came from other parts of the country, primarily from the Midwest.

Paley, Schneider, and Don Durgin grew up in Chicago; Stanton spent his youth in Ohio; Jim Duffy was from northern Illinois, Scott from Kansas City, Siegel from Denver, Goodman from Louisville, and Ev Erlick from Birmingham, Alabama. Rule, Jencks, and Wood were Californians. Only Bob Sarnoff was native to New York, and Goldenson was an Easterner from Pennsylvania. Of those who were in positions of authority during the fifties and sixties, virtually all had come east at a stage in their professional lives from another part of the country. Aubrey and Cowan came from Chicago; Jones, Dawson, and Shaker from Minneapolis–St. Paul; Reynolds from California; Tom

Moore from Mississippi; and Kintner from Stroudsburg, Pennsylvania.

There is no denying that an adjustment to New York City puts a veneer on a Midwesterner as he takes on the style of the Eastern businessman, but the acquired cosmopolitanism does not alter the essential character of the man. An ineffable Chicago quality predominated at the networks during the first two decades of television, and in the seventies the influence had become decidedly Western, Californian. Rule, Jencks, and Wood, and their coteries—men such as Ralph Daniels, Dick O'Leary, Dick Beesemyer, and others, who were moving up the executive ladders at CBS and ABC—imparted the tone and attitudes of their native region, metropolitan Los Angeles, to network management in New York.

Apart from that, to pierce the myth further if not to demolish it, television programs are purchased in New York and fed out to the country from the East, but in the vast majority they originate in California and are written and produced by persons who have migrated there from other parts of the country. If television programs reflect any specific regional values they are—God help us—those of the insular and unreal film community conveniently called Hollywood, which actually encompasses greater Los Angeles in that it draws its people from Beverly Hills, Bel Air, Malibu, Westwood, Brentwood, Pacific Palisades, and the other affluent suburbs.

Moreover, after accepting a series on the basis of a pilot, the network managements do not usually rule over the philosophical content of the individual program episodes; and the producers are practical men who (especially after the inquisitions during the McCarthy years) would not risk their careers and future contracts for an ideology, even if they had one. When a writer establishes a controversial situation in television it is usually just to be intriguing; invariably the matter is resolved in a routine law-and-order way. One way or another the Establishment prevails over the dissident or the dropout. With all its faults, it is a kindly and fair Establishment which through Christian tolerance eventually helps the wayward to see the error of their ways. The squares win, their convictions upheld. It is a code as tight as that which the movies once lived by: crime must *not* pay.

"Let's face it," an executive of one of the major studios said to me, "the squares have always been the television audience and always will be. If you don't play it their way, you're out of business."

Finally, the myth of network liberalism. In a comparative sense, considering the narrowness and rigid conservatism of a great many station managements, it may not be totally mythical. At stations in the smaller communities particularly (though not exclusively), with their limited spectrum of permitted ideologies, the networks do seem excessively free and even wanton in their criticism of the existing order, inclining to the urban melting-pot mentality, left of center, reformist, and determined to upset the pat and righteous Americanism of the provinces. Many of the stations are owned by persons of hard right-wing bias who are pillars of the local power structure and who believe their public service obligations to be met by promoting love for the flag. They would have networks concentrate on spreading patriotism and rallying the country to the war effort, and they would keep the air waves free from the voices of dissent.

But, as national media serving the broadest swath of the citizenry, the networks are obliged to make a show of basic Bill of Rights idealism; and even in that they have displayed shameful insensitivity, in both advertising and program content, toward racial minorities and the economically underprivileged. Integration of the programs with blacks, beyond the token tap dances and guest singers, incredibly did not begin until 1968—and even then only after the networks were coerced by pressure groups, and the intractable stations by the FCC's belated strict construction of the Communications Act. Negroes were not kept off the air because network managements were consciously racist (they are not consciously anything but business-minded); they were not used because there seemed to be evidence that they would not *sell*, that is, that they would drive away audience. It was not their own prejudices they were acting from but rather those they fancied existed within the great television audience.

Where entertainment programs are concerned, the networks and their Hollywood suppliers are only as liberal as Nielsen's rating sample. In that they are misled, for as even they are aware the rating surveys of the black ghetto communities have long been inadequate, to say the least.

The rating services, as discussed in Chapter 2, have explained that illiteracy, lack of telephone service, vandalism, and other problems have made the installation of electronic meters and the placement of diaries in the black communities difficult. And for their part, neither the networks nor the ad agencies raised any significant complaint over this lapse in the democracy of ratings. The reasons: ghetto families were by and large low-income families, many of them welfare families, and not the consumer that commercial television was particularly eager to reach. Thus, although there is evidence that ghetto homes are among the heaviest users of television, they have historically received a short count in the ratings and have not had a proper vote in the popularity of TV shows.

Such has been the liberalism of the networks, on the practical level. And as for the political level, which primarily is what the conservative affiliates were exercised about, the network managements were seriously misjudged.

To be sure, the political labels of *liberal, conservative,* and *moderate,* the fashionable ones of 1970, are imprecise for most individuals who do not first adopt the designation and then conform to its doctrine. But through the decision-making echelons of the three great bureaucracies of broadcasting—from the level of network president upward—there is not a person who I would judge is a liberal in the sense that, say, Senators McGovern, Fulbright, and Javits are considered to be, although there were several who identified with the Western conservativism of Ronald Reagan. The ruling powers at the networks are decidedly Establishment in their politics and in general closer to the right of the political center than to the left.

With the possible exception of Paley (Republican) and Stanton (Democrat), no high official of the networks has worn his political affiliation on his sleeve. Whatever their partisan alignments as citizens, the men in television are not political creatures, merely believers in laissez-faire, sympathetic to any Administration that is good for business.

As operators of networks they do what is practical, and frequently their deeds are inconsistent with their political inclinations. Wood, for instance, as an avowed conservative, was actively separating CBS from the rural comedies which idealized the heartland and was steering the network toward urban-centered program series which acknowledged many of the depressing social problems of the times. Superficially, under his design, the character of the CBS schedule was taking on a more liberal appearance.

But it was not really the entertainment programs that troubled the affiliates. It was news. And station managements who were fixed strongly to the right in the political spectrum would not accept glib arguments about who did or did not control the immensely powerful national media. The corporate managements did influence the network news but in pragmatic or politic ways, rather than, as many grass-roots affiliates suspected, ideologically.

Big broadcasting has always had its lines out to the federal government. Largely through the connections of certain company officers, NBC was well wired to the Kennedy Administration, CBS was very thick with Lyndon Johnson, and ABC was closest of the networks to Richard Nixon. Nor were Presidents above making use of their network contacts. Bill McAndrew, the late president of NBC News, received a call at home late one evening and heard a secretary announce, "Just a minute, sir, the President is calling." McAndrew thought it was *his* president, his boss Bob Kintner. It turned out to be Lyndon Johnson.

News was sometimes "adjusted," compromised, and even censored to please a President. It was probably no coincidence that all three networks declined live coverage of the huge Vietnam Moratorium demonstration in the capital on November 15, 1969, knowing as they did that the President wished it to be ignored, but at the request of the White House all three networks carried some part of the "Honor America Day" patriotic festivities in Washington on July 4. Similarly, on October 31, ABC cut away from the field during the half-time show of its regional telecast of the Buffalo–Holy Cross football game when the State University of Buffalo marching band staged an extravaganza titled "Give Peace a Chance," which was critical of the war in Vietnam, racism, and pollution. But several weeks later it broadcast the half-time show at the Army-Navy college football game, which honored those who took part in the American raid on a prisoner-of-war camp near Hanoi and featured Admiral Thomas H. Moorer, chairman of the Joint Chiefs of Staff. Roone Arledge, president of ABC Sports, explained that the pro-peace show in Buffalo was blacked out because it was political in nature. Apparently, the network did not consider the pro-war show to be out of line as a partisan comment.

It was not uncommon for stories to be discreetly killed or softened by corporate officers at White House request, and Presidents were in some instances also given the privilege of hand-picking their network interviewers for televised question-and-answer sessions. Obviously, they chose those whom they felt would not be hostile.

After the blistering criticism of the Eastern press by Vice President Agnew, ABC adapted many of its news policies to conform with the Administration's prescription for "better" journalism. In light of that, it seemed not altogether coincidental that ABC, when it acquired newscaster Harry Rea-

soner from CBS in December, chose to substitute him for
Frank Reynolds on the evening newscast and not his co-
anchorman, Howard K. Smith. Reynolds had been an irritant
to the Administration with his commentary, Smith one of
the TV newsmen most popular with it.

ABC became close to the Nixon Administration through
corporate relations vice-president Jim Hagerty, who, before
he joined the company, had been press secretary to President
Dwight D. Eisenhower. Nixon, of course, had been the Vice
President then. During 1970, Hagerty was spending more
time in Washington than in New York, and reportedly it was
he who alerted the President to the fact that one of his
scheduled speeches in prime time would interrupt a televised basketball game. Rather than antagonize the sports
fans, Nixon rescheduled his speech for a later time that night.

President Johnson had had a personal relationship with
CBS corporate president Frank Stanton long before he won
the highest office (politics aside, as owner of television station
KBTC in Austin, Texas, Johnson was a CBS affiliate), and it
had been expected throughout his Administration that Stanton would receive a cabinet appointment. He did not, but the
friendship was unaffected.

Closeness to government and concessions to Presidents,
which might well worry the citizenry, were not what concerned anxious members of the network families. Indeed,
those political alliances were comforts. What troubled them
was the general tenor of network news, the viewpoints and
values seemingly expressed in the day-to-day reporting. By
and large, the everyday news judgment was not dictated by
corporate managements but was left to the professionals.
And by the nature of their profession, men trained in journalism tend to a humanitarian viewpoint and progressive
attitudes.

Journalists deal in change: a thing that does not change
usually is not a story. They deal in morality: evil is news.
And they are sensitized to human rights by their own professional rights under the First Amendment to the Constitu-

tion. With a heightened awareness of both the changing and moral conditions of their times, and frequently confronted with the bitter irony of law prevailing over true justice, much of the time journalists will be at some variance with businessmen in the matter of values.

And this is where the thought content of network television, meager as it is, and often constituting nothing more than news judgment, comes into conflict with the beliefs of some local station operators.

The mission of news is not to preserve the status quo but to document change. News is subhistory. To select for coverage only the stories that do not threaten the power structure, or to report fact out of the context of truth, is a blasphemy against the public's right to know which brings news perilously close to propaganda.

The earnest practice of their profession by network journalists was one part of what conservative station managers construed as Eastern liberalism. There was another, and it was the only real basis for their suspicions.

Richard Salant, Reuven Frank, and Elmer Lower, the presidents of CBS, NBC, and ABC News, respectively, had one thing in common—an adoration of the *New York Times*, which *is* Eastern and some would also say liberal. Nor was it a devotion peculiar to them; their predecessors had also been avid followers of the *Times*, and their corporate superiors no less than they.

The *Times*'s influence on network journalism in America is twofold: it is first the model, the textbook newspaper, from which the network news shops derive their standards for news judgments; it is secondly the supreme evaluator of their performance. Its favorable recognition of a network news effort is a source of elation within the company and held up as proof of distinguished achievement, its criticism a cause of anguish.

The *New York Daily News*, with the largest circulation in the country, counts for little in its approval or disapproval of a network news special. All the newspapers in the country could gang up on a single news broadcast, but if the *Times* liked it the network was vindicated. Since high ratings are not usually expected for news specials or documentaries, the practical value of the effort is the prestige that might accrue from it. And since a favorable notice in the *Times* is largely what is meant by prestige, certain network news producers studied the Jack Gould reviews and aimed at turning out the kinds of programs that would please him, for that was the way to glory. (Gould has since relinquished the reviewing chore to concentrate on commentary and think-pieces.)

Once, to NBC's Reuven Frank, I made the observation that all three network newscasts were much alike and that with all the news stories available on any single day in a large world it was surprising that the networks seemed to cover the same ones and in roughly the same order.

"Why is that surprising?" Frank snapped. "Look at the *New York Times.* They give the same importance to the same stories we do." As if to say the *Times*'s news judgment proved the validity of their own.

A news producer admitted to me that often he was guided in his decisions by what he expected would be on the front page of the *Times* the next morning.

Shortly after he returned to the presidency of CBS News in 1966, following Fred Friendly's departure from the company, Dick Salant told me he was dropping music from all the network's news presentations, even Aaron Copland's *Appalachian Spring*, which had long been the theme for *CBS Reports*. Music, he said, was show business and improper in a news broadcast.

I suggested that theme music was effective for identification and said I did not see how, if used for that purpose, it violated the principles of journalism.

"The *New York Times* doesn't play music," he answered.

Sometime later, when he was concerned about the brevity of television news and its lack of depth with regard to the details in news reports, Salant had a full evening's script set columnarly in newspaper type, and he pasted it on the front page of the *Times*. To his despair, the television script covered about one-third of the page. He would have had better luck making the comparison with a tabloid, but CBS News did not identify with tabloid journalism.

Elmer Lower, of the three news presidents, privately acknowledged the effect of the prestigious New York daily on the thinking of network news executives and expressed some regret to me a few years ago that, unlike newspapers, the network news divisions did not operate under differing journalistic philosophies.

There was no Hearst, no Scripps-Howard, no *Chicago Tribune*, no Pulitzer, and no *Post-Newsweek* style in network news. There was only the *Times*, the nearest equivalent in the realm of news to the Nielsen Company's influence in entertainment.

McGannon's plan to truncate network prime time was the surface issue at the 1970 affiliate meetings; the hidden (though not secret) issue was news.

NBC's two-day meeting in New York, May 21 to 22, was in part a celebration of the network's powerful program schedule which promised to make rating leaders of most of its affiliates, and outwardly there was a show of harmony and fellowship between network officials and the station clan. But after the screenings and presentations of the first day, in the customary private meeting of the affiliate body, the divisive question came to the fore.

Was the network's news biased?

By a hand vote, with approximately 60 per cent of the affiliates in the majority, they declared that it was—specifically, that it was slanted against the war in Vietnam.

On the following day, the affiliate board confronted NBC corporate president Julian Goodman with the charge, and he requested time to answer it. Goodman, who had been a professional newsman before he became an administrator, was being given instructions in his craft by men who were thoroughly business-minded, anxious to preserve their licenses, and in the majority unschooled in journalism and insensitive to its proper function in society.

This humiliating confrontation pointed up one of the saddest and most dangerous truths of the American broadcasting system. In awarding licenses to operate television stations the FCC indiscriminately made news publishers of all comers, and as if that did not present serious enough hazards on the level of local communities, the same men collectively had the power to muzzle the dedicated practitioners of electronic journalism nationally. For it is, after all, webs of stations which are networks and not three businessmen in New York.

There are, as only luck has it, a sizable number of local TV operators with an intuitive understanding of news, if not actually a practical background in reporting, who have been more than equal to the journalistic function in their local situations. But whether or not there are more of their opposite, far too many publishers of the air waves, who have been entrusted with the responsibility to inform the people, have not the qualifications for the job, or a respect for truth, or a feel for communications beyond the level of propagandizing or selling.

There was some discord over news at the CBS meeting, too, surfacing after the Walter Cronkite evening newscast of May 6, which was broadcast from the convention before the entire affiliate assembly. That program carried a Vietnam report from correspondent Gary Shepard, who was interviewing troops scheduled to fly to Cambodia for the controversial invasion, several of whom expressed in strong terms their reluctance to take part. After the broadcast, one affiliate stood up to criticize the dispatch as an example of slanted news. He received a round of applause.

Cronkite responded with a strong defense of network news practices, pointing out that whatever is news has to be reported whether or not it fits anyone's preconceived notions of what the news should be. Shepard was not inventing the story he was covering, Cronkite said, but was letting the rest of us know what was happening in a remote place where he was an eyewitness. The applause for the reply was at least equal to that for the querulous affiliate, but it was demeaning to the newsman to have to explain to his publishers something as fundamental as normal professionalism.

The surfacing of the news issue was no surprise; both CBS and NBC had expected it. For months, through private communications, officials of both network news divisions had weathered charges that they were biased against the war in Vietnam, the Nixon Administration, and the conservative point of view in general, and that in their quest for provocative stories and dramatic news film they were being gulled by intransigents and demonstrators into giving them undue and disproportionate air time. The criticism resonated Vice President Agnew's first attack on the broadcast media, made in November 1969.

These were the first formal affiliate meetings since that speech, and the agitated response to it among the broadcast licensees had not subsided.

The telling sign of where the station sentiments lay and whose side they were on was made the day following the Vice President's explosive address from Des Moines on November 13. From the networks came statements deploring the government's attempt to intimidate the news media and to deny television the freedom of the press; from the printed press flowed outrage and wide concern over a new era of repression. The speech became a subject for debate in legislative and academic circles, and overnight an uneasiness over "Agnewism" fell over much of the country. But from the television stations there came a profound silence.

In faint voices a paltry few station men defended the networks, but the vast remainder were taciturn and indicated by that a desire to be divorced from the taint, if not indeed tacit agreement with Agnew. They were letting the networks take the rap.

It was not the first time the networks failed to receive vocal and moral support from their member stations in a controversy over journalism. After the 1968 Democratic Convention, when the networks were accused of gross distortions for cutting back and forth between the nominating speeches and the street riots, a resolution was put before the convention of the Radio and Television News Directors Association to back the networks' coverage under difficult circumstances against the accusations by government figures of malice aforethought. The resolution was voted down.

If the Vice President was trying to turn public opinion against network journalism so that it would be forced to become a conduit of government policy instead of an interpreter and occasional critic of it, he succeeded probably beyond his own imaginings because, intentionally or not, he enlisted the support of the rank-and-file stations which give the networks their circulation. Some sided with him from political conviction, some because he spoke their own ancient suspicions of the Eastern liberal establishment, but most responded from fear, or, putting it positively, in the interest of self-preservation. The government, not the network, can perform the favor of a broadcast license, and it can also grant it in virtual perpetuity or take it away. For a licensed businessman who is pragmatic, and who has never made a religion of news freedom, there is better sense in allying with the government than in quarreling with it.

"The purpose of my remarks tonight," the Vice President had said, "is to focus your attention on this little group of men who not only enjoy a right of instant rebuttal to every presidential address, but, more importantly, wield a free hand in selecting, presenting, and interpreting the great issues in our nation. . . .

"Is it not fair and relevant to question [the] concentration [of power] in the hands of a tiny, enclosed fraternity of privileged men elected by no one and enjoying a monopoly sanctioned and licensed by government?

"The views of the majority of this fraternity do not—and I repeat, not—represent the views of America.

"That is why such a great gulf existed between how the

nation received the President's address and how the networks reviewed it."

Significant in Agnew's speech was that it appeared to exempt the stations in concentrating its attack on the "fraternity" in New York. No less significant were the remarks of FCC chairman Dean Burch following the speech, calling it "thoughtful and provocative" and deserving of "careful consideration by the industry and public." Addressing the industry he helped to regulate, Burch said, "Physician, heal thyself!"

The combination could not fail to turn the stations against their networks on the issue. Agnew had not implicated the individual licensee, and when he spoke of monopolies it was in reference to the networks and not to the media barons who control powerful groups of stations. When a government that craves loyalty raises the question of media monopolies it behooves the broadcaster with multiple licenses to become loyal in a hurry. And when an FCC chairman tells broadcasters that the Vice President has dispensed good advice, it is well for them to take it to heart, especially if the Commission chairman has a history of hostility to broadcast news dating to when, in 1964, he had been Republican national chairman and assistant campaign director for Barry Goldwater's unsuccessful run for the presidency.

(In his postmortem on that campaign, Burch, in a document called "The State of Our Party as of February 1965," described a communications complex "highlighted by a handful of influential pundits that exposed our campaign to a running critique barely within the bounds of responsible and objective journalism.")

After Agnew's speech, instead of an industry-wide affirmation of the principles of journalistic freedom, there was disunity in television and a widening of the chasm of mutual distrust between network managements and the operators of stations.

The entire episode was fraught with irony. All three networks had carried the Vice President's speech simultaneously in the belief that they would be ventilating an issue, and this had the effect of force-feeding it to the viewer. In televising it, they gave the speech the credibility of their medium and news judgment; and they brought it to the screen from a rigged environment, a Republican Party conference in Des Moines, where the on-camera reception would be fulsomely favorable, the generous applause cuing the audience at home in the same way the laugh machine tells them when something is funny in a situation comedy. Then the networks allowed the speech to air without rebuttal. Except for CBS, which took a few minutes merely to read the official network answers to Agnew's charges, they cut right to the programs in progress. The result was that much of the TV audience could easily believe that everything Agnew had said was true and beyond challenge.

The networks themselves magnified the importance of Agnew's speech. Up to that point the Vice President had not been taken very seriously as a spokesman, and it is probable that if the speech had received the standard excerpting for the newscasts the issue might have bubbled briefly and subsided. He thus became the beneficiary of the news judgment of that "tiny, enclosed fraternity of privileged men," and like "the loudest and most extreme dissenters on every issue" whom Agnew accused television of popularizing, he and his denunciation of network news became "known to every man in the street."

A higher irony, verging on comedy, was that many of the stations which would later agree with Agnew that network news is politically slanted did not carry the Vice President's speech in the choice evening time when it was broadcast. Many played the tape of the speech at 11:30 that night and some delayed it for a couple of days to weekend fringe time. Why? Because Agnew gave his speech during a rating week for local stations, and assuming that the Vice President's address would depress their numbers, and therefore impair their ability to sell, they bumped it from prime time and substituted entertainment programing.

What apparently had provoked Agnew's peroration (which, incidentally, had been written by one of President Nixon's speech writers, Pat Buchanan) were the commentaries and "instant analyses" that followed the President's November 3 address on Vietnam policy, a speech he evidently hoped would have the effect of unifying the country and defusing the moratorium movement. That it did not was blamed on the commentaries and particularly on one network's use of former Paris peace negotiator (and Democrat) Ambassador W. Averell Harriman as guest analyst. Harriman's views were at considerable variance with Nixon's, and it displeased the President that he was given the right of rebuttal. Interestingly, the network involved was the one least watched by the viewers when there is common coverage of news events and otherwise most co-operative with the Administration, ABC.

Compounding that irony is that stations within the ABC affiliate family which carried the Harriman post-address commentary were owned by such politically conservative companies as General Tire, Hearst Corporation, Storer Broadcasting, the Dallas News, the Outlet Company, Capital Cities, the *Washington Star*, and the publishing empires of Newhouse, Annenberg, and Scripps-Howard.

If the Administration had really wanted to finger the responsible parties who by their own acts of omission had allowed the networks to become unlicensed monopolies, Agnew might have directed his wrath at the individual stations which should be capable of providing the kind of regional commentary reflecting regional attitudes that the Vice President had found lacking on television.

Any broadcaster who did not agree that Harriman should have been the one to rebut Nixon on Vietnam was privileged—indeed required—to discontinue the network feed at that point in order to supply its own commentator or panel of analysts; and of course the same held for any who felt that John Chancellor on NBC or Eric Sevareid on CBS were incapable of being fair in assessing the President's

speech. That they did not can only be attributed to their in-
dolence and love of economy; it takes time and money for a
station to do a program of its own, even one as simple as a
news commentary.

Through the entire episode the individual stations behaved, as said earlier, as though they were merely the vic-
timized newsstands that sell the papers, presumably trusting
no one would notice that under law they, as licensees, had
full responsibility for what was broadcast over their facilities. Whatever its failings, the communications law specifies
that a broadcaster's responsibility cannot be delegated—
and that means to an advertiser, a network, or a politician.

Agnew spoke of television news as being controlled by a
"small and unelected" elite. To the contrary, the networks
are in effect elected by the stations, which in turn are elected
and re-elected by the seven-member FCC for three-year
terms. And these stations are controlled by individuals whose
locations and commitments run the entire geographical and
ideological gamut of the United States.

Spared by the Vice President, the television affiliates of
CBS and NBC would in both subtle and overt ways push the
networks toward such news "reforms" as were prescribed by
Agnew. They were no more interested in taking over the responsibility for news analysis than they were in programing
the extra half hour of prime time that probably would be
returned to them.

The second of the affiliates meetings—ABC's—had
barely begun when the FCC by a 5 to 2 vote passed the three-
hour prime-time rule, which it chose to call the prime-time
access rule (and which the trade continued to call the Westinghouse rule). But although it had finally become a regulation after a dozen years' pending with the Commission in a
variety of forms, the new measure still seemed only a nuisance and not a permanent fact of life for broadcasters, and
few believed it would survive long enough to meet its effective date, September 1, 1971.

One reason for this was that CBS and NBC had both vowed to their affiliates that they would challenge the constitutionality of the rule in the highest courts; but another, which suggested that legal recourse might be unnecessary, was the strong opposition to the regulation by no less than the chairman of the FCC. Dean Burch was one of the two who had voted against it, and in his dissent he called it a "Pollyanna" rule, an unrealistic and impractical means to achieve a broader range of programing for the medium. He expected that it would spawn only cheap talk and quiz shows instead of public affairs and higher forms of entertainment, and after the Commission's vote Burch called for petitions from the industry which might present sufficient hard facts to convince the government agency to reconsider the measure. There was in this a strong hint that before too long—perhaps soon after President Nixon appointed a Republican to replace the intellectual Kenneth Cox, a Democrat whose seven-year term was expiring, thereby putting conservatives in a 4 to 3 majority at the FCC—Burch would call for another vote by the Commission to rescind the rule.

It was fair to assume that Cox's replacement would initially take his cue from Burch on the questions before the Commission, and it would then be necessary for one other commissioner to reverse his vote to rescind the rule. That would hardly be difficult, since Commissioner Robert E. Lee had always been friendly to the existing system and seemed to enjoy his popularity with the broadcast establishment. Lee was a commissioner with a single cause, to make the UHF band more viable in the television market place. Strong UHF stations would make possible additional networks to compete with the big three; it was his all-purpose cure for the multifold ailments of television. Lee had voted for the three-hour prime-time rule for a single reason, which he had made explicit; it would, he felt, somehow benefit the UHF stations. The broadcast establishment was prepared to demonstrate that, to the contrary, the rule would hurt UHF. For when the powerful commercial stations had new prime-time periods to program, they would gobble up the best that was available in syndication, taking those programs away from UHF. Lee would be a pushover for a conversion.

NBC and CBS filed petitions to the FCC, as did the affiliate organizations and such major producing companies as MCA, Inc. (Universal TV), Warner Brothers TV, and Paramount TV, along with a number of independent producers and talent unions. All sought to corroborate Burch's view that the new rule would tend to inhibit rather than stimulate greater diversification of program types and sources of supply. Most of the petitions requested at least a year's postponement of the effective date because program development for September 1971 was already under way on the old scale for the customary prime-time requirements. Thus enforcement of the new measure prior to September 1972 would create confusion and cause economic losses both to the networks and to the studios.

Meanwhile, the networks proceeded with their development plans for the 1971–72 television season as though there were no rule.

On August 7 there was an astonishing development. The Burch Commission declared that having considered the petitions it would stand by its original vote. The sole concession to the petitioners was a small one: the effective date would be extended not one year but one month, to October 1971. Case closed.

Immediately, CBS opened the legal battle, filing in the Second Court of Appeals in New York a brief contending that the FCC prime-time dictum was in violation of the First Amendment through its unprecedented interference with the freedom of TV licensees to choose programing from any source based on its merits, and in violation of the Communications Act of 1934 in attempting to regulate the networks. It is the stations which are the licensed entities, and not the networks, and the Commission's actions must address themselves to station conduct. Never having had authority over the networks under the Communications Act, the FCC has, however, held them in check indirectly through its regulation of the stations that comprise a network and particularly over the stations that are network-owned.

The prime-time access rule—in specifying that the networks may no longer retain ownership in programs they did not themselves produce and in ordering them to desist from syndicating programs as an adjunct to networking—was pointed at CBS, NBC, and ABC and not the stations and therefore, as the CBS legal argument went, was a case of the FCC overstepping its authority. Several of the stations also went to the courts individually.

Still needing explanation, in the meantime, was the reason for the FCC's sudden refusal to reconsider the rule. *Broadcasting* magazine surmised that the Commission was swung by the advocacy of a single industry figure highly respected by the FCC, Sylvester L. Weaver, Jr., one of network television's early luminaries who, like many another displaying some genius in the medium, was cast out by the system. Pat Weaver had been chairman and president of NBC from December 1953 to December 1955, rising to that height through his remarkable contributions in the programing sphere. He had introduced the television special (then called *spectacular*) and conceived of the NBC *Today* and *Tonight* shows, the perfect formats for live television from which all the other desk and sofa talk shows descend. It was said, when NBC fired him, that he was a creative person who should never have been made chief executive (not his mistake, certainly); nevertheless, there was no putting him back to a lesser job, and he went on to become an industry pariah in trying to promote subscription television in California, unsuccessfully as it proved. By 1970, he was representing clients at the networks for an advertising agency.

As it happened, Weaver was one of several to come out in favor of the prime-time access rule, and lacking a better explanation for the Burch Commission's surprising reaffirmation of its decision, the house organ for the radio-TV establishment, *Broadcasting*, ever in search of scapegoats and enemies, pinned it on him.

Variety, however, came upon a more plausible reason, a letter from the Justice Department to Dean Burch advising him of its antitrust division's interest in the matter and of its concurrence with the Commission majority on the prime-time access rule. The letter, dated July 15 and signed by Richard W. McLaren, assistant attorney general in charge of the department's antitrust division, in effect warned Burch that it had the authority to take action if the FCC should decide to overturn its original decision.

McLaren wrote: "We have previously expressed to the Commission our conviction that the networks' control over television programing which appears to have arisen primarily because of their effective control over access to the nation-wide television audience raises serious questions under the antitrust laws." He described the networks' control over programing as "dangerous" and said the letter was written "in view of the antitrust division's frequently expressed interest in supporting the Commission's efforts to maintain strong, independent sources of television programing other than the three nation-wide networks."

Then he delicately laid in the punchline: "These comments are not intended to preclude the Dept. of Justice from taking any appropriate action under its responsibilities for antitrust enforcement," citing the 1959 precedent of the *United States* versus *RCA*, a case involving an exchange of stations which helped to establish the Justice Department's primary jurisdiction in broadcast matters pertaining to antitrust laws. Under the circumstances, it would have been politically unwise and probably futile for the FCC to do anything but uphold the original decision.

11

Molting Season

Late in June, Mike Dann submitted his resignation at CBS. A week later it became known that Paul Klein had given his notice at NBC. By an astounding coincidence these antagonists, the two most spirited competitors at the networks, who jousted endlessly for rating supremacy and scraps of company prestige, within a single week had abandoned the Beautiful Business, Klein after ten years to form his own company in the cable television field, Dann after twenty-one to become a vice-president of the Children's Television Workshop, which produced *Sesame Street,* at about one-fourth his CBS salary.

Journalistically, which is to say in simple fact, the departures were unrelated; poetically, however, they were of a piece. In a new era, when salesmen and attorneys had ascended to the command of companies that had been run by showmen, firebrands were out of vogue. Dann and Klein, although of unquestioned value as experts in strategy, were nevertheless sources of embarrassment to their managements for their intemperance and flamboyance. Both were all too aware of being distrusted, and at the same time neither found joy in the new, conservative network style. Journalistically neither was fired; poetically both were cast out.

Each professed to have reached a point in his life when he desired to make a meaningful contribution to society. The reader may make what he will of the fact that two men with great influence over the program matter of the most pervasive and powerful communications forces in all history were giving up the office from a desire to do something *important.*

As an intellectual, Klein derived limited gratification from his professional achievements or his salary, which with bonuses and other perquisites, came to more than $50,000 annually. Bereft of community among his colleagues—intellectuals being scarce in television—he felt, perhaps more than most, oppressed by corporate bureaucracy, fighting up channels constantly to convey a new idea and often dependent on an alliance with corporate information vice-president Bob Kasmire or press relations vice-president Bud Rukeyser to give the idea the credence of their sobriety. Not an all-purpose executive, Klein had held the same job for ten years and knew he would never be promoted to another. His superiors seemed to prize decorum over talent, which was not unusual in large corporations. People who have original ideas are off center, and companies have a way of valuing conventional behavior which is dead center.

It was not surprising that Klein's private venture would be in the new field that had caught the fancy of the medium's most ambivalent critics, cable television. Typically his enterprise had a futuristic sound, but Klein maintained that it was no more than a year away from being operational. Briefly, it involved program retrieval by means of two-way cable linked to a computer. The consumer in a cable home could select from a catalogue of video cartridges any of some twoscore programs, including first-run movies and shows for specialized interests. If practicable, the concept had revolutionary implications on the existing television system in that it would turn the viewer into his own programer, and it threatened to make obsolete the network theories of sequential programing.

Dann, too, had reached the end of the line at his network. With Jack Schneider positioned to succeed Bill Paley as chairman of the corporation, there was no hope of realizing his ambition to become president of the network. Dann had once been close to Schneider, but Wood was closer, and Dann's encounters with Wood on policy had served to alienate him from both men. Besides, he was not of the fraternity, not of the crisp, stylish group which had hustled television at the ad agencies during the fifties.

The celebrated incident with the Smothers Brothers during the spring of 1969 provided a signal that Dann might be out of his time. When the young comedians were waging their war on CBS for its extreme caution with their topical material, causing them to charge censorship and to splatter the issue in the press and in Washington, Dann in his counsel gave them to believe they could exploit their case without fear of losing their Sunday night berth on CBS. They were winners for the network—stars by virtue of their 33 share against the toughest family show on television, *Bonanza*—and the first to compete successfully for CBS at nine o'clock on Sundays in years. When Wood, who was then the new network president, issued a warning to the Smothers Brothers, Dann advised that it was not to be taken seriously. Two weeks later, the brothers lost their mooring in the fall schedule.

It was the beginning of a new time.

Dann's authority in the program area had begun to erode. Having lost the Smothers Brothers show, and with it an effective CBS challenge on Sunday nights, he tried next to liberalize CBS standards and practices so that he might acquire some of the more sophisticated movies for the network. He was thwarted, and on the movie issue a number of the company's elder statesmen were aligned against him.

During the program meetings in February, Dann's plea to preserve the shows that would keep CBS a winner lost out to president Bob Wood's plan to modernize the network and build for the future. Wood won over to his side the next two in the chain of command, Dick Jencks and Jack Schneider, and finally also the chairman himself.

More than a defeat, it was a repudiation of all he had stood for—the fourteen consecutive years of CBS supremacy in the ratings, the last five of which he personally had jockeyed home the winner, and his own Operation 100 campaign which was under way at the time to win the laurel a fifteenth time for CBS and a sixth by his devices. Worse, the schedule that would represent CBS in September was not of Dann's making, and it would be difficult for him to live with it. If it proved a winner, it would not be his to enjoy, but if a loser he would feel the humiliation.

Yet, even after failing in debate with Wood, Dann would not concede that his era was ended. If through Operation 100 he was to succeed in inching past NBC to victory in the Nielsen averages he was certain that that would rekindle Paley's pride in being Number One and would reawaken the competitive drive that went to the essence of the network.

For what it was—a maniacal surprise offensive—Operation 100 was a masterpiece. Not only was the network a winner once again, its late rating drive carried a majority of the affiliated stations to first place in their local markets in the spring Nielsen and ARB sweep ratings, assuring them of bountiful sales for the duration of the year.

"You'll be interested in what happens at the affiliates meeting," Dann told me at peak exhilaration over his triumph. "I've gotten word that they're planning to do something for me this year out of gratitude for Operation 100."

This is what happened. Wood, in his state-of-the-network speech to the affiliates, tokenly acknowledged the victory and then said, "We are determined that we will resist being sucked into the annual ratings rat race where long-range advantages are sacrificed for short-term gains. We are going to lift our sights from the narrow focus of next week's rating report, or next quarter's, or next season's. Our major concern will be what is good for CBS and for our affiliates over the next decade."

Wood's message was an outright renunciation of Dann and was warmly received. Later when the warrior from programing was called to speak and there was no hero's welcome, no ovation in tribute, Dann, who every year jocularly ad libbed half an hour's worth of tales about the program wars in a barracks idiom, soberly delivered a minute-long introduction to the program pilots that would be screened, and left the rostrum.

His isolation was complete—first Wood, then Schneider, then the elders, then Paley, and now the affiliates.

In a sense, Dann was Klein's victim. For it was Klein who, as the apostle of the demographic approach to ratings rather than the old-fashioned nose count, had conducted a successful campaign to indoctrinate the entire industry (broadcasting as well as advertising) to the idea that a profile of people viewing a given show—as to age, income level, education, etc.—was more important than the old mass-viewing criterion that Nielsen had reported as "Homes Viewing." One of Klein's tactics in dealing with CBS had been to alter the rules of the game just when his opponent had the advantage, and his push for demographics was timed to diminish the importance of CBS's dominance in the ratings by the old standard of total circulation. The measure of his campaign's success was that it forced CBS to change its operating philosophy and to discard high-rated established shows for new programs that would deliver a younger audience. Dann fought the principle at CBS and lost. The wags had sport with the idea that it was Klein who programed the CBS 1970–71 schedule.

A few weeks after the affiliates meeting I met Dann in an elevator at Black Rock.

"You've heard the rumors about me, I suppose?" he asked.

"Yes, and also the denials."

"Depends on the rumor. I'm denying that I'm going to Universal or anywhere else on the Coast. Would you be surprised if I were to leave commercial television entirely?"

"A little surprised," I said. "Where you going?"

"As soon as it's firmed I'll let you know. I won't blow your deadline."

"Who's going to succeed you? Perry?"

"I'm recommending Freddie."

"Will he get it?"

"Who knows with these guys?"

"Why don't you tell me where you're going, and I'll sit on it," I said.

"I promise you'll be the first to know."

As a matter of fact I was not. The first to know was Steve Knoll of my staff, who flushed it out from another source.

Dann and Klein, by another odd coincidence, had been the only two from the commercial television sphere to volunteer their time and skills to the Children's Television Workshop, Klein to provide audience research and Dann counsel in negotiations. Although they had still not met, not even in the offices of Workshop president Joan Ganz Cooney, each separately had offered his services to the preschool *Sesame Street* project because both hoped for its success. Although creatures of the system, each was painfully aware that the television medium had not realized its utilitarian potential.

As it happened, *Sesame Street* was branching into foreign adaptations and product adjuncts such as books, records, and toys, all to be developed for the disadvantaged, just as Dann had come at last to realize that he no longer belonged at CBS. Mrs. Cooney asked him to join at $25,000 a year, and he accepted.

Most executives leave the networks for bigger jobs in the business world, but Dann had worked at high salaries for the better part of twenty-one years at NBC and CBS, and his investments had left him (his word) "comfortable." He told me that he took the lesser job because his wife and three children were all engaged in one or another form of volunteer work for social causes, and none of his family was particularly proud of the work he was doing at the network. They were pleased that he had associated himself with *Sesame Street*.

A week after he had joined the Workshop, Dann called to tell me how delighted he was to be working with people who were dedicated to the project and not dollar-oriented, and who did not work in a climate of fear. "They're turning down millions in product licensing offers, because they don't want to exploit the name of the show for profit and because they want to be sure that the people in the ghetto will be able to afford them. When did you ever see that in commercial TV?"

Late in August, I spoke with him again.

"You'll never believe what I'm doing these days," he said. "Reading. I read every night. I have to in order to keep up with these people. They're up on everything. You know what's the matter with the people at the networks? They never read. I always used to say I never had the time. But the truth was the only thing I ever enjoyed reading then was a rating book."

It was Irv Wilson who introduced me to Freddie Silverman. We were all in Chicago then, about 1962, I running the bureau there for *Variety*, Wilson making a name for himself as general sales manager of the independent station, WGN-TV (he has since, with detours to two networks, become an agent engaged in packaging TV shows). There was at the station, he told me, an extraordinary young man who was too good for the Chicago league and frustrated as fifth man in a program department which considered him a nuisance, even though he was responsible for the only two shows that were competing successfully against the networks. Freddie's on fire and the rest of them are not, Wilson said.

He arranged our meeting. Silverman was a boy not long out of college, unimpressive if one were to go by appearances, introverted though not shy, and obviously impatient with his rate of progress in the business world. My own feeling was that he was rather far along for his age, then around twenty-four, and should have been satisfied that he was not in the mailroom, which is the way many young college graduates break into broadcasting. But there being few people I liked or trusted more than Wilson, and Silverman having a similar bond to him, we began our relationship felicitously.

Freddie was not intellectual but was scholarly about television. For his master's thesis at Ohio State he had analyzed

ABC's program schedule from the time of its merger with Paramount Theatres in 1953 through the end of that decade, noting why it succeeded when it did and why it went wrong where it failed. The manuscript, I'm told, is still floating around at ABC and was much admired when he submitted it in 1960 as an argument for a job with the network, but he wasn't hired. After being rebuffed in New York he took the job at WGN as a program department functionary left to make something of the drabbest film in the station's library, the dregs that were forced on a station when it purchased front-line movies.

By the pragmatic standards of the TV trade, Silverman's achievement in Chicago was remarkable. An independent station is one without a network service and therefore, *per se*, the fourth alternative for the viewer, a lowly local operation forced to scramble for an audience against the big-budget, star-laden, nationally promoted schedules of the powerful chains. Baseball games and children's shows were an independent's staples, old movies helped in prime time and later at night, and there were tolerable rating numbers to be gotten from off-network reruns, that is, film shows which had been canceled. After four o'clock, most independents had the appearance of yesterday's network.

WGN-TV, without other independent competition in the market (New York had three and Los Angeles four independents, but this was before UHF increased the number in all three cities), was one of the better, wider-ranging operations—possibly, at the time, the best of its kind—but had taken to striving for the easy economics of a network station and therefore favored the expedient over the imaginative solution to the program problem. Against the current, Silverman created two series for WGN from some of the most useless film in the vaults, one under the title *Zim Bomba*, the other *Family Classics*, which were triumphs of resourcefulness. By way of preface, motion pictures on a local station were usually scheduled late at night, in the heart of prime time, or in the late afternoon—and always they were aimed at adults. Juvenile films were therefore relegated to Saturday or Sunday mornings, where the advertising was scarce and came at low rates anyway, so that they were little more than fillers.

Silverman's *Zim Bomba* was merely the old *Bomba, the Jungle Boy* (sub-Tarzan) string of antique Hollywood potboilers dressed up with a dramatic opening for the credits, with jungle drums on the sound-track, and edited down to a television hour (52 minutes or less, to allow for the commercials). Presented as a new program series early Tuesday evenings, it found an unexpectedly large audience. As memory serves, *Bomba* overtook at least one network show in the ratings during its run and at times even two, so that for a cheap hour of programing it was handsomely profitable. The problem was that only ten *Bomba* films had ever been made, so that the TV "series" played once, repeated itself, and was finished.

Even more successful and far more lasting—at this writing it is still running on WGN—was *Family Classics*, nothing more than an anthology of movies of the *Tom Sawyer*, *Little Women*, and *My Friend Flicka* stripe, hosted by one of the station's kid-show personalities, Frazier Thomas, who gave it a reading-by-the-fireside introduction suggestive of a cultural offering for the young. In its first year it led the Chicago ratings on Friday nights, surpassing all three networks, even Bob Hope, who then had a weekly series on NBC.

Because it credited Freddie's ingenuity, my article on WGN's unique prime-time successes was far from celebrated at the station. "The kid has been impossible to live with," a representative of the station said to me. "What's he going to be like now, with all this recognition?"

Months later, over lunch at the Wrigley Restaurant, Freddie announced to me that he would soon be leaving the station to look for work in New York. I recall telling him it was poor strategy to look for a job while out of work, wiser to stay at WGN while making periodic trips to the East to survey the opportunities. He nodded at my advice but quit anyway. A few weeks later I read in *Variety* that Fred Silverman had become a program executive at the New York independent WPIX. And less than two months later the startling news, startling not only to me in Chicago but to the entire trade: an obscure young man of twenty-five, virtually unknown in New York, with no network experience, had been appointed by Michael H. Dann as the new director of daytime programs for CBS Television.

Daytime television may not have the glamour and prominence of prime time, but it was not a trivial part of the schedule and, at CBS particularly, was not to be entrusted to an amateur. At CBS the position had been associated with such knowledgeable and proficient programing technicians as Oscar Katz and Larry White, who had helped to build it into the greatest profit center at the network. CBS more than dominated daytime; it lorded over it with as much as 40 per cent of the regular daily audience and ten of its programs in the top twelve of the Nielsen daytime ratings. As long as CBS maintained such pre-eminence in the numbers it would take far more millions out of its morning and afternoon service than it could possibly get in the evening.

The economics of daytime television are gorgeous. Five episodes per week of a typical soap opera (the practitioners use the term *dramatic serial*) cost less to produce than a single half-hour prime-time film show, and the quiz and panel shows are even cheaper. Shot on tape as though live, with few production frills and a minimum of rehearsal, a full week's worth of studio melodrama carries a typical budget of $60,000 (costs for a nighttime situation comedy on film are $75,000 per half hour, and upward). Given the healthy ratings CBS had been getting, the six commercial minutes in the daytime half hour would sell for an average of $10,000. Thus the revenue in a single day covers the production cost for a week, and after the commissions to advertising agencies and compensation payments to the stations, all the rest is profit, or, as they say at the networks, gravy.

The soap and packaged-food companies invest heavily in

daytime television because the costs are favorable and the viewing audience almost pure in housewives who do the marketing for the family. Daytime viewing levels range between 11 and 15 million homes daily, with total circulation calculated on an estimate of slightly less than two viewers per home in the daylight hours, and most of that number are women in the age range of eighteen to forty-nine years. Daytime at CBS had been more profitable than all the other facets of a broadcast week combined.

In view of that, it seemed chancy and even reckless to turn over the responsibility for the gold mine to an untried and relatively inexperienced young man. Dann chose Silverman, an outsider, over the men in his department because he had read the master's thesis on ABC and found it "a brilliant diagnosis." Recalling it years later, he said, "Reading it I could see the kid had instincts that were unbelievable. We were so strong in daytime and had so few problems there that I felt it was a good spot for a bright young man to learn the ropes."

By the time I was transferred to New York, early in 1965, Silverman was meeting the test, for NBC again was starting to make rating gains by day, with one of Silverman's predecessors, Larry White, masterminding the schedule. CBS made a number of program alterations and strategic shifts to cut off the threat, and Silverman was rewarded with a vice-presidency.

By then, advertisers of products for the very young children—toys, candy, and breakfast foods—had discovered that their targets could be reached as effectively on Saturday mornings as in prime time, and much more cheaply. A new profit center following similar economic principles to weekday television was forming, addressing itself to juveniles, and as the advertising concentration increased there the networks found a diminishing need for child-oriented programing at 7:30 in the evening and began gravitating to programs of a general character. Since the Saturday morning demographics were specific and constant, the race was for bulk numbers, and Silverman demonstrated he knew better than his competitors how to get them. He developed and purchased first-run animated cartoon series that quickly won the children, and CBS became as entrenched there as on weekdays.

During the summer of 1967 Freddie and I were in Hollywood at the same time and met each other at the pool of the Beverly Hills Hotel. It was on a day when broke promoters and wishful producers were particularly profuse at poolside, buying each other drinks and having themselves paged for the phones, the familiar charades to appear successful and important while playing to fall in socially with someone who might be the salvation of their careers. There sat Freddie at the sparse end of the pool—the only one around that day with real credentials, who had the power to put any of the desperate, swaggering hustlers into business on a very profitable scale if he would but buy their show—alone, unnoticed, looking so young as to be taken for the son of a person wealthy enough to stop at the Beverly Hills.

"I'm out here to look over our animation for next season," he said to me. "We've really got some exciting stuff. When we get back to New York I'll show you the storyboards and the art."

A day or so later I had a visit with Joe Barbera, who took me on a tour of the Hanna-Barbera studios.

"We're doing monster stuff mainly," he said apologetically. "Comic-book fiction, super heroes, and fantasy. Not out of choice, you understand. It's the only thing we can sell to the networks, and we have to stay in business."

He reached into a file of drawings and pulled out a large color illustration of a beagle and a Siamese cat. "This was a sweet idea for a cartoon show, middle-class family life seen through the eyes of their pets, and the dog and cat having their own conflicts and adventures. Can't sell it, though. They say it's too gentle. They want out-of-this-world hard action."

"You mean violence?"

"We try not to use the word."

Back in New York, Silverman followed through on his
invitation to brief me on his new Saturday morning line-up.
Holding up, like valuable prints by the masters, three-foot
illustrations of his new stars—grotesques and thing-people
who lived in space or under water or thousands of years ago,
with gibberish names—he put me through the story concepts.
There were *Shazzan!*, *The Herculoids*, and a raft of others,
but I had trouble following because I was more interested in
Freddie's high excitement over each new creature character
and his absorption in the dramatic garbage he was detailing.
Since I was not paying attention, I will here have to simulate
the names of his dramatis personae and their peculiar talents.

"This," he said, "this is Airplaneman. He flies. Isn't this
a great rendition? He looks like a plane, yet he's handsome
like a man. Now this one is his mortal enemy Ack-Ack, who
fires shrapnel through his eyes, really cruel but clever and in
love with Airplaneman's girl, Prettyfanny, so we have that
situation going. Here's Prettyfanny. Cute. But she doesn't fly.
Airplaneman has to carry her. Or sometimes his friend does.
Here's his friend, Mongoloi, the comic relief. He has this
magic carpet. Now it all takes place on the planet
Whirla. . . ."

At first it was hard to believe that a grown person had
such a passionate involvement in a program that was meant
only to exploit the young, but that, I realized, was Freddie's
peculiar gift. Since television was his only interest, it was to
him more real than the world, and whatever he might contribute to the mass culture in the pursuit of first place was to
him as important as work could be.

"Fred, I consider myself forewarned," I said, when he
had finished taking me through his new schedule. "My own
kids will be spared Saturday morning television."

He seemed hurt and, unless I'm mistaken, perplexed.
"The kids are going to love this. We're going to cream the
competition this year."

He was right, but then in mass-appeal programs I have

never known him not to be. Whenever he made an important change, whether in a daytime serial or the Saturday morning kids' bloc, the outcome was invariably as he predicted it, and I soon came to realize that it was more than luck. Freddie had an extrasensory perception about the television audience that was uncomplicated by conscience, taste, idealism, or a personal life.

He was a bachelor specializing in programs for children and housewives, and no father or husband knew better than he how to serve those majorities. Dann, who once confessed to me that he did not know what was on CBS's daytime or Saturday schedule and would not recognize the name of a show if you asked him, had given Freddie the freedom to make all the necessary decisions in his area. "Freddie's my expert," he said, "and if he wants to drop a game show or go with soaps all day long that's okay with me."

In time it became necessary to promote him. At thirty-two he had stopped making progress and was concerned about it, indicating also that he was tired of being a daytime specialist. Dann gave him the new title of vice-president of eastern program development, but was somewhat at a loss to describe his specific duties. That was in the spring of 1970. A few months later he became Dann's successor.

No one questioned that Silverman had the skills for Dann's job, only whether he could keep a staff together and whether he and Wood would get along. After he was appointed, his first instinct was to fire half the staff. He wanted from his department nothing less than the fervor he brought to the job and no less dedication. Freddie was one of the few important network executives I knew who really watched television, watched it and analyzed it, and as the daytime vice-president he fiercely drove producers and writers to keep the production level high and the story lines lively. When a soap opera slipped in the ratings, people were fired, new creative teams brought in, characters written out and new ones introduced, revisions made until the show was nursed back to a winning pattern. He intended to deal with his inherited staff the same way, but Wood counseled him to proceed slowly.

"Bob and I will get along," Freddie said to me. "I don't know why some people think we won't. He's the boss, and I intend to give him what he wants. There isn't going to be any trouble."

Still, under Dann, Silverman had had virtual autonomy with the daytime schedule and was accustomed to having his own way. In Wood he had a president who, with little experience in programing, had become enamoured of that function and seemed determined to make the decisions. It was, of course, easy to understand why. Programing is more fun than sales and infinitely more glamorous. Wood had had a taste of the celebrity treatment in Hollywood, as only the big names can administer it—invitations to their homes, dinners at Chasen's and The Bistro, recognition as a peer, deference, respect, and favors. When Wood gave a party at the Century Plaza, name performers and producers made a point of being there. As long as it was he who determined in the end what would play on CBS and what would not, he would have immense importance with the celebrity colony in his native Los Angeles.

Given that situation, it seemed only a matter of time before the two would clash over a well-thought-out program maneuver of Silverman's which for reasons of his own would be vetoed by Wood.

In July, Wood and Silverman went to Hollywood together, the purpose being to introduce the new program chief to the producers who were preparing shows for the CBS fall schedule and to look at the rushes and rough cuts of films already shot. At the same time it gave them an opportunity to discuss the course CBS was taking and Silverman's uppermost thoughts about it. His first observation was that the new schedule was worse than it should be and that it could function more effectively for CBS if six shows were moved about.

Dann had been a good enough strategist to see the mistakes, but when Wood cut him down in February and made the schedule his own, Dann lost all interest and also felt no desire to contribute to the glorification of the president. Some of the errors were elementary: *Beverly Hillbillies* was clearly not a proper bridge between *Storefront Lawyers* and *Medical Center*. The audience for the latter two would be essentially the same, but *Hillbillies* had a different appeal and obviously did not belong between them. Nor did *Green Acres* belong in the middle of an evening flanked by *Mission: Impossible* and *Mannix*, if there was to be any hope of maintaining an audience flow from the beginning of the evening to the end. The new *Mary Tyler Moore Show* could not survive as a freshman with *The Don Knotts Hour* and *Mod Squad* as its competition.

Wood returned from the trip before Silverman and made a surprising disclosure. The schedule would be revised immediately, in midsummer, with six shows changing places on three different days, which meant that all sales in the programs would have to be renegotiated, the producers and affiliates informed, and all the promotional materials revised at a large cost.

Changes in the schedule on such a scale had never before been attempted so late in the year. In particular at CBS, the schedule published in February had traditionally been immutable, as though cast in bronze. Wood risked a loss of face in admitting the mistakes, but found that prospect preferable to letting the blunders stand, where they would impair CBS's competitive chances. *Beverly Hillbillies* and *Green Acres*, with almost identical appeal, were grouped together as the new opposition to *Mod Squad* and Don Knotts. *To Rome With Love* was moved to the 9:30 half hour on Tuesdays, displacing *The Governor and J.J.*, which in turn moved to Wednesday, to provide a more feasible link between *Storefront Lawyers* and *Medical Center*. On Saturdays, *Arnie* was moved up a half hour into the *Green Acres* slot to be followed by the Mary Tyler Moore comedy.

Their first time as a team, Wood and Silverman worked well together.

Silverman then proposed a project he had hoped for years to develop at CBS—family movies, much on the order of *Family Classics*, his prize brainchild at WGN-TV. And since they were no longer being made by the picture companies, CBS would commission their production by independent producers and would make several of them. There were, foreseeably, two ideal spots in the schedule for such a ninety-minute show: Fridays, precedented at WGN, which would give CBS a double feature for the evening, the family film at 7:30 followed by *Friday Night at the Movies;* or Sundays, as competition to NBC's indestructible *Disney's Wonderful World of Color*, especially since both *Lassie* and *The Ed Sullivan Show* seemed to be on their last legs at CBS. Wood gave his approval, and Silverman proceeded.

A month later Wood called it off and canceled the project. Economic conditions were unfavorable, he said. The country was in the grip of a business recession, and CBS was feeling it at least as severely as most other companies. Besides, the network would be losing $50 million in cigarette billings after the first of the year, and the fall of 1971, under the new FCC ruling, would find network prime time shrunken to twenty-one hours a week from what, practically speaking, had been twenty-five. The networks would be divesting themselves of programing rather than adding substantially to the schedules.

Silverman's project represented over-all a $20 million program risk.

It's a great idea, but the wrong time, Wood said.

Freddie said he agreed.

Paul Klein was replaced by Bill Rubens, an able numbers man who was also most acceptable to NBC management as a low-pressure and altogether malleable type; but he was not succeeded in a real sense, for Klein was more than a researcher and a juggler of statistics. He was a creative executive who worked out new solutions to new problems, and it was his old adversary Dann who observed that the industry was losing him at the time his vision and his dexterity to meet changing needs and conditions were most needed, when the established system was seriously troubled by economic uncertainty, harassments from Washington, and the threats of new technology. Not only was Klein a lost resource in the crisis, he had joined an enemy camp—cable—and he and Dann, who went into public television, were applying their talents and skills in areas that were operating against the commercial television machinery.

Their absence would in time affect not only the style of network competition and the decisions on programing—both were, for instance, advocates of the television special—but also perhaps the order of things in the hierarchy of networks.

It was the last of nine summers on the Federal Communications Commission for Kenneth Cox. For seven of them he had been a commissioner and the first two as head of the Commission's broadcast bureau. His term had expired, and while President Nixon might in good conscience have reappointed him—for he was surely one of the few knowledgeable and diligent members of that seven-man body, and probably the most respected by the industry he helped to regulate—there was never a doubt, even though the President was slow getting around to it, that he would be replaced.

He was, despite his qualities, cast out by another system, political patronage. Cox was a Democrat, and Nixon was privileged to appoint one of his own party. Besides, the broadcast elite, many of whom supported the President in his campaign, made it known that they wanted a more conservative Commission, which presumably would be more sympathetic to their business interests. Nixon had already given the broadcasters two who seemed to favor the status quo, the new chairman, Dean Burch, who had been conspicuous in the conservative movement of Barry Goldwater, and one of their own number, Robert Wells, a station operator from Kansas. Together with the veteran bureaucrat Robert E. Lee, they comprised the Republic minority on the Commission. Re-

placing Cox with a Republican appointee would for the first
time since the Eisenhower Administration give that party a 4
to 3 majority at the FCC.

While it had never been true that the commissioners
voted unfailingly in political blocs, still the broadcast industry felt more secure with a Republican-dominated Commission than with a Democratic one, since the latter party tended
to produce the reformers and idealists who sought change.

Until Dean Burch's appointment, the FCC had seemed to
many in broadcasting rigged against the existing structure,
even though the head of the Commission had been a Republican and a career bureaucrat, Rosel Hyde. The oldest member of the FCC, Hyde had been appointed its chairman by
President Johnson, who yielded up a patronage opportunity
to pacify the broadcast community (of which he was, in private life, a member—in his wife's name). But Hyde was
a peaceable man who generally preferred to leave well
enough, or poorly enough, alone; and since he was not a
strong leader the FCC was never really the Hyde Commission, but rather the Nicholas Johnson Commission, marked
by the radical energies and brilliant language of its young-
est member.

Nick Johnson, an Iowan who took his law degree in Texas
and taught for a time at the University of California at
Berkeley, was named to the FCC by President Johnson in
1966 at the age of thirty-two. He had been previously with
the Maritime Commission, where in two years he established
a reputation as a maverick and troublemaker, and the Washington scuttlebutt was that the President had been impor-
tuned to relieve Maritime of the hotly outspoken young man
who wanted to correct all the wrongs at once. A man of stunning intellect, young Johnson was a passionately partisan
Democrat and obviously an outstanding member of the
party's new generation, but he was an overspirited colt who
needed to learn political patience and the ways of compromise. It is possible that he was assigned to the FCC in the
belief that his fierce idealism and indomitable litigiousness

would be contained and more than offset by the dull men who would be his fellow commissioners, and that in time he would be tamed. If that was the reasoning, it was ill-reasoned.

Taking his trust more seriously than any previous commissioner, Johnson immediately set about learning the American broadcasting system and the workings of the government agency that regulated it. Within a few months he was calling for drastic reforms at the FCC, representing it to the whole country as an inert body of appointed officials who in their lethargy were serving the private interests of businessmen ahead of the public interest. That, of course, did not endear him to his colleagues, but he seemed not to care and continued his campaign of criticism until he embarrassed the Commission into coming alive, at least to the extent of considering issues that had conveniently been ignored or pushed aside for years.

Shortly after he joined the Commission, Nick Johnson called to have lunch with *Variety*'s president, Syd Silverman, and me, as I suppose he called other publishers and editors to present himself in person and open the lines of communication. In our experience, no new appointee to the FCC had done that before. It was evident that Johnson was tuning up the press. Our conversation at lunch was fairly innocuous— he searching out our attitudes on certain broadcast matters, and Silverman and I searching out his on the same and others, although knowing that he was still new to the questions—but it was possible to tell even then that he would be a vigorous commissioner and a newsmaker.

At the left end of the FCC's ideological spectrum, Johnson was frequently a lone dissenter in cases before the Commission, but many of his dissents rang with logic and forceful rhetoric, and he did not leave them to the musty FCC records, making sure they reached the interested public. He was the FCC's vocal minority, using his gift of language and the receptivity of the print media to activate civic groups to issues on which he had been outvoted. His resort to the press first irritated the broadcasters, who accused him of headline-grabbing at their expense for the presumed purpose of running for office, and later alarmed them; for the issues Nick Johnson promulgated were those of concentrated media power (cross-ownership of newspapers and radio and/or TV, or multiple ownership of broadcast stations in a single market area or across an entire state) and public access to the public air waves, the latter illuminating the denial of voice by the licensed media to ethnic and social minorities—blacks and youth, for instance—and to the full range of political opinion, including those in disagreement with the established order.

He then campaigned, through speeches, magazine articles, and a book, *How to Talk Back to Your Television Set*, to alert the citizenry to their rights to challenge a broadcast licensee at license renewal time—as it were, to "vote" against or for his continuance as a station operator—which was, within the trade, the most unorthodox and unpopular thing an FCC commissioner had ever done. Groups of broadcasters called for Johnson's impeachment on grounds that a commissioner was supposed to work quietly at regulating and not go before the public as a critic of the industry. But when the Vice President of the United States was critical of the networks in a televised speech, the same broadcasters defended his right to speak his mind as a citizen. And if a public official as high on the scale as Spiro Agnew had the right to speak critically of an aspect of broadcasting, so then must a lesser official like citizen Nicholas Johnson, and that ended the impeachment movement.

But this was supposed to be about Kenneth Cox, the scholarly commissioner—possibly the best commissioner since the advent of television—whose term had run out. And the relevance of Nick Johnson to the story is that Cox had been his nearest ally, although unlike Johnson he was mature, reasonable, pragmatic, and unflamboyant, and respected by broadcasters, although most would have preferred having him off the government agency because he saw too clearly the failings of radio and television and was an advocate of change. When Cox voted with Johnson he gave credence to the view, for Cox was not of the rebellious generation; he was not a hothead and hardly a radical.

Sometimes joined by a third Democrat in the voting, Robert Bartley (nephew of the late Speaker of the House, Sam Rayburn), especially on the matters of media concentration, Cox and Johnson were strong factors in a number of decisions with jarring repercussions. The three of them were the hard core in frustrating the merger of ABC with International Telephone and Telegraph, in the proposals to break up the concentration of media ownership, in trimming network prime time to three hours, and in the decisions against stations which were ignoring the broadcast needs of the black citizenry in their communities. Some stations in cities whose population was 30 per cent black or even more—licensed as they were to serve the interests of their specific communities —had no black on-the-air talent or employees above the rank of janitor who were not Caucasian, and they broadcast little or no black-oriented programing. Their actions prompted coalitions of black organizations to demand reforms at the local stations, and they had a measure of success.

Cox and Johnson were opposed to the FCC's routine renewal of station licenses, and their concern as to whether a licensee had properly fulfilled his local obligations had the inevitable effect of making a majority of stations try harder. Cox did not leave the Commission until he saw through the passage of one of his pet proposals, at the final meeting he attended on August 29, that the renewal application for a station license list the major issues in the community it served and specify how the station dealt with those issues and met the informational and emotional needs of the community under those circumstances.

Station operators for years had come to expect automatic renewal of their licenses every three years, and the Nicholas Johnson FCC suggested for the first time that renewals might have to be earned. My own feeling is that the FCC had but to take away a single license for the right reasons—indifference to community needs in a blind dedication to the pursuit of profits—to shock every station from coast to coast into a more responsible communications service, and although a number of licenses were in jeopardy for such reasons during the Cox-Johnson-Bartley era of the FCC there was never the fourth vote to make it happen. WHDH-TV in Boston had lost its right to broadcast, but not for the reason of indifferent service.

President Nixon had been under some pressure to appoint a black commissioner as Cox's successor and, from other quarters, to name a woman.

On July 22 he gave the job to a forty-two-year-old loyal Republican with no broadcast or communications background, Sherman Unger, who had been serving as general counsel for the Department of Housing and Urban Development. A Midwesterner, Unger had worked with Dean Burch as a special assistant when Burch was Republican national chairman in 1964, had been an advance man for Nixon in his 1960 presidential campaign, and was a co-ordinator in the briefings for Nixon and Agnew when they were the Republican candidates in the 1968 campaign. He would tilt the balance of power on the Commission to the Republicans and strengthen Burch's chairmanship.

But Unger's nomination by the President never went before the Senate Commerce Committee for confirmation. Senate approval was held up for five months while the White House investigated allegations of tax irregularities in Unger's past, and in December Unger withdrew from consideration.

Cox, whose term officially ended June 30, stayed on through the end of August and then joined the Washington law firm of Haley, Bader and Potts and at the same time became senior vice-president of Microwave Communications of America, Inc., a firm that provided specialized microwave transmission facilities to businesses. That left the FCC a six-man Commission from September through December, and on a number of matters, including the multimillion-dollar merger of Corinthian Broadcasting with Dun and Bradstreet, it was deadlocked in a three-three split along political party lines.

In December, the President named Thomas James Houser, deputy director of the Peace Corps and a political associate of Illinois Senator Charles Percy, as an interim appointee for a six-month term, with full voting powers on the FCC until the Senate returned to session after its winter adjournment to consider the nomination. Houser, forty-one and with no association with radio and television beyond membership in the same Chicago law firm as former FCC chairman Newton Minow, would be the tie-breaker on a number of complex issues before the Commission.

Rather than comforting the broadcast establishment, the appointment of Houser was disquieting. For although, like Unger, he was a Republican, his connections were with the liberal wing of the party whereas Unger's were decidedly with the conservative. It was another instance of the ambiguity of the Nixon Administration's dealings with radio and television. On one hand it purported to be sympathetic to the industry's economic interests, on the other it was the source of new forms of suffering for the broadcaster.

The paradox of Burch's administration during the first year was that it seemed more radical than conservative, and that was unsettling to operators of broadcast stations who had expected kinder treatment as businessmen from a conservative government. Under Burch the FCC initiated a raft of changes: the cutback of network prime time; the approval, after years of suppression, of over-the-air pay television (called STV now, or subscription TV, because the theater owners' organized campaign had made a bad word of pay TV); the full-scale release of cable television for expansion into the major cities, with conditions specified by the Commission; and the tentative adoption of the one-to-a-market rule, which in its 1970 form prohibited the owner of a newspaper from acquiring a broadcast property in the city his paper served, or the owner of a television or radio station from acquiring a companion station in the same city.

Then there was the license fee, a levy upon the operators of stations based on the size of their markets to help defray the operating expenses of the Federal Communications Commission; and finally the decision that the congressional opponents to the Administration policies were entitled to free air time to respond to the President's prime-time speeches, in the interest of keeping the executive branch of government from attaining excessive power through television.

But what had appeared to be a new activism by the FCC under Burch was really the result of the chairman's desire to clear the calendar of long-pending issues so that his administration could begin afresh. The irony was that he had pushed the issues to the fore while he was still working with a Commission predominating in Democrats. Had he waited until a Republican replaced Cox, decisions on the same issues might have been made with no important changes in the existing system. Word circulated through the industry that, having cleared away the backlog, Burch would be respectful of the venture capital that had helped to build American broadcasting and that he would guide his decisions accordingly. With four Republicans constituting the majority, broadcasters in theory would have less to fear from radical reforms.

And that was why the President's appointment of Houser created some uneasiness in the industry. Would the new commissioner, as a short-term appointee, vote obediently in a bloc with the other Republicans, or would he tend to vote as a liberal? Would he, as a young man, lean to reforms or align himself with commissioners Robert E. Lee and the former broadcaster Robert Wells, who were given to rubber-stamping license renewals and seemed eager to preserve the broadcasting business as it was? Would he try to make a name for himself, in the manner of the irrepressible Nick Johnson, or be content to be a faceless bureaucrat like the Democrat H. Rex Lee? Unger would have been a gift to the broadcast industry, assuring it of four commissioners who were all to the right of the political center. But Houser, if he inclined at all to the idealism of Johnson, could throw the industry into a state of chaos.

Johnson, in the meantime, served notice that he would not be silenced as the radical voice and would not give up his commission appointment until his seven-year term expired in 1973.

12

The Summer People

Not from any cultural conviction but because it proved to be good business, the radio industry gave full voice to the new folk poetry of the mid-twentieth century. Radio stations that programed music according to the trade popularity charts were led by the young consumer of the rich variety of folk and rock recordings into making a clean break with the routinely mass-produced ditties of Tin Pan Alley.

Throughout history, culture has been handed down from older generations to the young; radio reversed the course. Desperate for an audience in the fifties in the face of television's dominance, many radio station operators gave up their own ideas of radio programing to follow the market for recorded music. And since it was the young who purchased most of the records, the music they preferred, bad as it was initially, overwhelmed radio and became the popular music of the country. Culture was being handed up.

For teen-agers and new adults, the old audio medium was the communications link with their own generation and their emerging rock culture. A new recording made its metaphorical statement in Cleveland one day and within a week would spread across the country and even the oceans. Miraculously, the radio industry which had been imperiled by television now stood opposite the glamorous and more faceted medium with newfound strength in the market place. For radio had what television both craved and needed for its business growth—the young audience.

If television's economic growth was to continue at a rate faster than the gross national product, it would have to win back in the seventies its own disaffected youth. This would require a change in the content and language of the medium as well as in the style. Many of the advertisers who were the heaviest investors in television were interested primarily in reaching the "young marrieds," persons in the 18–34 age range, the rock generation.

The young people who had been raised before the set, the first TV generation, had broken the silver cord and, in their early adulthood, were spending TV's prime time in pizza parlors, drive-in restaurants, or more worldly gathering places—or at the movies, or listening to radio. Not all were indifferent to television, but most no longer depended on it as they had when it was their electronic Mammy. For many in their late teens and twenties, TV was the window on the Establishment; and for those who had dropped out of the mainstream, it was the meretricious huckster of the plastic world they were rebelling against.

Basically unchanged in either content or form from what it had been when they were growing up, television came to symbolize the dry surrogate parent with nothing important to say, the one-eyed Polonius relentlessly pushing a single precept: Want Something and Buy It. To idealistic youth, returning to TV was regressive.

And this once dedicated faction of the viewing public which had been weaned on *Hopalong Cassidy* and *Howdy Doody*, and around whom nearly two decades of program strategy had centered, was now, or soon would be, the most desired component of the audience, the one the advertiser was most eager to reach. Curious how a single generation has had the fate of being TV's eternal target. It would not be won back with the old shows and the old attitudes.

Television would have to express youth's point of view, often an anti-Establishment view, somehow without alienating its long-loyal constituencies.

The networks' September premieres were to be a beginning. Fantasy, escapism, slapstick—idioms that had seemed baked into the medium—would be supplanted where practical by a new, grittier and more socially contemporary idiom. It was Wood of CBS who had supplied the word for it: relevance.

Television would begin to speak for its own time, would involve itself with the explosive issues that were splitting the country, and would express the "nowness" of the American scene appropriate to a medium that had the capability of making the world witness to men walking on the moon.

During the summer, CBS brought to New York the producers of its new program series to explain to the press their new direction in fiction. *Storefront Lawyers*, Leonard Freeman testified, would be about idealistic youths giving their energies and legal skills to the downtrodden, following a true-to-life phenomenon in the society. "The lawyers are trying to change society and make it better, but within the rules," he said. Of the seven filming days for each episode, four would be on location in the streets of Los Angeles, not just for the appearance of realism but for the inspirational value of taking the series off the sound stage and setting it in the real world.

The Interns, according to its producer, Bob Claver, would be about young people struggling against authority in trying to change the Establishment from within; it would not be another medical melodrama but a story of five young people who incidentally are doctors. Andy Griffith's new series, *Headmaster*, would have the contemporary relevance of a school setting, rather than as before—in the series he originated which became *Mayberry R.F.D.*—an idealized mid-

American small town. Its producer, Aaron Ruben, told of its "now" subject matter: student militancy, marijuana, sex education.

Even the new comedies would be of the same school. As producer David Swift described it, *Arnie,* the new Herschel Bernardi show, would portray an average man coping with the Establishment, showing up the impersonal and sometimes fatuously arrogant ways of the corporation. Jim Brooks vowed that *The Mary Tyler Moore Show* would not be foolish comedy but one built upon real people, set in Minneapolis for realism ("We've heard rumors that there's something between New York and Los Angeles")—although of course it would be filmed in Hollywood—and centering on a newsroom at a fictional TV station. The newsroom, Brooks said, "will help keep us honest." So would the absence of the laugh machine.

Rock theme music, film montages using the modish fast-cut techniques, and slogans in the language of the young— "CBS Is Putting It All Together"—characterized the summer-long promotional campaigns at all three networks. In style, the tune-in announcements were a telling departure from the conventional preseason trailers, conveying an implicit message to the wayward generation that the television networks were with it. In the flashes of scenes was other evidence: young men with long hair, mod costumes, blacks, hints of disturbing social themes.

The Big Sell was on, and it had never failed.

There were, however, the betrayals of television's natural establishmentarianism. In April, President Nixon called a conference of network and Hollywood studio executives requesting that they use their most persuasive medium to help the government in its effort to stem the spread of the drug menace. The President had but to ask, and within months nineteen different prime-time series and three daytime programs were in production with episodes dramatizing the hazards of experimenting with drugs and the horrors of being hooked on them. Narcotics addiction as a "bad scene" was to be one of the prevailing themes of the new TV season.

Meanwhile, local TV stations, ever in search of one-sided and therefore noncontroversial issues for their editorial attacks, and eager also to perform the kind of public service that would please the government by whose sufferance they held their licenses, pledged themselves to a massive all-industry drive against drug abuses (an interesting business euphemism not to disparage all drugs, least of all those advertised on television) in their public service efforts.

The drug problem was, of course, relevant to the times and a serious rent in the social fabric, but drug culture was also threaded into youth culture and was symbolic of the rebellion. To the generation at whom the networks' rock promotional spots were aimed, it was clear they were being seduced into a typical series of Establishment sermons.

Their summer schedules revealed that the networks were not fully committed to pursuing a younger audience. Either they were hedging their bets or simply could not give up the old formulas that had always worked so well in the capture of the two most loyal age groups in the TV audience, juveniles and what the industry called the geriatric set. Of an unusually large number of summer programs offered by the networks amid the customary reruns, a few might have been regarded as earnest overtures to elusive youth, but the majority were distinctly backward-looking.

Although it had always been a logical time for TV experimentation, since audience levels are down in the warm-weather months, summer rarely brought anything new to the medium for the reason that there were great profit opportunities in reruns. Second-run film is cheaper than first-run by as much as 75 per cent, while advertiser rates drop only slightly less than half. Thus the mark-up is much better than during the regular season, and audiences have demonstrated over the years that they are content to watch the same shows again.

That fact has played an important part in the television

economy, since some programing is so expensive it can hope
only to recoup its costs during the original exposure and
needs a repeat cycle to make any money at all.

During the late sixties, however, the mad spiral of program costs was driving the networks into a search for effective, low-expense series. There were first some efforts at as-
similating British filmed shows into the American schedules,
that country having finally come up to a production standard
acceptable to the American industry. Production quality had
been one reservation; the other was the British accent, which
Yankee TV practitioners felt was too taxing on the mid-
American ear for the immediate acceptance that shows
needed in the television economy here (the American accent
apparently poses no such problem in Britain).

It was Sir Lew Grade, London's master showman and a
canny observer of the American market, who found the solution: programs whose leading players spoke a *neutral* English, without the slurring and other qualities of enunciation
which grass-roots Americans tended to reject as high-
falutin'. As head of Associated Television in England, Grade
produced adventure series for both sides of the Atlantic at
once, and since he could recover much of the expense in his
own and the Commonwealth countries, he was able to offer
them to the United States networks at prices that were irresistible.

A number of Grade's film shows won a modest following
in the States—*Secret Agent, The Saint, The Prisoner,* and
The Champions among them (his competitor, Associated
British Pathe, exported *The Avengers*)—but the rating
scores were never really large enough to satisfy the networks. It was not enough for the programs to be profitable;
they had to be functional in terms of the over-all rating levels
the networks sought to maintain and so competitive as to take
audience from the competition.

The romance with Britain's television film cooled when
NBC entered into co-production with Grade on two series,
The Strange Report and *A Bird's Eye View,* neither of

which, when completed, the network found suitable for its schedule. Both were put aside as reserve programing and were finally inserted in the schedule in the spring of 1971 as fillers.

But Great Britain continued to be represented in the United States during the summer months with variety shows that crossbred performing and creative talent from both countries; and again co-production was an economy measure rather than an attempt to broaden horizons. *The Kraft Music Hall* became *The Kraft Summer Music Hall,* from London, headlining the popular British personality Des O'Connor. *The Dean Martin Show* became *Dean Martin Presents The Golddiggers,* featuring American comedian Charles Nelson Reilly and an English comic, Marty Feldman. The summer replacement for *The Andy Williams Show* was produced in Canada under the title, *Andy Williams Presents The Ray Stevens Show???*

As chance hits of the 1969 summer, later to enter into the regular schedules of ABC and CBS, *The Johnny Cash Show* and *Hee Haw* were the inspiration for the increase in summer tryouts during 1970. But, pointing up their confusion over the proper course of television, the networks hedged every bet on the future with one on the past. So while CBS ventured a new program of modern satirical sketches by a bright young cast of unknowns headed by Robert Klein, titled *Comedy Tonight,* it also fished for the dear old audience with a hark back to the musical comedy styles and material of the thirties in a variety series titled *Happy Days,* purporting a nostalgic escape from contemporary relevance. And the summer program for which Bob Wood and other CBS officials had highest expectations was a Hanna-Barbera cartoon series, *Where's Huddles?,* another variation on the old cartoon success *The Flintstones,* which later imitated itself in *The Jetsons* and was based in the first place on the Jackie Gleason–Art Carney relationship in *The Honeymooners.*

Similarly, NBC, in testing the acceptance of the blend of

contemporary popular music and far-out comedy in the Ray Stevens show, stepped back in time with the Des O'Connor *Music Hall*, which was a standard old-time variety hour. As for *The Golddiggers*, it was an established concept with new faces. ABC's summer offerings likewise reflected the dichotomy: the Smothers Brothers resurrected the hour of topical satire that was successful on CBS up to the time they were fired and, in a safer vein, *Johnny Cash Presents The Everly Brothers Show* made a conventional bid as another country music hour.

Any of the tryout programs which maintained a 30 share in the ratings over the course of the summer would earn its way into the regular schedule, either as a January replacement or as a new entry the following fall. ABC had other plans for the Smothers Brothers. If their deportment, which had led to their dismissal at CBS, was manifestly improved —their political barbs made gentler and their response to network censorship more compliant—they would be leading candidates for the network's talk-variety program, which was faring poorly in the ratings under Dick Cavett.

In fact, the Smothers Brothers did mute their satire and were careful not to be insubordinate, but the summer ratings contained a jolt. Theirs were the lowest for all the new shows. Well before the summer ended, they had dropped out of ABC's outline for the future.

As a group the summer originals fared poorly. *Where's Huddles?* looked as though it might succeed at first, but its audience, to their credit, quickly began to slip away. With one exception, the other shows were unable to rise to a 30 share and were of no further use to the networks. The summer viewers indicated, through the numbers, that they preferred a second exposure of the existing popular programs to new shows without star power.

Only *The Golddiggers* performed well in the Nielsens, placing in the top ten for the summer. It introduced a British performer to American audiences, Marty Feldman, who eclipsed the American, Charles Nelson Reilly, for whom

Golddiggers was to have been a showcase. A former *That Was the Week That Was* comedy writer who turned performer, Feldman, seeming to have incorporated in his physical style aspects of the silent film funny men, displayed the zany turn of mind that makes droll occasions of commonplace situations. He was so well received by American viewers that Greg Garrison, producer of the *Dean Martin Show* as well as its summer replacement, optioned his services for television in the United States. On the strength of Marty Feldman's summertime popularity, ABC bought a series to be built around him packaged by Garrison that was to begin in the fall of 1971. It was deferred to the following January.

The only other series to make a perceptible impact on some part of the American viewing audience during the summer was actually one that was in its rerun cycle, *The Forsyte Saga*, the serialization for television of John Galsworthy's sequence of novels spanning the Victorian and Edwardian eras in England. Produced by BBC-TV several years before, it had been one of Britain's greatest popular hits and an artistic achievement as well; one of those rare programs whose devotees declined social engagements in order to keep up with the episodes.

But the American TV networks deemed it too highbrow for their audiences, and all three rejected it. A second failing of the series, from their standpoint, was that it was finite; they preferred series which had no end and that could serve as keystones for an infinite number of future program schedules. Also it was in black and white and therefore unworthy of any commercial network in America.

(The superb BBC production of Chekhov's *Uncle Vanya*, which had starred Sir Laurence Olivier, had also been turned down by CBS, NBC, and ABC because it had not been produced in color; eventually it played on educational television in the United States.)

National Educational Television was the only remaining avenue for *The Forsyte Saga*, and there it was the unquestioned adult hit of the 1969–70 season, *Sesame Street* being counted a children's show. Since many viewers discovered the serial late, it was repeated during the summer, where it continued to attract new enthusiasts who, as in Britain, gave it priority over social and even business activities. A family we know was so addicted that the parents had to summarize the weekly episodes in letters to their sons at summer camp or risk finding them back at the doorstep.

At that, *Forsyte*, a literate soap opera, had what the commercial trade would call a negligible audience for its American run. Educational television does not subscribe to the Nielsen rating service, and so there are no estimates of how many viewers it played to cumulatively or in any given week. Two special surveys conducted in Boston and New York by the Corporation for Public Broadcasting found that the British serial was receiving about 4 per cent of the audience, which was a decided improvement on the 1 per cent usually estimated for educational television fare, but still in no way a competitive threat to the commercial networks. Yet the series made its impact on American television. There were no series like it on the commercial networks, none which so involved their viewers, gave them so much in return for their dedication, and had cultural value besides. Nor did the merits of *Forsyte* elude commercial television's program suppliers.

Several studios turned to the American novel as new source material for TV series. Universal TV, which had already purchased Fletcher Knebel's best-seller *Vanished* for a four-hour presentation over two nights, began negotiations for TV rights to several popular novels in hopes of creating series that would run in six or seven installments.

It was hit novels and not classic fiction the studios were working with, but it was a new idea for commercial TV, and *Forsyte* was the source of it.

Business had not picked up, the general economy was still recessive, and it was clear that television profits would not only decline in 1970 but, with the impending loss of more than $220 million in cigarette advertising, probably would slip even more in 1971.

Bob Wood had not so much declared as demonstrated that CBS would cut back severely in special (*i.e.*, one-time only) programing. A Kodak-sponsored special starring Dick Van Dyke and Bill Cosby, scheduled for CBS in the fall of 1970, suddenly defected to NBC. Soon afterward, a Carol Channing special for Monsanto followed. Somewhat bitterly, the agency vice-presidents involved in the placements told of CBS's loss of interest in specials, indicated by its unwillingness to provide the specific dates and time periods requested by advertisers. NBC, on the other hand, welcomed both shows and made every effort to accommodate the requests for time periods.

In the differing attitudes toward the special, the two networks were beginning to grow apart. It would be a distinguishing characteristic that NBC scheduled them lavishly and CBS only sparsely, that NBC was willing to interrupt its week-to-week program series frequently and CBS only rarely. Wood's aversion to the special was chiefly economic in a year in which faltering business threatened nearly every company's profit performance. Businessmen were effecting austerity programs, and one of Wood's was to cut back TV shows which did not offer the maximum profit potential.

There are two kinds of specials: those created or purchased by the networks and those brought to a network by a sponsor. Except in the realm of news, the first were virtually out of consideration at every network during 1970 because they tended to be high-risk shows that seldom earned their money back. This was no year for eleemosynary service. As for specials provided by a sponsor, the terms most often were that the advertiser paid the network only the basic time charges and underwrote the full cost of the show itself. While there was no risk involved and the network was compensated for its time, the fact was that more money could be made with a program series the special would be pre-empting. In a weekly series, the commercial minutes can be sold at a profit over and above the time charges.

But the main economic argument against the special was that it displaced an episode of a regular series which in effect is prepaid by a network. When the networks contract for twenty-six episodes and twenty-six reruns of a series, the purchase is firm, whether or not the episodes are used that calendar year. When a special is inserted, one of the fifty-two episodes is a net loss to the network, which means that for every program pre-emption it will play one fewer rerun. As has been noted, the reruns invariably are more profitable than the first runs.

A half-hour TV series may cost the network $80,000 per episode. With healthy ratings it might be sold at around $50,000 per commercial minute for the three allotted in the half hour. Out of the mythical $150,000 grossed must go payments to the stations carrying the show—approximately 12 per cent of their own time rates—and a 15 per cent commission to the advertising agencies. The repeats come much cheaper, but the reduction in ad rates is not as great. A rerun of the same $80,000 show might cost $20,000, but the $50,000-a-minute commercial rate would drop only to $30,000.

Therefore, when profits are what matter, a network has much to gain when it does not disrupt the regular weekly grind of twice-told tales spilling off the Hollywood belt lines.

Finally, there is a theory, which originated at CBS during Jim Aubrey's tenure as president, that the hard-core viewing audience is happiest when the shows are in the same place every week without interruptions and that therefore the rating levels for such shows are more secure. Aubrey recognized the heavy consumer of television as a creature of habit who laid out his own viewing schedule for the week, and it was his belief that each pre-emption for a special served to break the habit pattern and tempted the viewer to try a rival series. Wood subscribed to the same theory, but it was not now as valid as before. Because the heavy viewer was most often an old person or a very young one.

Don Durgin, Wood's counterpart at NBC, saw greater advantages in the opposite application of the same theory. If there are habit viewers, there are also those perpetually in search of new fare on television. In addition, there are the occasional viewers who could be drawn into an evening of TV on the promise of a single special. Those persons, Durgin reasoned, were the elite of the audience, the young or middle-aged and, very likely, the better-educated and more affluent consumers.

With careful planning, specials that were presold to sponsors before they were scheduled probably would not impair a network's profit potential. One device was to cut back in the production of series episodes from twenty-six to twenty-four, allowing for four pre-emptions a year without causing the loss of a rerun. Another employed by NBC was to couple hour-long specials in a time period normally reserved for a movie. Since movies are leased on long-term contracts and do not have to be played off on rigid schedules, their pre-emption for specials imposes no penalty.

There would be close to one hundred specials on NBC during the 1970–71 season, more than the combined quantity on CBS and ABC.

The notable casualty of the austerity in specials was original drama, *CBS Playhouse* and NBC's *Prudential's On-Stage*, both having lost their underwriters in the business recession. Neither had been profitable even in the best of times, for although General Telephone and Electronics was the sole advertiser in *CBS Playhouse*, the dramas were actually produced at the network's expense and had never found a single advertiser who would cover the full bill.

Hallmark Cards was continuing its long-running *Hallmark Hall of Fame* on NBC, but it was not a series given to dramas of controversial or even contemporary subject matter. That sponsor's offerings over the years have had a way of blurring into a pastel wash of conventional classical literature, usually mildly inspirational but seldom pungent.

Except for the Hallmark efforts, the commercial networks had eschewed original drama throughout the first half of the sixties and probably would have continued to ignore the form but for the precipitous act of one man in 1965 which led to a curious, even comic, stampede by the networks to exceed one another in the presentation of drama.

In 1965 Leonard Goldenson *had* to win the Distinguished Service Award of the National Association of Broadcasters. The president of ABC, Inc., was the highest-ranking official of a major broadcast company not yet to have received the honor; and although it was difficult to find reason to cite him for industry statesmanship, each year he was denied it only served to emphasize his lack of stature in broadcasting. Paley, Stanton, both Sarnoffs (General David and his son Robert), and Kintner had received it, and so had Edward R. Murrow and Bob Hope. Even the head of Westinghouse Broadcasting, Don McGannon, had beaten Goldenson to the honor.

An effort was made with the Association's board to bestow it on the ABC president in 1965, with the promise that his acceptance speech would vindicate the selection of him, since with it Goldenson would project himself into a leadership role.

In his address to the convention on accepting the award, Goldenson decried the medium's lack of creative growth, deplored the networks' relentless imitation of their own program successes and announced there and then that his network would lead the way to new concepts for the medium by inaugurating a new series with an immense budget dedicated to experimentation in prime time. It would begin in September of 1966 (needing eighteen months to be formulated and to set the production apparatus in motion) and would be titled *Stage '67*. He promised it would produce a new literature for the medium and vowed to continue it over several seasons without consideration to ratings.

The rival networks took seriously ABC's bid for prestige

and cultural leadership, and CBS in particular made an effort not to lose ground to Goldenson's network. In May of 1966, CBS presented a revival of Arthur Miller's *Death of a Salesman*, with the leads of the original Broadway production, Lee J. Cobb and Mildred Dunnock. Its high ratings were such a surprise that CBS was encouraged to plan a production of Miller's *The Crucible* and then to engage Hal Holbrook's *Mark Twain Tonight*. The fever became contagious. NBC would offer *Othello*. ABC would dramatize Katherine Anne Porter's *Noon Wine*, CBS Tennessee Williams' *The Glass Menagerie*. That prompted ABC to announce a series of eight two-hour drama revivals for a new showcase, *Sunday Night at the Theatre*, to occasionally supplant its *Sunday Night at the Movies*.

During the war of announcements, CBS acquired a new president who was almost as obscure to the trade as to the outside world, John Reynolds. A shy man and short on personal charisma, he would have to be given an instant identity as an advocate of some worthwhile television cause. The field was wide open for a champion of contemporary TV drama by serious playwrights, and CBS quickly moved Reynolds into that vacuum. He would be the man who revived the long-mourned *Playhouse 90* on an occasional basis, calling it *CBS Playhouse*, and through it he would propose to draw back to the medium the artistic producers, directors, and writers who had left it.

When good things come to commercial TV, the motives for them are usually base. Documentaries had a renaissance when a new FCC chairman called television "a vast wasteland" and frightened the industry. The scandal over rigged quiz shows brought on weekly news anthologies. Violence became a caution when Senators evinced their concern. And original drama came back to television to put a face on a faceless network president.

When I interviewed Reynolds about the new project, he had Mike Dann at his side, and it was Dann who fielded all the questions about the kinds of plays envisioned. In a short time it became apparent that Reynolds knew little about the theater and had no genuine conviction about bringing drama back to the medium. He was merely submitting to the myth-making process.

Since 1966 was a year of great prosperity, the networks could afford to vie with each other for prestige. ABC answered the CBS entry into original drama with the announcement that it would open *Stage '67* with an original, *The World of Barney Kempinski,* featuring Alan Arkin (who was then relatively unknown), and NBC with the disclosure that it would wipe out a week of prime-time series in the spring for a full week of original drama.

Reynolds then declared that CBS would compete with Broadway for playwrights and would pay as much as $25,000 for important scripts. NBC countered by paying $125,000 for William Hanley's *Flesh and Blood,* snatching it from a Broadway producer who was hopeful of mounting it for the stage. That was the high point in the whole absurd affair, and the end of the line.

Flesh and Blood turned out to be an artistic disaster that would probably have closed in one night on Broadway. Moreover, it was a clear betrayal of network ignorance of what had literary merit and what had not. ABC's *Barney Kempinski* won little praise, and the whole *Stage '67* venture failed to live up to Goldenson's promise, including the promise that it would run several seasons regardless of ratings. After a huge loss the first season, with little advertiser or affiliate support, it was canceled the second. NBC's proposed full week of drama also fell through for lack of sponsor interest, and ABC's *Sunday Night at the Theatre* folded because neither the ratings nor the criticism was overwhelmingly favorable. And, so far as is known, CBS only once paid the publicized $25,000 for a *CBS Playhouse* manuscript and never exceeded three productions in a season.

NBC corporate president Julian Goodman said he could

not understand why critics found a shortage of original drama in television when there was good drama every night in the hour-long adventure series.

In the final shake-out, by 1969, there were only the occasional original dramas sponsored on NBC by Prudential Insurance, the perennial *Hallmark Hall of Fame,* and the few *CBS Playhouse* offerings sponsored by General Telephone and Electronics.

Each production of *CBS Playhouse* represented an investment of nearly half a million dollars by the network, and since each was accorded the respect of dignified institutional sponsorship and fewer than the customary number of commercial breaks there was practically no chance for total recoupment. The value to CBS had been in the response from prestigious sectors of society and in the fallout of praise, the mail, and critical applause that were rarely experienced for ordinary TV efforts. That had begun to wane even in 1968; and when dramas, whose practical function was to heap praise on the networks, failed to achieve that result the money began to seem ill-spent.

Of course, the quality of the plays had everything to do with the public response. But network managements, few of whose members had any particular interest in serious theater, resented the fact that the effort itself of presenting a profitless drama, good or bad—the sacrifice—was not hailed by the critics each time out.

Wood, in a press conference during the summer of 1970, stated that the elimination of *Playhouse* was at least partly attributable to the lack of good scripts to choose from. It was true, of course, that very little serious literature was now being written for the electronic media, there being practically no market for it, but there must surely have been many worthy unproduced plays for the stage which could have been adapted for television if anyone had wanted to seek them out. More probable was that the shortage was not of available material but of plays the networks would be *willing* to present. A good play usually is the personal expression of an individual. But networks are concerned with the expression of a corporation, and if the artist does not express what is safe for the corporation to put on its air waves then his work is not acceptable.

An anti-Vietnam War drama would, of course, be out. Anything seeming to take a position on, or expressing a feeling about, any of the current issues over which the country was divided would not be produced. The safe topics for social drama dealing with the contemporary world were drugs and ecology, and there was a limit to their dramatic possibilities. Besides, they were receiving ample treatment in the regular potboiler melodramas.

In a way, the drama met the same fate as the news documentary. If it was controversial, or if it presented an honest minority view, it subjected the network to attack from special-interest groups or from either side of the political center. If it was cautious and equivocal in its statement, then it became punchless and barren, and there are no awards or cascades of praise for such drama.

American television had reasonable fears about performing a free society communications function, but original drama might not have been banished from the medium if anyone in the network hierarchies had the background in the humanities to appreciate that something important had gone out of the medium.

There was no longer a profit to be made from professional football either, the rights having leaped beyond what TV might feasibly charge for an advertising minute, but it was considered a necessary part of network service.

Rather suddenly in September, just before the new season opened, CBS moved *The Merv Griffin Show* to Hollywood.

The transfer had been considered all summer, but it was checked by the network's $2 million lease of the Cort Theatre on West Forty-eighth Street in Manhattan as the originating studio, and the additional million that went into remodeling it as the Merv Griffin Theatre. In the economic trials of the year, it was a sum not to be wasted.

Still, against the CBS investment in Griffin himself and against the ultimate consequences of losing its affiliates for the late-night period, CBS could ill afford to let the program continue to perform unaggressively in the ratings. After a year, the show was going nowhere against NBC's Johnny Carson. There was still a year to go on Griffin's contract, which guaranteed him and his production company $50,000 a week. Disillusioned, a number of affiliates had dropped the show and returned to movies. Something had to be done.

Admittedly, the move west was made in desperation, but it was not without a rationale. With three late-night shows emanating from New York, and all of the same type, the rating leader understandably had first choice of guests while the other two built their marquees on the remainder of the Eastern talent pool. In Hollywood, Griffin would tap a different celebrity vein and for most of the year would have exclusive access to the Western star colony.

It had become no secret in the halls of CBS that network officials had lost faith in Griffin as an interviewer. Since they were committed to him for another year, they decided that the only hope for improving the program's fortunes was to steer it from the desk-and-sofa conversation format toward a straight variety presentation. To doctor the show, they would engage a top-flight producing team which specialized in TV variety, Saul Ilson and Ernie Chambers, whose credits included the successful Sunday night *Smothers Brothers* show, and that was a second reason for moving to Hollywood. Ilson and Chambers had other involvements there.

A third was to stem affiliate defections from the CBS late-night service. By redesigning the program and moving its base of origination, the network could hope to keep its affiliates interested at least until there were clear signs that the show would not add substantially to its audience, and by then CBS would be prepared to take the drastic step of buying up the contract and replacing the host. The important thing, in the meantime, was to keep the affiliate line-up intact; once dissipated it would be hard to rebuild to a competitive size.

Late-night television was potentially the most gorgeously profitable area of the broadcast day. Since it was outside of prime time, the networks were not restricted to six commercial minutes per hour, and the production economics were highly favorable. Yet neither CBS nor ABC (with *The Dick Cavett Show*) was drawing profits from its venture at anywhere near the potential.

NBC had been entrenched with *Tonight* long before the other two networks entered the competition, and it was realizing between $10 and $15 million a year in net income from that single program in spite of Carson's fabulous salary of close to $1,250,000 a year, along with other perquisites. The program's budget was $125,000 per week for five ninety-minute shows, not much above the cost of a single episode of a prime-time situation comedy. For its eight commercial minutes per program, NBC's open rate was $17,900. On a theoretical gross of $143,200 per night (theoretical because of frequency discounts and sundry advertising plans devised by the sales department), *Tonight* met its weekly expenses in a single broadcast. Most of the revenues for the rest of the week, then, were what network presidents like to call "keeping money," that is, after the payment of station compensation.

As the late-night leader, *Tonight* was a boon to the NBC affiliated stations, providing them easy income without effort or investment. It had the effect, moreover, of increasing the audience for their newscasts that were scheduled just before the Johnny Carson show, and the evening news was a large source of station revenues.

Unlike prime-time programs, the late-night show gave the affiliates more than station compensation. Alongside the network's eight commercial minutes per night, the stations received ten minutes to sell locally, so that in every ninety-minute broadcast there were eighteen minutes of commercials, spotted in three interruptions each half hour. And since the program had glamour and proven popularity, it was seldom difficult for the stations to sell their own allotment of minutes at relatively high rates.

Such late-night riches could also have been CBS's or ABC's if they but had competitive ratings. With such economics, it was possible to show a profit on ratings of 2 or 3, but no network was content to settle for a meager amount when a sumptuous income was possible.

In truth, CBS had been reluctant to do battle with Carson while he was clearly in his prime, but had been driven to it by its member stations, which were covetous of the easy money the NBC stations enjoyed. For years the CBS affiliate family had done admirably against Carson, or his predecessor Jack Paar, with local movies purchased in the syndication market. Under a pattern established by the network's owned stations division, a majority of the CBS outlets had invested heavily in motion pictures, circulating each title between an *Early Show,* a *Late Show,* and a *Late, Late Show.* With multiple exposures to amortize the costs, movies were handsomely profitable—until the networks began to program them in prime time. After that, the choicest films were at least twice exposed on television before they were sold to the local stations, and that served to diminish the stature of the *Late Show.*

At the CBS affiliates meeting in 1968, a number of stations made it known that they desired a late-night network service. Tom Dawson, who was then president of the network, told the group that if a sufficient number of stations pledged to carry a nightly program so that it became economic for the network to feed one, CBS would provide it. By fall, Dawson received his mandate. CBS hired Bert Berman from Universal Television at $42,000 a year to work at developing a new nighttime show to compete with *Tonight.* He had perhaps a dozen formats under consideration when, in May of 1969, at the next affiliates meeting, CBS management promised that the new show would be on the air that fall.

Six months is considered short lead time in TV programing, and it fell on Mike Dann to deliver something from Berman's development stable which would compete effectively with Carson. As a veteran reared on the fail-safe principle, Dann ignored Berman's projects to secure a ready-made show. Learning that Merv Griffin's contract was up for renegotiation with Westinghouse Broadcasting that summer, he moved swiftly to steal him away for CBS.

Griffin had one of the most successful shows in syndication at the time. Playing in more than 170 markets at whatever times of day the stations chose to slot him, his show produced the desired commercial result in the morning, afternoon, and even prime time. Dann was buying what the trade called a *known quantity*, a performer whose acceptance by the viewership was established and who had long experience in conducting a daily ninety-minute talk-variety show. The unknown factor was his appeal with the late-night audience, vastly different as it was from the daytime audience in sophistication and demographic composition. There was no record of Griffin's success in syndication when programed against Carson at night, but there had been a few scattered instances of failure.

CBS courted him with extravagant terms and a firm two-year contract, and Griffin gave up the security he enjoyed in syndication for the prestige of network stardom. Losing him was a blow to Westinghouse Broadcasting, and although that company signed David Frost to replace him in syndication it was with the knowledge that his English accent would be a handicap and that the program might never become as popular or profitable as Griffin's had been. As it proved, it took a year for *The David Frost Show* to line up enough stations to operate in the black.

ABC had preceded CBS in the late-night derby by almost a year and had had modest results with Joey Bishop in a program that originated in Hollywood. At the same time it was grooming a new find, Dick Cavett, a witty and immensely likable TV personality who was a favorite of the critics but who had not yet caught on with the masses.

Cavett failed with a morning conversation program, although it was admired by a discriminating audience, and during the summer of 1969 he failed to ring up acceptable rating numbers with a thrice-weekly off-season show in prime time. Still, ABC maintained its faith in him, and on the theory that his natural audience would be of an age and sophistication to stay up with television after 11:30, the network bought up the remainder of Bishop's contract and gave Cavett the job in New York.

Neither Griffin nor Cavett proved a match for Carson, whose ratings remained larger than those for the other two combined. Whatever either tried by way of innovation, however often they changed producers or other creative personnel, they seemed in fixed rating orbits. Cavett began to show marked improvement in the numbers during the summer of 1970, fanning network hopes that he was at last catching on, but when school began again he fell back to his previous rating level. Clearly he had some appeal with the young viewers, but that was not enough for a competitive showing. Television popularity, even late at night, requires a more general acceptance, a universal charm.

Griffin's move to California did not immediately inspire new interest in the program, and even after four months there was no evidence of an uptrend in his audience. Evidently, the viewership had been conditioned to thinking of him as a daytime personality, and it was possible that the faithful audience he had cultivated with his syndicated show was of the demographic stripe that did not stay up for late-night television.

At the end of the year, *Tonight* was averaging a 30 share, Griffin hovered at a 23 share, and Cavett was at 12.

In cities where there was a fourth station, its movies were in second place and sometimes in first.

Fred Silverman had a plan to replace Griffin with a new program concept for the late-night competition. He proposed original ninety-minute nightly studio dramas produced on video tape, which he felt would be a stronger attraction than old movies. His experience with soap operas in the daytime sphere proved to him that they could be turned out rapidly enough and on a reasonable budget to be a feasible entry. Having discussed the project with outside producers, Silverman was persuaded that the dramas could be produced for no more than $80,000 each, which with a repeat play would bring the program costs to about $40,000 per night or $200,000 per week. While that was considerably above the $125,000-a-week budget for the talk shows it was still very agreeable economics if it enabled CBS to overtake NBC's *Tonight.* Beyond that, the project would bring new writers and directors into the medium and reflect favorably on CBS.

A fine idea but the wrong year for it was management's judgment. The risk was too great in a business recession. Silverman, whose children's movie series had been shot down earlier for the same reason, took the frustration manfully.

In March of 1971, Merv Griffin was renewed through August of 1972.

ABC, which had a smaller prime-time audience than its rivals but one that was favored with the desirable demographics, released a study by an outside firm, Lieberman Research, Inc., which seemed to prove that younger people were substantially better marketing and advertising prospects than older consumers. CBS research promptly issued a rebuttal of the findings.

The Lieberman study, conducted in twelve markets with a sample of 972 adult respondents, indicated that younger people (1) more readily absorbed advertising messages than older people, (2) were more apt to try different brands while older persons were less given to experimenting with products, and (3) learned about new products more rapidly than older persons and, if they were not already using them, were more interested than their seniors in trying them. A fourth conclusion was that older people eager to express a youthful outlook would be attracted to products appealing to younger people.

It came out in the study that younger persons (18–49) were more retentive of advertising themes and slogans than the older group (50–64); that the younger used their current brands of products listed in the questionnaire an average of 4.3 years against an average of 6.5 years for older persons; that the younger were more aware of new brands and products on the market, especially the 1970–71 car makes; and that both generations believed new products were more likely to be used by younger people.

In its rebuttal of the study, the CBS department of economics and research pointed out that its own studies showed (a) the target audience for most products to be the 25–64 age group, rather than the 18–49, and (b) the 50–64-year group to be "far more valuable" to advertisers than the 18–24-year group. It cited a report by the National Industrial Conference which showed the 18–24 group to comprise 17 per cent of the population and to represent 12 per cent of the total spending power; while the 50–64 group made up 22 per cent of the population and 25 per cent of the spending power.

According to the CBS research, the young group (18–24) concentrated its spending in areas such as movie-going, records, and wearing apparel but played a "small role" in buying products of the type generally advertised on network television. "Faced with these data and the fact that its audience has disproportionately many of this 'low value' group, ABC has attempted to make them look better," the CBS critique stated.

Moreover, it pointed out, if young people really are able to retain advertising messages longer and identify them better than older persons, that does not necessarily have an effect on the purchase decision. Also, it argued, older people have been in the market place longer than young people, which probably was why the older seemed to use the same products longer. And lastly, it noted that the ABC questionnaire gave a list of new products and brands that were heavily slanted to the interests of younger people (suntan lotions, feminine hygiene deodorants, soft drinks, eye-shadow kits, tape cartridges, and the new Volkswagen-sized cars).

It was the opening gun of a new debate in television: Which was better for the advertiser, *older* young or *younger* young?

Up to the fall of 1970, the Nielsen demographic break-outs for adults had come in three categories: 18–34, 35–49, and 50-upward. Conventionally, the first group was taken to be most desirable and the last least desirable. Television's audience was heavy in 50-upward, and there had been the not unreasonable argument to Nielsen and the advertising industry that consumers in their fifties and sixties had purchasing habits that were much closer to persons of forty than to retired senior citizens. The age group of 50–65 was not to be dismissed as a consumer group, and it was unfair to lump them with septuagenarians and octogenarians.

Just ahead of the new television season, Nielsen disclosed that it would expand its adult demographic break-outs. The new groupings would be 18–24, 25–34, 35–49, 50–64, 65-upward.

The effect of this on the television industry was highly dramatic. Overnight, the game had new rules. If the networks and stations could persuade advertisers that 50–64 was a bigger prize than 18–24, the manic quest for youth might be over. One of the major sources of advertising which was most eager to reach the young, the cigarette manufacturers, was lost to the medium anyway after New Year's Day. The audience television had had all along might be the best means to the advertising dollar after all.

Early in September, less than two weeks before the new season's premieres, I met with Fred Silverman, who had just returned from another of his trips to Hollywood.

"Been working on program development for next fall, and I must tell you I like how it's taking shape," he said. "We've got some great things going. I think we're going to be very strong."

The voice quality was reminiscent of comedian Don Adams, but the idiom was pure Mike Dann, which was probably only natural.

I asked if he could tell me about specific shows.

"I can only tell you this," he said. "The emphasis is going to be on comedy."

"Comedy?" I said. "What happened to Bob Wood's relevance?"

Silverman hesitated. Then he said, "Well, that's this year."

13

The Fourth Quarter

Plotted in January and February, sold in March, pitched to affiliates in May, and promoted to the American public after July, the new television season opened officially on September 15.

Premiering eighty-one prime-time series (twenty-three of them new), all neatly time-packaged and preproduced so as to unspool precisely by the clock, week upon week, it was an event to rival the unleafing of trees, the bird migrations, and the return to school as a harbinger of longer and colder nights and a suburban return from the summer patio to the hearth.

In business terms, the new season was nearly half a billion dollars' worth of entertainment product competing for more than a billion dollars' worth of prime-time advertising over the next full year, the programs' overhead not including affiliate payments, agency commissions, staff salaries, promotion and advertising, line charges, equipment usage, and the electric bill. Compared to the rest of television, the prime-time profits, where there were any, would be slim; but prime time was the showcase for the networks and their stations, and supremacy there had values which filtered down through the rest of the network service. The winner would strengthen its affiliate loyalties and be respected for leadership in the market place. Investors in securities—and this was most important—would respond to the prime-time ratings in their trading. *Variety*, first to detect the correlation between the movements of the Nielsen digits and the fluctuations in the prices of broadcast stocks, framed the story in a classic headline in 1967: TV KEEPING UP WITH DOW JONESES.

Television's fourth quarter, the fiscal designation for the months October through December, gave itself to a single activity—watching the ratings. The die cast, a dozen episodes of each series already shot and past changing, there was nothing to do but chart the individual rating histories and analyze what, for future use, the viewership preferred and what it rejected. The selling for the first quarter, January through March, would begin in November, and the prices per minute would be based on the rating data to that point. Outright flops would be eliminated and replaced by January, if not before.

NBC had the first premiere night to itself, CBS began its season the following night, and ABC started up a week behind the others, on September 22. In all there were twenty-seven adventure melodramas, twenty-seven situation comedies, sixteen variety shows and seven movies (including the ersatz movies) regularly scheduled in a week of prime time. There were also two game shows, one weekly news anthology and one monthly, and a single weekly sports feature, professional football. By network standards it was a balanced schedule, nearly 100 per cent light entertainment.

During the first week it was evident that something was wrong; the viewers were not following the script. They were supposed to be so aroused by the advent of a new television season that they would return en masse to the thralldom of the medium. They were supposed to set aside their old favorites for three or four weeks while they tried (the researchers call it *sampled*) the newest offerings, and then by the fifth week they were supposed to have established their new viewing patterns, which they would settle into for the duration. Above all they were supposed to care that it was all happening again, and that the schedules were revitalized, with more than a third of the programs new.

The earliest ratings were nothing less than shocking. The return of NBC's Sunday night line-up, playing against the last of the summer reruns on CBS and ABC, failed to win the night. Repeats of *The FBI* outrated the fall premiere of *The Bill Cosby Show*, and later in the evening a vintage theatrical movie which had had a previous television exposure, *A Guide for the Married Man*, surpassed the initial installment of *The Senator* on *The Bold Ones*, an hour in which three series rotate. Not only irregular, it was ominous. By all previous experience, an evening of premieres should have scored ratings twice as high as those for competing programs that were in their second time around.

The strange behavior of the television public continued through the week. On Tuesday night ABC's reruns of *Mod Squad, Movie of the Week*, and *Marcus Welby, M.D.* beat everything that was premiering on CBS and NBC that night; but if that seemed to augur a bountiful year in the ratings for ABC it was misleading, because ABC's own premieres the following week bordered on disaster.

By the end of the second premiere week there was panic along Television Row. Each night carried more than a million dollars' worth of programing, and far from paying a proper respect the American public was receiving it all with utter indifference. In particular, the new shows were disregarded. Under the established rating processes, any new show that failed to attract a large audience at the very outset stood little chance of building in popularity as the season wore on. Programs having the promise of developing into hits had to score a 40 share in the opening weeks; any opening to less than a 35 share would have to be considered prerejected by the mass audience. Unsampled, it had scant hope for success.

Only *The Flip Wilson Show* received the kind of initial ratings that bespoke a hit. Five or six other fledgling series registered sufficient interest not to be counted out, but the remainder stirred minimal curiosity, and that meant trouble.

Since viewer apathy to the new season and the new shows was unprecedented, there were the inevitable attempts at the networks to explain it. The weather had been pleasant, much too mild for that time of year to expect people to commit themselves to the television set. The first three or four days of the new season predominated, moreover, in returning shows and presented few new entries, so that there was not a high excitement level to start from, no smash opening number. And there was baseball. In three of the major cities—New York, Chicago, and Pittsburgh—the National League teams were still in contention for the Eastern Division title, and in those metropolitan areas the night games were hard to compete with, many of them marking up ratings on independent stations that were worthy of program premieres.

All that was true, but those factors were not unique to the 1970 season. The sober minds accepted the mass indifference for what it was.

Marvin Antonowsky, vice-president of research at ABC, commented privately that it was a lesson to be learned, although a painful one. "Some advertisers have learned it before this," he said. "You can only kid the public so much of the time. We call it 'new, improved' every year, and when we're discovered in the lie, we have to pay for it. It's not really a lie, though. We really know the truth, but we hypnotize ourselves into believing what we wish were true."

In fact, there was nothing really new in the September line-up at any network and very little that might legitimately be called improved. Any show might have played on any network in any of the previous ten seasons.

NBC's wonderful publicity machine had given many to believe that Red Skelton, after seventeen years on television, would have a brand-new show. The comedian had fired his old creative team and hired a new one to devise a modern format which would be an appropriate companion for *Laugh-In*, but the new improved *Red Skelton Show* proved to be what it had always been, low comedy verging on the vulgar and hewing to the time-tested formula of broadly played sketches and painfully unsophisticated jokes. The 1970 improvement was only that it had been reduced in length by thirty minutes.

Nor were the Don Knotts, Tim Conway, and Flip Wilson shows new in concept; they were, in fact, the conventional comedy-variety series turned out by the same persons who produce, direct, and write television comedy-variety every year. Two who had made their way in television as second-banana comedians, Knotts and Conway, had been promoted to first banana with series under their own billing, and their established comedy identities were in conflict with the success betokened by their elevation. Although both were sketch players of the first order, they had, as comedy types, always traded on diffidence and on the pathos of being lesser men than heroes. Both lacked the insouciance and the image of social competency that were the prescribed attributes of a television host.

Breaking the mold should have been refreshing, but to work well a series with a new kind of host should have a correspondingly new format. Instead, both comedians were in standard comedy-variety shows of the old video tradition, and the weak characters they represented could not support the conventional requirements.

Flip Wilson enjoyed far better luck. Establishing itself quickly and decisively as the season's new rating hit, even against the competition of a long-popular CBS series, *Family Affair*, the new series was nevertheless no more original or inventive than the others in its framework.

Why did Wilson catch on, and not Knotts and Conway? First, because he had never been a second banana and could conduct a show of his own without seeming out of character.

Second, because his source of humor was not white society but black, and in that sense it *was* original for television, other Negroes in the medium having had to pretend the races had a common culture. Third, he was a one-man repertory company, having developed two characters outside his own stand-up comedy identity, the Reverend Leroy of the Church of What's Happening Now and the Harlem chatterbox Geraldine Jones, both satirical types and so distinctly Negro they had no credible co-ordinates in white society. Fourth, his comedy was not an ethnic argument; rather than sentimentalizing Negro-American culture it seemed to mock it. And fifth, it did mock it.

The last may well have been the key. Wilson had performed his act before black audiences in segregated clubs and theaters for many years before his first television exposure and, within the group, the satire was appreciated for the healthy reasons. Irish can satirize the Irish, Jews the Jews, and Italians the Italians. Within the respective ethnic circles the stereotypical truths, although embarrassingly amusing, have a way of strengthening an individual's identification with the group and heightening his pride in belonging to it. But on television, with its vast and heterogeneous audience, the honest kidding of ethnic types becomes something else, tending to validate the stereotype as a true representative of a whole people and in that way contributing to prejudice.

Amos 'n' Andy was very popular even in television when the players were black (whites created the series for radio and did the voices), but it was driven off the air finally because its portrayal of Negro life fed, rather than dispelled, racial bigotry. Whites can be represented in comedies as bumbling, shiftless, or ignorant, and no one would conclude that all Caucasians are of that kind; but when the only series on black life in all broadcasting portrays the characters in precisely the way bigots imagine black people to be, it is insidious.

Flip Wilson's character Geraldine was funny because

she yielded to her impulses and, in her shrill way, always explained her waywardness with the running line, "The debbil made me do it." It was dependably the big laugh line. And the Reverend Leroy, taking up collections in the church, had his funniest moments whenever he had to explain away his possession of valuable goods, such as Cadillacs.

Flip Wilson was liked by the mass TV audience for positive reasons, because he was a lively and prepossessing personality, and loved for negative ones, because he substantiated a racist view of blacks. The show was defined a hit because the audience for it was great in size, and many who were drawn to it for negative reasons undoubtedly believed that their hour a week with a Negro, filtered through a TV screen, manifested their tolerance, their essential goodness as Americans.

But the Flip Wilson 40 per cent share of audience was accompanied by this curious development. Two television series headlined by blacks which had been popular the previous season suddenly and unaccountably lost their following. In the very year that Flip Wilson vaulted into the television top ten, Bill Cosby—who had been TV's favorite black the previous season—dropped to the bottom quartile of the ratings and was averaging only a 25 per cent share of audience. What made it harder to explain his decline in popularity was that his competition had not changed from the year before; it was still Ed Sullivan and *The FBI*. Experiencing a similar drop in the ratings was *Julia*, the first television situation comedy with Negro stars, Diahann Carroll and Marc Copage, which had done well for two seasons; and worth noting here was that it was losing to the most Southern cracker show on the networks, *Hee Haw*. The other Negro show in prime time, *Barefoot in the Park*, a new ABC entry, was a rating flop—and deservedly—from its first installment.

Flip Wilson had become the new pet Negro to a television populace that apparently could embrace only one at a time.

NBC moved quickly to cash in on its runaway hit. Between the premiere and the middle of November, the network raised the advertising rates in the Flip Wilson show four times. The charter advertisers paid $46,000 per minute, and by the fourth increase that rate was up to $65,000 a minute, equal to that of *Laugh-In*. For the January wave of buying, there was yet another raise, to almost $80,000 a minute.

ABC had had high hopes for *Barefoot in the Park* because the pilot episode tested well, with both blacks and whites—which perhaps contains its own comment on the value of program testing. The pilot, which aired as the first episode, was no more than white humor in blackface, an artistically calamitous attempt to convert the Neil Simon stage hit of the same title into a continuing TV series with blacks as the principals. The rendition was true neither to Simon nor to the mentality of modern blacks, and if it had been done with a white cast it would have been every bit as unreal and irrelevant.

All during the production of the first dozen episodes reports circulated of strife on the set, described in whispers as racial clashes, with one of the series stars, Scoey Mitchlll, mentioned repeatedly as the most rebellious member. Some witnesses to the quarrels said that Mitchlll's racial thrusts were merely a camouflage for the "star-ego thing" and that the real source of the problem was his desire to have the series retitled *The Scoey Mitchlll Show*.

Days before the premiere, Mitchlll was fired from the cast for punching the production manager for Paramount Television, Ted Leonard. In his own defense, Mitchlll later said that his fury had been brought on by the "idiotic dialogue" that had been forced upon the cast by white producers, writers, and directors.

To the extent that the pilot show was about an attractive young couple settling into a New York loft, the man eager for the middle-class attainments and the wife romantic about the economic struggle, the show followed Neil Simon's broad outline. But in the opening program the couple is pushed down the social scale, temporarily, when circumstances find them hiring out as maid and butler at a fancy dinner party for wealthy whites. The young man is an attorney just hired by a stuffy law firm—and who, in the world of situation comedy, should be a guest at that very party but his new boss! Since everyone is in black tie, the comedy is supposed to derive from the young man pretending to be a guest while serving the champagne cocktails. This kind of nonhilarity dates to the early talkies. Not to defend Mitchlll's unprofessional behavior, but an actor's distress over such demeaning comedy ploys might be understandable.

A number of years before the historic arrival of *Julia*, Harry Belafonte was on a television talk show on which he was sharply critical of the misrepresentation of Negro life on television and of the unrealistic portrayal of the black man.

I remember commenting in *Variety* then that he was undoubtedly right but that he was concerned with only part of the sin. For it was equally true that television habitually misrepresented white life and, moreover, that it was guilty of an unrealistic portrayal of the whole human race.

The situation comedies were as slick and nitwitty as ever, for all the putative efforts at making the genre more sophisticated and respectable.

Arnie was one that threatened to rise above its class, and the premiere episode hovered uncertainly between a richer and more mature kind of humor than was customary in the form and the hackneyed sight comedy that had been depressingly typical of it. As a comedy based on character (if its producers had had the courage to allow it to become that) the series' prime resource was its star, Herschel Bernardi, an accomplished actor whose television projection as an amiable, ordinary fellow was excellent. Arnie is a blue-collar worker of immigrant Greek parentage who, rather implausibly, receives a promotion to the white-collar executive tier of the corporation. Even if improbable, such promotions are possible and, given the situation, a warm and perhaps meaningful series might have evolved from it if the writing had concentrated on the peculiar conflict of a man who on the one hand is flattered by the promotion and happy with its emoluments but on the other feels a certain sorrow and perhaps guilt at having deserted his caste.

A comedy does not have to be funny all the time, or even at all; warmly human and joyful can be sufficient. But in the life-and-death climate of commercial television, producers and writers operate in the belief that the program is dying if there is no laughter—even if only artificial laughter created by the laugh console and dubbed onto the soundtrack —and *Arnie* fell victim to the television of fear.

It had a promising start. Arnie's inability to sleep the night before he begins his new job and his family's admiration of his new executive appearance as he sets out for work were semblances of truth. In the family appraisal, his empty briefcase swings too freely and is judged to need contents. The nearest thing at hand is a brick. His secretary, unpacking his bag (do secretaries unpack briefcases for their bosses?) is startled by what she finds. To cover his embarrassment, the new executive feigns eccentricity and says, as reasonably as if indicating a trophy, "That's my brick." Inoffensive comedy business, and mildly amusing.

But then come the shopworn mechanical gambits of the comic strips. The brick accidentally slips from Arnie's hand, falling out the window. And who does it fall on—not to kill him but merely to break his leg in good video fun? Well, that's the punchline for the episode, the boff laugh. The victim is the unfriendly fellow who had opposed Arnie's promotion.

The second episode would tell. Does *Arnie* become a series about a lovable Greek-American or about bricks falling out of windows? There is a moment when it seems the former. Arnie's secretary is fat and bossy, but the fact of a secretary, as a symbol of his new status, entrances him. It is a new relationship ordinary men do not easily adjust to. Up to this point, the situation and its comic embellishments are believable and pleasant. At home, his preoccupation with his secretary upsets his wife, played by a good comedy actress, Sue Ane Langdon, who must not be blamed for what happens next. Suspecting a romantic involvement she makes Arnie hire a new secretary. And who, unfailingly, must it be in any show that is driven to being contrived nonsense? An abundant sex goddess, of course. No need to describe how it ends.

The Odd Couple and *The Mary Tyler Moore Show* were more artistically successful (the latter in the ratings as well) because they resisted such hackneyed plot gambits and drew their comedy chiefly from the interplay of characters—Jack Klugman and Tony Randall in *The Odd Couple*, and Miss Moore and Ed Asner in the other. Still, neither was so fresh or distinguished a series that it could be said to have uplifted situation comedy as a form.

The Partridge Family was in the old motif of "heart comedy" (parents and children) with the added feature of music, one of those hybrids created from crossing two or more hits of the past, in this case *The Monkees* with *Family Affair* and the several shows of its stripe. As with *The Monkees*, a rock music group was manufactured to create recordings of songs that would be introduced on the show, so that there were dual benefits, the program promoting record sales and the recordings in turn promoting the series. In the twenty-year commercial history of the medium, this technique of parlaying the money possibilities was but a minor episode and probably no more serious an offense to the viewer than the counterfeiting of family life in America by all the situation comedies descended from *Father Knows Best* and *Make Room for Daddy*.

I knew a young couple whose marriage was deeply troubled because the woman was not able, for all her trying, to have a domestic life that measured up to what she believed to be the norm. Ridiculous as it may seem, television families were real to her, and they were never invaded by ugly quarrels or deep, debilitating distress over the conduct of the children. Television houses were orderly and uncluttered, the children precocious and never runny at the nose, the dog gifted with human insight, the husband-father even-tempered and for all his bumbling nature an incredibly good provider, and all the problems cute. There is no death, no disease, no emotional illness, no sex anxiety, no real financial insecurity, no religious doubt, and no personal unfulfillment in TV's antiseptic households, and so the irony is bitter when the consumer watches from an environment of cracked plaster and roaches, sniveling tots and a dog in heat, and a husband-father twisted into a grotesque by his job, his bills, and by having read the evening papers.

The measure of how far television family fiction had progressed in September 1970 was that Danny Thomas' *Make Room for Daddy* had returned as *Make Room for Granddaddy*, after a six-year hiatus following an eleven-year run. In texture it had not changed from the original, except that with the children grown up the new central relationship was between Thomas and his fictional grandson, Michael Hughes. As for wisdom and wit, it contained about as much as a TV commercial.

Among the new series there was also *Nancy* on NBC, one of the networks' tentative steps toward relevancy, not a program about ordinary, insignificant suburban people but about a President's daughter—a princess, as it were, with real-life counterparts in Tricia and Julie Nixon, except that Nancy longs for an ordinary, insignificant small-town life. For all the insulation of a chaperone and her Secret Service guards, she meets and falls in love with a young country veterinarian, who does not find out until later that she's the President's daughter. In typical make-believe film fashion, that bothers the lad and momentarily jars the romance, but then it all resolves itself in more typical make-believe film fashion. After one episode the viewer might well have wondered where the series would go from there. Some shows were meant to be small movies and not endlessly running series. *Nancy* was one.

In the ratings there was a curious valley between *Iron-*

side and *The Dean Martin Show* on Thursday nights. Both
were getting winning shares, but the half-hour program between them was not, which meant that in millions of television households an effort was made to tune out *Nancy* even
though thirty minutes later the viewer tuned back to NBC. If
Nancy was dull as entertainment it was interesting as a video
view of politics. Nicholas von Hoffman, writing in the *Washington Post*, saw it as a sop to the Administration: "At first
this surprising choice of profession for the hero (veterinarian) is mystifying, but then it becomes clear. The intention is
to associate the White House with everything that's warm and
cuddly. Instead of aircraft carriers, high taxes, Black Pan-
thers, when we think of the White House we're to imagine
baby lambs, puppies, and tiny, weeny little kitty cats. . . .
The real everything disappears in this program, the real
city, the real suburbs, and we're given Wasp small-town
America circa 1938. . . . In [this] case the results aren't
likely to be serious. Anybody who accepts that view of the
White House will coast through life undisturbed by truth in
any form."

He probably gives the program too much credit. I doubt
that it had political intentions, only economic ones. Sidney
Sheldon Productions, Screen Gems, and NBC all saw money
in the old princess and the pauper fairy tale if it were given
the contemporary American trappings, and as for the warm
and cuddly view of the presidency, it was probably less a
gesture to Washington than an attempt to appeal to the presumed twelve-year-old mentality of the viewership.

At any rate, a minority of the Nielsen population accepted the view, and for the second year only a minority accepted another situation comedy built around politics, *The
Governor and J.J.* on CBS. It was a favorite of the high-
ranking officials of the company, their idea of a sophisticated
program, and they attributed its rejection by the audience to
the chasm between their own refined tastes and that of the
general public, or, more bluntly, to the ignorance of the
masses. But for their belief in its worth, *The Governor* would

have been canceled after its first season under the going rules of Nielsen numbers and program viability.

The series used actual governors in supporting roles and starred Dan Dailey (the whilom song-and-dance man who picked up in Hollywood where Senator George Murphy left off) and Julie Sommars. Its distinctive characteristic was that none of its characters spoke dialogue. Ingeniously, the story moved along on flippant cracks and comic one-liners. The view of politics from here was that it was full of popularity crises and laughs, but the series was not without a philosophical level.

Opening its sophomore season was an innocuous episode whose crisis had what might be called relevant overtones. The governor has to cancel an appearance on television with one of the medium's coarse, sensation-seeking interviewers because of laryngitis. His daughter is allowed to appear in his place to talk about the governor's ecological programs. Although never shown, the TV interviewer is as though caricatured by Vice President Agnew, a disreputable character who will not give an elected official an open forum to sell his political image but rather will prod him with embarrassing questions to pry out something of news value. Such journalistic enterprise is deprecated as disrespectful.

The daughter, J. J., has the interview and creates a minor scandal that could be politically ruinous to her father. In response to the interviewer's unpleasantness, she hauls off at him with a four-letter word. For that a governor could lose an election, and there is a scene of his aides in despair. But then the mail begins to come in, and the silent majority allays their fears. They forgive the girl her indiscretion, noting—and this is important—the provocation. *Suddenly the mind hurtles into the real world, Chicago in August of 1968 and Kent State in the spring of 1970.* The lovely young girl who called a television interviewer a bad name was provoked into it by bad manners, and so it was justified, an understandable lapse in civility. Moreover, the mail tells the governor that his daughter did what most of the writers had wished to do as television viewers, namely to tell off the mongrel interviewer. A gentle show, full of sophisticated one-line jokes.

The new season brought one other program centering on politics, *The Senator*, a new alternating subseries of NBC's Sunday night trilogy titled *The Bold Ones*. What was bold about the Senator, played by Hal Holbrook, was that he was going to fulfill his promise to speak at a university in spite of a threat to assassinate him on the premises. The question never answered was why anyone would want to kill this particular Senator, since apparently he stood for nothing controversial and seemed uncommitted on any of the true-life issues that surfaced for discussion in the program. Judging from the positions not taken, he was either a conservative-liberal or a liberal-conservative, perhaps even a militant-moderate. Whatever, he had the haunted look of one who took his legislative responsibilities seriously and who would risk losing an election to stand on his principles. It became an intriguing mystery story, but not in quite the way the script writer intended, for the real mystery was where the Senator stood.

While he has no real political identity, real matters swarm all about the Senator—political assassinations, campus unrest, the Vietnam War, marijuana, the omnibus crime bill, pollution, re-election, political deals. He has the appearance of an activist, but he is always circumspect, wanting to examine all sides of a question before taking a position he almost, but not quite, divulges. There is a method to his caution: it is not to fractionalize or polarize the Nielsen constituency.

And in his debut on September 15, the first night of the new television season, *The Senator* became the symbol of television's newfound relevancy. Sounds and fury signifying nothing.

On September 23, Sunday afternoon football became a Monday prime-time event. Many another American institution had fought television and its disruption of its traditions, but professional football, through the vision of its young commissioner, Pete Rozelle, readily adapted itself to the commercial exigencies of the medium. Football was overtaking baseball as the national spectator sport, and its willingness to change its rules for television purposes was a major reason why. The money NBC and CBS were paying for football rights on Sunday afternoons had reached the feasible limit. To get more from the medium Rozelle had to involve a third network and create a special schedule of games in prime time, knowing that was where the programs scaled highest.

ABC had lost many millions for several years in its fruitless attempts to program competitively against the well-entrenched CBS and NBC Monday night shows. *Gunsmoke, Lucy, Mayberry R.F.D., Doris Day*, and *Carol Burnett* were a powerful line-up for CBS, and *Rowan and Martin's Laugh-In* coupled with a two-hour movie gave viewers the logical light entertainment alternatives on NBC.

There seemed no way for ABC to penetrate that domination of the audience until Rozelle offered his package of evening football games.

Television is a medium for real events. From the very first, it was a miracle that could show to the eyes what previously had to be read about or heard described on radio. On a continuing basis, with the added advantage of its escapist values, there was nothing better suited to television than sports. And football, because it is an action game, an acting out of war, with form—violent, competitive, full of strategy, marked with surprise—was the consummate television show.

In all prime-time television during the 1970–71 season there would probably be no better-written or better-performed dramatic scene than one that occurred in the fourth quarter of the first game in ABC's new prime-time series. The game was between the Cleveland Browns and the New York Jets, and with only minutes left to play the Browns were leading by three points. Perilously close to their own goal line, the Jets had the ball, and the team's superstar, Joe Namath—loved for his prowess on the field, otherwise despised for his nonconformity—was laboring on ailing legs to move the ball some ninety yards against the clock. With his incredibly precise passes he had many times accomplished the breath-catching storybook finish, and as millions watched he proceeded to do what they knew he would do—throw a succession of short passes to move up the field, and then lay one high in the air and deep to a brilliant receiver such as George Sauer, who would take it across the opposition goal. This of course was not drama but high melodrama.

Namath's eruption of short passes was about to begin. Back-stepping with the ball to spot his receivers, trained to execute his art in desperate seconds before the tons of uniformed gristle upended him, he issued the confident toss. Intercepted, it was run the short distance across the goal line, and the Browns had the decisive points.

The poignancy of drama is not what occurs climactically but what happens afterward, not the outcome of events but how the outcome affects the protagonist. The cameras dwelled a long time upon the figure on the sidelines as the extra point was being kicked, the cocksure Joe Namath in the anguished moments of his own imperfection, his head down and his body shuddering.

It was an honest moment in television, and an affecting one. The announcers were mute, but in the silence something was being said of the death of kings.

Whatever television relevance, or relevant television, was—topical, issue-oriented stories with a veneer of documentary realism, perhaps—it was a bust.

This was evident in the early ratings and confirmed by the so-regarded "definitive" Nielsens of November. None of the new programs purporting to social concern ranked in the top half of prime time's eighty-one programs, evidence of a massive rejection by the audience. Industry analysts would cite this as proof that viewers turn to television for escape and not for a confrontation with society's problems.

Furthermore, far from satisfying the viewers who wished for a more significant fiction from the medium, television's version of socially consequential programing was only a betrayal of the commercial industry's inability to deal honestly with life and of its ingrained commitment to a dead-center Establishment point of view. Whatever the social question, its resolution in the melodrama pointed up a single video truth: the existing order was always right.

Fault-finding youth was conceded its points: there were wickedness, injustice, and unreason, but they were the sins of individuals and not of the system. The script writers echoed some of the anger of the young, but their stories invariably went on to demonstrate that they were captives of their unripe passions and misled by sinister individuals among them who played on their passions. Implicit in virtually every story was the message that teen-age and post-teen rebels eventually would recognize the error of their ways and take their proper places within the system.

In *Storefront Lawyers*, three swaggering young attorneys fresh out of law school will not give the rich and stodgy firm that employs them the benefit of their minds unless it sponsors their part-time efforts to assist the poor from a storefront office in the ghetto. Although this reflects an actual phenomenon of legal recruitment today, the reality is vitiated by the absurdly glamorous representation of it. Two of the young advocates, Sheila Larken and David Arkin, look pure-insincere-1940-Hollywood-pretty, and the third, Robert Foxworth, is left the burden of credibility as a person of some intellect and conscience who feels concern for the underprivileged. But more than from the miscasting, the program suffered from its style, which was derived from television advertising.

The three youths move between the patrician and poverty worlds to a rock music score, seeming choreographed rather than directed. "Let's go to court!" one shouts and, joining hands, they spring from the plush office building into the street, gaily exchanging glances as they weave through the traffic, and deftly take their places in a happy red convertible. Here, the climactic commercial pause would not have been jarring; one could have expected them to reach for their cigarettes, bounce their three packs of L&Ms against each other, and after a knowing smile go soaring off on a cigarette high, the Pepsi Generation bound to do its condescending thing for the ignorant poor.

Through helping a simple man driven to vengeful murder, in the premiere installment, the three youngsters expose and destroy a white-collar criminal who by one of those marvelous coincidences happens to be a large and powerful client of their parent law firm. Now in the real life of law and business, a wealthy client comes before the idealistic mischief of trainees; new members are supposed to help the firm make money, not lose it. But the bosses of the storefront lawyers, after some soul searching, condone the investigation and look with pride on the youngsters as they devastate the paying customer in court and ring up a no-fee for the case.

The implication is that they are learning to be fine young attorneys who will be equipped to pay their way in the future when they pass through the callow phase and move up in the firm. Although in their token way they are outside the Establishment now, they are destined to join it. That, in reality, was the series' message to the young, and the clue to it was that Foxworth, who seemed so right for the role both to producer Leonard Freeman and to those who approved the show at CBS, had come to their attention as the protagonist in *Sadbird*, an original drama for *CBS Playhouse* in which he played a hippie who took a job in the toy industry and reformed, becoming in the end reclaimed by society. It is a subtle point, perhaps, but his "rightness" for the role among all the actors available for it was conditioned by his association in television with a previous role in which he played the outsider who comes inside.

(The first episode, incidentally, was the pilot that had everyone at CBS wild when it arrived in January. After the early ratings, however, it was almost impossible to find anyone at the network who did not claim to have warned everyone else the show would fail.)

ABC had a similar new series, *The Young Lawyers*, which was probably the best of the social involvement shows, a well-written and particularly well-performed legal melodrama. The title was something of a misnomer since its principals were Zalman King, young, and Lee J. Cobb, not young. A second *young* lawyer, a black girl named Judy Pace, had occasional scenes of some consequence, but practically speaking she was a secondary character. There was also this odd item: the young male lead portrayed a character named Silverman, a Jewish name for sure, making him in all probability TV's first Jewish hero in a nonethnic series. That presumably was for realism. Here, too, through the patience and indulgence of the older generation, the young were being led from the morass of discontent to the salvation of social adjustment.

During the first week of television's relevance cycle the new stereotypes were established. In the fashion of the old movie Westerns which marked off the heroes by their white hats and the villains by their black, TV's social adventure tales presented the redeemable young as stylish mods with long hair and full sideburns and the heavies as unwashed hippies. Typical was the criminal in the pilot of *The Interns* on CBS, telegraphed in one of the earliest scenes by his preoccupation with smut. Crude-speaking, seedy, and having a distracted look suggestive of being stoned, he sells to a terminal patient looking for the means of committing suicide an *injection* that does the job.

He is not a philosophical dropout of the system but an old-fashioned psychopath, and here was another sly deceit of the production-line dramas that were spilling into prime time as meaningful encounters with (in Wood's words) "the gut issues of our time." Ideological types, as they were depicted in TV shows, had little resemblance beyond the external trappings to their objective counterparts in the real world. The psychopath looked like a hippie but was not in any philosophical sense a hippie. Yet the message was: beware the hippie, within lives a psychopath.

In other shows, militants were not angry revolutionaries but paranoiacs or agents of hostile countries; draft evaders not really opponents of the war but neurotics rejecting their fathers in return for having been rejected by them; bigots not true haters but merely persons who lived too long in isolation from other races; drug users not the disenchanted but victims of ghoulish weirdos and organized crime. Television faced the gut issues with false characters, and instead of shedding light on the ailments of the social system and the divisions within it the playlets distorted the questions and fudged the answers.

The script writers had merely found new vestments for their old, reliable evildoers.

A classic instance of an ideological clash which had the appearance but not the substance of objective reality, and therefore was irrelevant, was that between a hawk and a dove on the question of the Vietnam War in the season's premiere of *Bracken's World* on NBC. Forrest Tucker portrayed an aging cowboy actor of intense right-wing sentiment making a film with a brash, left-leaning young man, Tony Bill. But neither's views had more than an effluvium of the real-life doctrines they fictively espoused, and their debate had less to do with ideas than with their differences in personality. The program seemed to be tackling head-on the most divisive issue in America in 1970 while in actuality it was running skillfully around it. In the resolution, both the hawk and dove are shown to be wrong, but a nonpolitical soldier who has lost both legs becomes the argument to finish the war for peace.

As in the TV commercials, nothing in television's relevance cycle was represented quite as it really was. The police were gracious, thoughtful, and efficient, with here and there a bad apple to soil their image. Doctors and lawyers desired nothing more for themselves than the satisfaction of knowing they had served honorably in their professions, although there was among them the occasional mercenary. Politicians were dedicated servants who prevailed against money power and their party machines because they had the support of honest people who recognized their goodness. And the business community, which seemed callous because it was busy, had a great sense of social justice when apprised of its oversights and was capable of legendary generosity and humanity.

For all their genuflections toward social awareness, the networks' intent was not so much to involve themselves with the real issues of the day as patently to exploit them for purposes of delivering up to advertisers more of the young consumers than before, without alienating the older habitués of the medium.

It was, in retrospect, naïve of the networks to think the young would be happily hooked by the rock music and pop slogans of their promotions. And there was no better evidence that the network-studio-advertiser nexus was out of touch with the alienation phenomenon in America than their innocence in supposing they could sell their plastic replicas of reality to the turned-off or awakened young.

In spite of the networks' slow start and the public apathy to the new offerings, television viewing had not decreased from the previous year but, according to Nielsen statistics in late October, was growing at a somewhat faster rate than the population expansion. More people were spending more hours before the television set, even if it seemed they were less involved than ever with the programs they were watching. In large part this was an effect of the growing unemployment in the land and the national economic pinch. Having less money to spend than before, more people were staying home, and staying home for many meant watching television.

But if the total audience was ample and it was not swarming about the new youth-angled social-relevance series, what was it watching? In the main, the established family comedies and a particular kind of melodrama—the police and detective stories. It was an interesting pattern, for the national rating trend was in perfect parallel with the political mood of much of the American middle class in 1970, the yearning for law and order.

The FBI was having its best year in four seasons on ABC, and *Gunsmoke* had lost none of its popularity to the new competition. High in the ratings also were *Hawaii Five-O, Adam 12, Ironside, Mannix,* and *Mission: Impossible* (a kind of CIA series), all in the standard law-and-order idiom of television, leading to the realization that the networks had probably misread the program they all copied, *Mod Squad.* For it, too, was maintaining its popularity, and it became clear that the series owed its success in the first place not to the anti-Establishment antics of its three youthful lead characters but rather to their function as police.

Since it is a reasonable assumption that a person's viewing choices have some correlation to his philosophical attitudes, or at least to his wish-fulfillment fantasies, the Nielsen reports had some validity as public opinion polls in the off-year elections held in November. What the Nielsens illustrated was that the mass public cared not so much about exploring the reasons for the troublesome upheavals in society as about the simplistic solutions to the problems, by capture and arrest—containment of disorder.

That the November elections were not a sweeping triumph nationally for the so-called law-and-order candidates did not necessarily diminish the value of the Nielsen ratings as a political indicator. A popular television program has two major competitors, a political candidate usually only one. The highly successful law-and-order TV shows were popular with substantially more than one-third of the viewership; the law-and-order candidate, to win his election, needed the votes of more than one-half the electorate.

Relevance may have been the shortest program cycle in the history of the medium. By November, decisions were being made to replace certain programs of the new vogue with more traditional fare in January. Others would be altered.

To preserve *Storefront Lawyers* for at least the remainder of the season, CBS and producer Leonard Freeman worked out a number of revisions for the seven episodes that had not yet gone into production. These included the addition of a new character, an older man (Gerald S. O'Loughlin) who would play mentor to Foxworth, and the diminution of the other youth roles as well as of the gimmick storefront law office. Thus, the series would lose its resemblance to *Mod Squad* and adopt the basic central character relationships and story accents of such successful series as *Marcus Welby, M.D.*, *Medical Center*, and *The Bold Ones*. With the February 4 episode, *Storefront Lawyers* would have a new title, *Men at Law*.

Andy Griffith, the rural favorite who had essayed a "relevant" comedy drama in his return to the medium in September—a half-hour school show, *Headmaster*, in which he dispensed platitudinous advice to kids who were in the new orbit—also at the behest of CBS abandoned the social story lines and reverted to his old specialty, small town comedy. At mid-season, Griffith would continue in the Friday half hour with a new cast, a different concept (his old one for CBS), and a new title, *The New Andy Griffith Show* (which meant the *old* Andy Griffith show).

In normal seasons—and 1970 was not one—the networks made strategic changes in January for the purpose of strengthening their competitive performance. But with the imminent loss of cigarette advertising adding to the distress of a faltering general economy, the mid-season emendations of their schedules were made strictly with a view toward trimming the overhead.

NBC pulled out the loser *Nancy* and replaced it on

Thursday nights with a program from Saturday, *Adam 12.*
Ingeniously, the network did not fill that vacant time period
with a new show but extended the Saturday night movies to
two and a half hours. The longer movies in its library would
be scheduled for Saturday nights, starting at 8:30 instead of
9:00 P.M., and would be stretched out with fillers where
necessary. *Bracken's World* would yield to a British-made series, *The Strange Report*, which was already paid for and
had been sitting on the shelf. Otherwise, NBC's only other
mid-season change was to flip-flop *Julia* and Don Knotts in
the Tuesday night line-up, in hopes that the change in time
slot might be beneficial to one or both of them.

ABC needed a prodigious overhaul. Nine of the twelve
new series it introduced in September were at the very bottom of the rating order, and the Tom Jones variety hour,
which had been brought back from the previous season, had
still not caught on. Furthermore, the football season would
end in January, and the Monday night games would need a
replacement. It would be devastatingly expensive to make all
the necessary repairs in the schedule.

Luck was still with Elton Rule, however. The FCC's three-
hour rule, which would force the networks to cut back prime-
time programing by thirty minutes every night starting October 1971, was his *deus ex machina.* Since network service
was going to have to be reduced anyway, ABC determined
that it would start trimming back immediately. Seven programs were canceled and were replaced by only four, and a
movie was inserted for football. ABC gave back to the affiliates, for them to program in their own ways, an hour on Sunday nights, two hours on Saturday nights, and a half hour on
Thursdays.

In withdrawing three and a half hours a week from the
prime-time competition, ABC suffered a loss of face, but it
conserved an estimated $6 million in program inventory.
Furthermore, its owned stations figured to make substantially larger profits from scheduling their own local movies in

the periods returned by the network, so that the parent company, ABC, Inc., would benefit two ways.

The network's replacement shows in January were a new situation comedy with Henry Fonda, *The Smith Family*; a Western, *Alias Smith and Jones*; a new variety hour with Pearl Bailey; and a half-hour game show, *The Reel Game*. Old-fashioned, time-tested, unventuresome formats.

CBS had two casualties at mid-season—*The Tim Conway Show* and *The Governor and J.J.*—and both were replaced with programs that required no new investment by the network. Precommitted to the Yorkin and Lear series, *All in the Family*, CBS scheduled it in place of *The Governor*. Conway's successor was, of all people, Jackie Gleason. The network owned the repeat rights to all of the late-vintage, hour-long episodes of *The Honeymooners*, which it acquired when it bought out Gleason's production company a few seasons before. They had already performed summer replacement service several times, and some of the episodes had had as many as *five* previous exposures, but the thinking was that they were bound to do at least as well in the ratings as Conway. At about the same time, CBS engaged Gleason to develop a new half-hour comedy series possibly to begin in the fall of 1971.

Had the reruns scored unexpectedly well in the late Sunday night hour Gleason might have made his comeback in the same year in which he was canceled. But there was no surprise ending. The old *Honeymooners* barely equaled Conway's scores. Months later the scripts were submitted for two different situation comedy vehicles for Gleason and both were rejected.

14

The Public Service

A new fourth network—there had been others—made its debut on October 5. It would survive, where the earlier Dumont, NTA, and Overmyer networks did not, because it was noncommercial and had the pledged economic support of the federal government. It also had a ready-made and sufficient family of stations desirous of a national service, 186 educational and otherwise noncommercial TV outlets whose limited finances and facilities precluded major production and full-time operation.

Theoretically, the new Public Broadcasting Service (PBS) was the realization of a decades-old dream for an alternative system to commercial television, a government-ensured system unrestricted by the market place and free from the tyranny of ratings, somewhat comparable to the BBC in Great Britain or to other enlightened state-operated systems carefully insulated from politics. American television critics and communications analysts, watching how the creative goals of commercial broadcasting grew progressively narrow, had prayed for such a new network to enrich the resource of the national air waves.

With a three-hour prime-time schedule five nights a week, Sundays through Thursdays, and a six-month advertising budget of around $500,000 (a gift from the Ford Foundation) administered by a top-flight advertising agency, Wells, Rich, Greene, PBS set out three weeks after the commercial network premieres to establish itself as a new broadcast entity.

Although it employed promotional techniques borrowed

from the major networks and in spite of an attempt at counterprograming the commercial opposition, PBS scarcely made its existence felt with the mass audience. With its impact on the viewership faint, PBS posed no threat whatever to the well-being of the commercial chains.

It was natural to take the competitive failings of public television as a reflection on the American audience; indeed, persons in commercial television took it as proof that they knew more about public tastes than their critics. That PBS's *Realities, Homewood, The Advocates, San Francisco Mix, Book Beat, Civilisation, NET Playhouse, The French Chef, World Press, Flickout,* and the TV classic *Kukla, Fran & Ollie* stole nothing from the established networks in the Nielsen ratings justified their hackneyed melodramas, situation comedies, and vaudevilles.

The new network's programing was at very least agreeable, some of it was even distinguished, and it had the virtue of cutting a wider geographical swath than the commercial system would permit itself, wedded as it was to Hollywood and New York production. Four of the PBS series emanated from Boston; two each from San Francisco, Los Angeles, and Chicago; one each from Washington, D.C., Pittsburgh, and Lincoln, Nebraska; and six from New York. *Civilisation* originated in England.

But to capture the fancy of a public conditioned to commercial slickness and escapism—and thus to become a new force in communications—it was not enough to spread out a selection of likable or even culturally worthy offerings, it was necessary to project an independent spirit and a sense of new creative ferment. What PBS offered was little more than a continuation of what used to be called educational television, and so it was as easy for the television multitudes to ignore as was its precursor.

Civilisation was surely the most remarkable program series in American television during the fall of 1970, and the most aesthetically satisfying and, as it turned out, more pertinent to contemporary life by far than anything CBS, ABC, and NBC proffered as "relevant," but it was only one series and not a product of the new network but an import from abroad. PBS was a last resort for *Civilisation*. It was placed there by Time-Life Films as a gift from the Xerox Corporation only after the three major networks had rejected it. But while it was a jewel in the PBS diadem, Sir Kenneth Clark's thirteen-part history of the human adventure illustrated by man's artistic creations was hardly a program to tempt the seeker after painless entertainment except possibly for a single admiring visit. Whatever else, it was not the adult *Sesame Street* indicated for a new alternative to the existing system whose example would set new standards for the commercial networks to meet.

At a close look, the PBS programs on the whole were marked by the intellectual prudence, the social cautions, and the feigned creative vitality that were hallmarks of commercial television in America. The new network spoke in a somewhat different language but ultimately for the same Establishment.

So PBS was not the second coming of television in this country, nor in truth did its guiding forces intend it to be (although the Public Broadcasting Act of 1967 meant it to be), nor did the fraternity of TV critics who had watched a noble idea disintegrate in three years expect it to be. PBS was not even in a fair sense a *new* network, its arrival not so much a birth as a usurpation, for it had taken over the programing and distribution function that had previously belonged to National Educational Television. So little was really expected of PBS and so modest were its aspirations that when its debut stirred scarcely a ripple of excitement, it was to absolutely no one's disappointment.

After the premieres, PBS principals and advocates praised the schedule as a service to the cultural minorities who could not be accommodated by the commercial system, and they seemed to take it as a mark of success that PBS made no discernible inroads into the commercial ratings. The public television system did not seek after ratings, they said; the whole point was to be above the battle for mass viewing and to make program decisions without regard to the Nielsen quantitative evaluations.

All very well, but if the service was designed for an elite minority and did not care to reach numbers of people, in what sense was it a public network?

Perhaps only in a Madison Avenue sense. "Public" serves nicely as a euphemism for "government-supported." An indication of the public the new network sought to reach was its selection of advertising media in New York for the 1970 premieres. The daily tune-in advertising was concentrated in the *New York Times*, the newspaper of greatest influence with professionals of all kinds, including educators, heads of foundations and corporations, and with government officials in the capital. Nominal space was purchased in the *New York Daily News* and the *New York Post*, which are not elitist papers but popular dailies with the working middle classes. The *Daily News*, with the largest circulation in the country, charges a great deal for its ad space, but it would be considered good value by a network that wanted to reach the masses.

As before, when it was known as educational television, public TV was more interested in prestige and in the sources of its operating monies than in the attentions of the lower classes.

Something went wrong in public television between its conception and its realization. Partly it was inauspicious timing: first, the financial drain of the Vietnam War making funds for a new television system scarce; second, the ideological polarization in the land seeming to make every contemporary issue a sensitive one and every non-Establishment or minority voice inflammatory. There was the promise of a government subsidy but not the long-range fulfillment, and there were philosophical divisions among the persons in public TV, clashes between the left and the right on the political scale, and between the zealous young producers and their more pragmatic elders.

Having watched the movement from its practical inception, however, I would trace the untracking back to the recommendations of the Carnegie Commission on Educational Television submitted to President Johnson in January 1967. Its proposal for a noncommercial system followed too closely the supposedly democratic structure of the American commercial system, which obviously was not working in the public interest—*obviously* because if it had worked there would have been no pressing need for an alternative system.

The key to the Commission's recommendations was the primacy of the local stations over the national or network service, the supposition being that strength at the grass-roots level would open the medium to regional issues, and to local spokesmen for the various points of view, and that it would create a sturdy foundation for a system oriented to public needs. That is precisely the theory on which the commercial TV system was established. It would be for the local broadcaster to determine whether a national program was appropriate for his viewing area or whether the locale might not be better served with one of local origin. This is almost the reverse of the British system, the BBC being a national service without local stations in England, hence without local options to carry or not to carry. In ideal terms, station primacy is the power to determine what is best and most useful for the citizenry of a city or region; in practical terms, it is the power of censorship.

Assuming the best about the operators of the local stations, it was a careless recommendation; and the dangers were compounded by the Carnegie Commission's conceiving public television (it coined the term) as an overlay on existing educational stations rather than as a prospectus for an entirely new body of stations. Their objectives and purposes having been established long before the Carnegie Commission was organized, the stations were bound to bend the new ideals of public television to their own separate selfish interests.

Once the Carnegie recommendations were converted into

law and the prospect of economic security was on the horizon, schisms developed within the public TV family. Given a voice within the new system, the local educational licensees produced too many voices. Suddenly an idea that had once seemed clear and concrete to everyone—independent, advertiser-free broadcasting—meant something different to each and, the Carnegie report notwithstanding, public television became a name without a concept. The one thing all the stations had in common was a desire for the government endowment, and even after the PBS network was launched the unifying factor within public television was not the public service mission or the lofty promises of the Carnegie Commission ("It will be a civilized voice in a civilized society"), but the pursuit of the congressionally authorized federal funds.

It should be mentioned that the Commission did a large share of its research during 1966 at the local station level— by its own report "ninety-two educational television stations in thirty-five states," or about two-thirds of those then on the air—and so it was natural that the recommendations would strongly reflect station interests and anxieties. The report stated: "From station to station the lament rises: so much that might be done, so much that needs doing, so receptive the small audience that is now reached, so little resources with which to operate."

And yet, when there were signs that the funds were forthcoming, the first priority for many of the stations was to buy new equipment for conversion to color.

After money, the second anxiety was New York.

NET was New York. There may have been a tolerance for radical or unorthodox viewpoints in New York, an acceptance of truth-searching journalism, and a sophistication with language, which were not shared everywhere in the country. As the principal source of national programing, NET was too progressive, too given to muckraking, and too willing to create controversy for the comfort of most station operators. They knew this: that the similarity between an ex-

posé and a chamber of commerce documentary is that neither would get a large audience, but the difference was that
the exposé would bring trouble and the other would win
praise.

Also centered in New York—we are now in 1966, when
the Carnegie Commission was performing its research—was
educational television's chief benefactor, the Ford Foundation, by whose generosity NET existed. And in that year the
Ford Foundation took on a new consultant in broadcast matters, Fred W. Friendly, who had recently left CBS, where he
had been president of the news division. To the alarm of educational station operators, he seemed determined to push
noncommercial television into broadcast journalism on a
scale to compete with the networks—nay, to surpass them
through the freedom from corporate restraints. Friendly
spoke frequently of wanting men about him "who had fire in
their bellies." They were precisely the kind most educational
operators tried to avoid.

An aggressive man with a great sense of his own chapter
in the history of broadcasting and rudely impatient with the
small-town mentality, Friendly marched into educational
television as though it had lain dormant waiting for a leader.
There were programs he could not wait to put into motion.
One was an interconnection of stations to create a new national network (programs were then being *bicycled, i.e.*,
mailed, from station to station) to deal with current affairs
with a frequency that was economically prohibitive for the
commercial networks and to examine issues the networks
feared to explore.

What Friendly may have known but chose to disregard
was that most educational stations had no more desire than
the networks to deal with those issues.

Through the Ford Foundation, he then rushed a proposal
to the federal government, before the Carnegie Commission
report was completed, for an interconnected noncommercial
network to be financed by means of domestic communications satellite. Calling it "the people's dividend," Friendly

envisioned a new public network interconnected by satellite free of charge. The commercial networks would pay for its use at rates to cover the fourth network's share.

And to demonstrate how the new network would perform, he established the Public Broadcasting Laboratory to produce a two-hour weekly program titled *PBL*, which under a Ford grant would be broadcast coast to coast over the conventional land lines. A news magazine of the air, it would prove the value of a free interconnected service. Friendly scheduled the program for Sunday nights.

Each of Friendly's acts pointed to the goal of a national network that would lord it over public television, relegating the stations to the status of carriers except in the non network hours. Neglecting to acknowledge their useful existence or to make them part of his proposals except as outlets, Friendly earned the animosity of the station operators, and he added to the offense by staking out Sunday nights for *PBL* as though the hours were his, or the Ford Foundation's, to claim. The hours actually belonged to the licensees.

His tactical errors were costly. When, in its research, the Carnegie Commission called on the selfsame educational broadcasters Friendly had alienated—people anxious to preserve their professional existence who by then had developed serious doubts about the value of a regular schedule of national programs dictated from New York—the argument for the strengthening of local stations was overwhelming.

Friendly also came to represent a threat to NET, since his new creation, *PBL*, was under separate administration with a separate board of trustees. Since NET and *PBL* were both national services, and since both were dependent for their budgets on the Ford Foundation, Friendly's build-up of *PBL* seemed ominous to members of the older organization. To preserve peace in what had become a chaotic time in public broadcasting, Friendly put the new project nominally under the wing of NET and withdrew—or, more aptly, retreated—from the forefront of public television to his office at the Ford Foundation.

By then nearly all the public television forces hoped the new *PBL* series would fail, including NET and most of the stations carrying it. Jack Gould of the *New York Times*, himself a force in public TV by dint of his newspaper's influence and by his long campaign as a television critic for an independent noncommercial system, seemed also to resent *PBL*. Five days before it premiered, on October 31, 1967, he led his review of another program with a gratuitous jab at Friendly's folly: "The program called 'NET Journal,' which has quietly gone about its reportorial business *without either disparaging commercial network efforts or proclaiming itself the ultimate renaissance in electronic journalism,* presented last night a calm and sober appraisal of Fidel Castro's revolution in Cuba." (Italics added.)

After that prereview, there was reason to suppose that Gould might not take kindly to the *PBL* premiere, but his severe panning of it the following Monday morning exceeded expectations. (For the record, *Variety* gave it a favorable notice.)

It lasted two seasons, as Friendly had pledged that it would, but *PBL* died as a factor in public television before it went on the air.

Ironically, it had a greater influence on commercial television. No sooner had it faded away than both CBS and NBC adopted its news magazine format, CBS for the biweekly *60 Minutes*, NBC for the monthly *First Tuesday*.

And in January of 1971, NET borrowed the format from the commercial networks and started its own Wednesday night magazine, *The Great American Dream Machine*, for PBS.

Friendly's main contribution to public broadcasting was to make the cause conspicuous. But if educational broadcasters were appreciative of that, they were unsettled by the nature of his forceful argument, which was that the built-in shortcomings of the profit-seeking system had made a national necessity of a free public TV service. It had been part of their unwritten code, in all their years of plodding toward

some manner of permanent federal subsidy, never to achieve
it at the expense of commercial broadcasting, never to wage
that war.

Instead, educational broadcasters had carefully cultivated an alliance with their affluent and powerful fellow
broadcasters. The Carnegie Commission may have divined
an *alternative* system to the prevailing advertiser-supported
television, but it had been decided by educational broadcasters long before that theirs would be a *supplementary* system.
The two systems would be facets of a single broadcast establishment.

Symbolic of the harmony is that both were joined in the
National Academy of Television Arts and Sciences, the parent organization of the Emmy Awards, and that in Chicago
the president of the local chapter was not from the commercial ranks but the program director of the educational station
there, Ed Morris.

The struggling, noncommercial industry knew better
than to tangle with the potent Washington lobby of commercial broadcasting and recognized, too, that the wealthy TV
stations were capable of generous favors in hard times. Many
of the educational stations received hand-me-down equipment, free programs, promotional assistance, and cash gifts
from their commercial brethren. Such was the spirit of co-
operation, moreover, that the noncommercial industry's aims
on Capitol Hill were supported, rather than opposed, by the
commercial television lobby, the National Association of
Broadcasters.

There was something of value in the alliance for the
commercial industry, too. First, having an educational station in the market meant one less commercial competitor, for
if an advertising-free station were to quit for lack of funds
the channel would quickly be applied for by a profit-seeking
operator. It was therefore in a commercial station's economic
interest to keep the educational station operating. Second,
having a full-time station to perform the cultural, informational, and educational functions removed some of the pres-

sure for such unlucrative services from the commercial stations. And third, by their co-operation and friendly relations, commercial operators might be reasonably sure that any proposal to tax them for the creation of a national public TV system would be vigorously opposed by their ETV colleagues. Which was so.

Thus it happened that when the Carnegie Commission made its proposal on funding the new system, the suggested source of support monies was not an impost on commercial television's vast profits—not, as Friendly had proposed, a "people's dividend" from those privileged to make money from the public air waves—but rather a special excise tax on television sets. The people would pay.

Although the rules by which they lived were somewhat different, the operators of most commercial and noncommercial stations shared an objective that was quintessential to their operating decisions: survival in their jobs. For the general manager of a typical TV station this generally meant keeping the ratings up and turning a larger profit every year while complying with the basic FCC license requirements. For his counterpart at the educational TV station survival was achieved by a successful fund-raising drive every year and by keeping the board of directors reasonably free from pressure.

In many ways, the ground rules for the commercial broadcaster were more heroic.

Admittedly, this is a generalization, but it is based on reportorial experience: the trick to running most public TV stations successfully is not to serve the public in the fullest but to serve the local board of directors, and in a majority of situations that is accomplished through an avoidance of controversy. And in times of strong ideological divisions in the country, it means muting the critics of the established order.

By and large, the boards of directors of the local public television outlets are made up of prominent representatives of industry, finance, education, and the professions—key figures in the local power structure, many of them with iron-bound political points of view and few with any real experience in communications or with a feel for the objective purposes of broadcasting. A station manager who too often allowed programs to generate shock waves of controversy in the community which would rebound on members of the board, who through exposés or discussion programs alienated large donors to the station, or who was given to disregarding the vested interests of board members, soon lost his job. And it was a job rich in prestige. The manager of a public TV station had the status of a publisher in his city and held a unique prominence in the academic and cultural communities as the man who could give television exposure to those who craved it. Further, since he was not a creature of commerce, he had a clergyman's dignity.

John W. Taylor, who could model the distinguished-looking, middle-aged man in magazine advertisements, was general manager of the Chicago station WTTW, a fairly typical unit of the educational television system on which the ideals of public TV had been superimposed. Before he became a broadcaster, Taylor had been president of the University of Louisville and then deputy director general of UNESCO. As an academician, he had had occasion to put a school course on Louisville television from the university, and that constituted his background as a TV communicator, up until his appointment as executive director of the Chicago Educational Television Association (the licensee of WTTW) in 1954. In *Who's Who in America, 1970–71* he continued to list himself as an educator rather than as a broadcaster, and his entry is lengthy with memberships in education organizations and on high-sounding commissions. As head of the public TV station, he was concurrently president of the Chicago City College board, one of several affiliations with the city government that made him part of Mayor Richard Daley's legendary web of authority.

Married to a socialite, the former June Cornell Fairbank, Taylor had virtual peerage with the socially prominent members of the station's board of directors who had served at

326 The Public Service

various times, Edward L. Ryerson, the former chairman of Inland Steel, who was responsible for Taylor's appointment, Mrs. Wesley Dixon, Homer P. Hargrave Jr., and Charles Benton. Thus, not only did WTTW hold strong ties to the Chicago political establishment but also to the city's social registry.

Others on the board were Irving Harris, a financier who earlier had headed the Toni Company (in the days of "Which twin has the Toni?"); Benjamin Willis, the former superintendent of schools; Robert Wilcox, a prominent lawyer; Alfred P. Stepan, president of Stepan Chemical Co.; Don Paul Nathanson, president of North Advertising; John Johnson, president of Johnson Publications, publishers of *Ebony;* and Bishop McManus of the Roman Catholic Archdiocese of Chicago. A neat cross section of the city's upper-crust and affluent middle-class strata.

With its chairman of the board, however, the Chicago station reached the height of broadcast prestige. Newton Minow was a famous name and still a myth in the cause of a more vital television system in America, tracing to his description of commercial TV as a "vast wasteland" in his initial speech as chairman of the Federal Communications Commission during the John F. Kennedy Administration. If Minow had seemed outside the Establishment then, he quickly rejoined it when he went back to the practice of law in Chicago, and even as he became a power in public television he numbered among his law clients the Columbia Broadcasting System. He also remained an active Democratic partisan, and so he, too, maintained a personal affiliation with the Daley machine.

Suffice it to say that with Minow's and Taylor's links to the local administration, not to ignore those of other board members, WTTW was not a station likely to be critical of city policies or to give generous voice to those who were. There was a meticulous caution over matters that might displease the mayor. As a veteran member of the station's staff related it, "We are not here to offend the powers that be. Our goal is harmony."

WTTW was not the exceptional public TV station but a representative one. New York's WNDT (before it became WNET in a union with National Educational Television in the summer of 1970) was similarly governed by a conformist board of social, academic, and business pillars of the community less concerned with the highest realization of television's potential than with fears of stirring up the populace or upsetting the power elite. The station took such a dull, dead-center course in its local programing that it failed to involve the public it was supposed to serve. Symptomatic of that was its history of struggling to raise its quota of funds from the community—the largest metropolitan community in the country.

WETA-TV in Washington, D.C., the showcase station for public television in the capital, where the money for the entire system would come from, was not as worried about displeasing the local administration as the federal, which it demonstrated through its censorship of NET programs that might offend federal officials.

Nor were these the worst examples of Establishment stations, or of broadcasting by fear. Many, in other cities, were supported by school systems and state boards of regents, and they were even more responsive to the will of the authorities and less inclined to venture beyond the regional mores and the conventional pieties because they stood in danger of losing their sources of funds.

A few stations, notably KQED in San Francisco and WGBH in Boston, were exemplary for their independence and courage, and both had built strong support in their coverage areas principally because their managements had vision and their boards of directors the character to fight the repressive petty battles. KQED lost an important local contributor in November of 1970 because its nightly program *News Room* was considered to have a left-of-center tilt. The school district in Richmond, a conservative bastion of the East Bay area, complained of *News Room*'s interpretive approach to journalism and objected in general to the station's liberal policies. A package of classroom programing for which the school board paid $15,000 a year lost its underwriting at KQED because the news coverage, which was not part of the education package, was deemed "thoroughly biased."

During the same month, a PBS documentary titled *Banks and the Poor,* which held the banking industry partly responsible for the perpetuation of slum conditions, and remiss in their social responsibilities, caused controversy all through the public TV system. The Texas Banking Association succeeded in keeping the program from being broadcast at several stations in that state, and there was strong opposition to the idea of the program by stations that eventually did carry it. All told, more than a dozen stations chose to forgo the program, and several that did carry it nervously invited local banking officials to prescreen it (but not representatives of the poor), with offers of rebuttal time.

The documentary had been produced for the public network by NET in New York and was approved by its attorneys, but—as the first probing and issue-oriented program to be offered under the new PBS banner—it was nearly canceled before telecast by the Washington-based network over an expressed concern that it might be unfairly negative in its portrayal of the banking industry. But it is probable that the real source of worry was the program's intimation that reforms in national banking legislation were scarcely possible while there were members of Congress with direct ties to banking institutions who disregarded a congressional rule that prohibits voting on legislation where there is a conflict of interest. While "The Battle Hymn of the Republic" played on the soundtrack, the documentary closed with a crawl that listed ninety-eight Senators and Representatives who were shareholders or directors of banks, including fifteen in positions specifically pertinent to banking legislation.

These congressmen, of course, voted for the funds for the

Corporation of Public Broadcasting, and one who was on the list, Senator John O. Pastore of Rhode Island, headed the Communications Subcommittee of the Senate Commerce Committee which *authorizes* the public television funds that the other legislators vote to approve. Pastore was a director of the Columbus National Bank in Providence. With public TV hungering for a federal endowment, it was no time to embarrass those who might grant the favor.

Although there was strong sentiment at PBS to kill the broadcast, there was really no choice but to proceed with it. To have suppressed it would surely have created a scandal worse in its effects on the noncommercial system than the mere discomfort of angering banks and congressmen. PBS officials, however, wired their member stations that it might be advisable to invite bank representatives to the screenings (contrary to a long-standing NET policy regarding controversial documentaries) and to address all complaints not to PBS but to NET.

Even more than commercial TV stations, educational stations feared their own New York network source, and some were almost paranoid in their distrust of programs fed over the national line. Again there was the suspicion that the Eastern liberal Establishment was visiting its wickedness upon them through its dominance over National Educational Television.

Numerous stations in the South would not carry nationally distributed programs with black principals or those dealing with racial issues on the grounds that they were not in the local interest or that they would inflame elements of the community; and, astonishingly, the program most celebrated in the entire history of educational or public television in America, *Sesame Street,* was rejected initially by a few stations because of its racially integrated cast.

As for nonracial shows, *The Banks and the Poor* was far from a lone instance of pusillanimous censorship in the public TV ranks.

In 1965, a NET documentary, *Three Faces of Cuba,* rattled a number of affiliates because it was not unswervingly critical of Castro and because it did not represent conditions in Cuba as all bad. Two programs on Red China from Canada's CBC were disparaged and rejected by some stations because they did not show Mao's China falling apart; and Felix Greene's documentary on North Vietnam, frankly propagandistic but not without informational value even on those terms, created a furor in the public television family as unpatriotic.

On similar charges, a number of stations (including Washington's WETA) declined to carry a NET program critical of American foreign policy and intervention in the emerging nations, *Who Invited US?* And the stations in Seattle, Philadelphia, Pittsburgh, Chicago, Jacksonville, and Austin, among others, refused an exclusive interview with black militant Bobby Seale, allegedly because it contained profane language.

Even the cultural area produced its share of strife. A production of Maxwell Anderson's *The Star Wagon* disturbed the Middle West because the dialogue contained that most explosive word in all television, "Goddam." And a series of cultural profiles of poets, painters, dancers, novelists, and other artists drew angry response from local educational broadcasters because some of the subjects expressed their political viewpoints and others, like Lawrence Ferlinghetti, "spoke dirty."

New York station WNDT killed a series that was to be a clinic for people desiring to quit smoking cigarettes because the proposed cure was not proven. The station manager reasoned that viewers who were not cured of the smoking habit by the series might be discouraged from ever trying to quit again, and therefore the project was dangerous. Maybe it did not influence his decision, but if not it was an embarrassing coincidence that the chairman of Philip Morris Tobacco Company, Joseph F. Cullman III, was a member of the station's board of directors.

A BBC documentary on homosexuality was declined by

several station operators because they found it "pro homo," and one would not carry a segment of the Consumers Union series, *Your Dollar's Worth*, dealing with gyps by television repairmen, because the head of the local TV repairman's association disapproved of it and threatened retaliation.

And upon such stations the United States built its system of public television to enrich the air waves and serve the needs of the people.

There was some soaring prose in the Carnegie Commission report, such as the paragraph next to the last:

"If we were to sum up our proposal with all the brevity at our command, we would say that what we recommend is freedom. We seek freedom from the constraints, however necessary in their context, of commercial television. We seek for educational television freedom from the pressures of inadequate funds. We seek for the artist, the technician, the journalist, the scholar, and the public servant freedom to create, freedom to innovate, freedom to be heard in this most far-reaching medium. We seek for the citizen freedom to view, to see programs that the present system, by its incompleteness, denies him."

An organization known as the National Association of Educational Broadcasters is to noncommercial stations approximately what the National Association of Broadcasters is to the television and radio business, a fraternity, an organization for self-regulation, a Washington lobby. At its general membership meeting in the fall of 1969 a resolution was passed, with a vote of 300 to 2, to establish a civil liberties committee to take action when threats to the freedom and independence of educational broadcasting arose. But the committee was never formed. At a meeting of the NAEB board of directors in May 1970, notwithstanding the mandate of the general membership, the decision was made to let the matter ride.

In the interval between the 1969 general convention and that held in November 1970, there were at least ten instances in which an NAEB civil liberties committee might have acted, at least to protest or condemn the threats to the professional prerogatives of broadcasting. As enumerated by the author of the original resolution, Dave Berkman, Associate Professor of Communication at American University in Washington, the threats were:

Vice President Spiro Agnew's impingement on editorial freedom in all broadcasting;

The FCC's fine against educational radio station WUHY-FM in Philadephia for language in an interview that it regarded as obscene;

The firing by WETA-TV in Washington of its news editor allegedly because his wife had taken a job as secretary to Attorney General John Mitchell;

The hesitation of the FCC to renew the licenses of the noncommercial, listener-supported Pacifica FM radio stations because of the free-speech programs they broadcast, specifically in giving vent to the bigotry of blacks;

The censorship by certain stations of the documentary *Who Invited US?*;

The refusal of certain stations to carry the interview with Black Panther leader Bobby Seale;

The two occasions on which the free speech radio station in Houston was dynamited into silence, after terrorist threats;

The movement in the broadcast industry to impeach FCC Commissioner Nicholas Johnson, whom Berkman called "broadcasting freedom's staunchest defender";

The pressures by the Texas Banking Association which led to certain Texas stations rejecting the documentary *The Banks and the Poor;*

And the FCC's four-to-three decision upholding the Alabama ETV Commission, which asserted its right to ignore the interests of the black population of the state (estimated at about 30 per cent of the residents) by refusing to carry national programs on black affairs.

NAEB maintained an official silence on each of the

issues, and on others of similar character, although even the National Association of Broadcasters, the FCC, and Frank Stanton of CBS issued statements deploring the bombings that knocked the Houston FM station off the air and appealing to the government to involve the Justice Department and the FBI in an investigation.

The NAEB executive board, Berkman said, "represents the interests of station management, which is, in turn, responsive mainly to conservative, legislative funding sources."

At the 1970 meeting of the Association, on November 11, Berkman once again introduced his resolution to the NAEB general membership, which had passed almost unanimously the previous year. This time, however, he called for the establishment of a Freedom of Broadcasting Committee to be formed within ninety days by mandate of the membership and secondly for censure by the NAEB of the Alabama Educational Television Commission for its disregard of the black population of its state.

This time the NAEB board openly opposed it, and the resolution was defeated by a vote of 119 to 67.

Only the crassest or most cynical of men would not have rejoiced when President Johnson signed the Public Broadcast Act in 1967. In that moment the new federally chartered but ostensibly independent Corporation for Public Broadcasting was born. There were two immediate gifts from the private sector to help the Corporation get started: one from the Carnegie Foundation, the other from CBS, both for one million dollars.

Then began the search for a chairman and a president for the Corporation, two men who would lead the second coming of broadcasting in the United States. One imagined, from the Carnegie Commission's prescription, fierce idealists steeped in the communications arts, courageous generals who once appointed by the President would keep the government at arm's length from the new public broadcasting service.

In February 1968, the search for a chairman ended with

the appointment of Frank Pace, Jr. A former secretary of the army, he had also been assistant director of the Budget and board chairman and president of General Dynamics Corporation. A year later a president was selected for the Corporation, John H. Macy, who had been chairman of the U.S. Civil Service Commission under Presidents Kennedy and Johnson.

Both were steeped in the ways of Washington bureaucracy, both had connections within the government, and neither had had any previous experience with broadcasting. As for a fierce idealism, it was never apparent in any of their speeches, which were, for all their volume, notably unquotable in news terms, and unfailingly unmemorable. If they were sound appointments for the fund-raising purposes of the Corporation—and that was not proved by the end of 1970—they were, however, dismally uninspiring men.

In April 1969, doubtless in response to station anxieties concerning the program judgments of NET, plans were laid for the Public Broadcasting Service as a new network that would make its base in Washington, superseding NET as the distributor. PBS would neither create nor produce programing but would select series from available sources, schedule the transmission, and feed them out over the network line. The board of directors of PBS would be elected by officials of the public TV stations, which at last gave them power over National Educational Television, reduced to merely a program supplier. Thus cushioned against NET's progressivism, which many found reckless, the member stations of public broadcasting had half their wishes realized. The other half was for economic security, which the federal government could make possible, and in a short time the stations made it clear that they would give up almost anything, including their First Amendment freedoms, for the subsidy.

Public broadcasting was a new bureaucracy and something of a monstrosity, tier upon tier of chairmen, presidents, boards of directors, and committees, infused with government influence at all levels, and particularly at the top—

the Corporation itself—which was meant to shield the system from practical politics so that it could be free.

Locating PBS in Washington put it under the eye of the federal government, which dangled appropriations and budget allocations like a carrot. Almost immediately, as the stations hungered for money, public TV set out to please the elected officials and in several ways demonstrated how the new noncommercial industry might serve their pet causes.

There was one interesting inconsistency in the role of the Corporation. Under the charter it was not to engage in the actual programing of the new system but only to secure funds and *administer* them to further worthy projects. But in its backing of projects for television the Corporation, in fact, was playing the crucial part—the role of the advertiser—in the programing of the new system. And since the officers and directors of the Corporation were to be appointed by the President of the United States there was the distinct danger of public television becoming a form of government television, or as one worried member of the public TV industry put it, "a domestic Voice of America."

The shortage of programing funds was next to critical during 1970, and yet the Corporation saw fit to allocate approximately $200,000 for six and one-half hours' coverage of the national ecology promotion, Earth Day, as a special event, and $158,000 for coverage of President Nixon's hunger conference. Out of its own strained budget, NET spent close to $160,000 to interconnect the stations for the President's State of the Union Message, also carried by the commercial networks. Then on July 4 there was the costly three-and-one-half-hour interconnection in prime time for the patrotic "Honor America Day" activities in the capital. And then, in line with the President's wishes, there was the formation of a Public Broadcasting Environment Center to produce a weekly program, under a Department of Health, Education, and Welfare grant, to be titled *Quality of Life*. This series, according to a fact sheet, "would employ various techniques (including the performing arts) to explore how the environment can be restored to healthy balance and preserved." The fact sheet also stated—and this has particular significance in point of pleasing the Administration—that "the emphasis will be on remedies and prevention, not predictions of doom."

Even before the Public Broadcasting Environment Center came into being and performed its research, it had a point of view, indeed a message, and it was leaning away from journalism toward propaganda.

One program was late premiering among the PBS debuts. Although initially it was scheduled to begin with the others the week of October 5, for reasons undisclosed beyond an official statement that it "required more time to unearth necessary source material" it was delayed a month. The new series was *The Nader Report,* a weekly half hour featuring the leader of the consumerism movement, Ralph Nader, and the young aides from his Center of Study of·Responsible Law who were known popularly as Nader's Raiders. The series was to be the prime showcase for the courage and freedom of PBS, demonstrating how the new network was able to deal with subjects which were off limits to commercial broadcasters, especially subjects that might alienate advertisers.

Reports from members of the program's staff, however, were that the curtailment had centered on two sequences which were to have been in the initial program, an examination of deception in advertising. Executives of Boston station WGBH, where the series was being produced, were hesitant about a segment questioning the nutritional value of popular breakfast cereals and another analyzing the claims of a Mobil Oil television commercial that its detergent gasoline made automobile engines cleaner and therefore contributed to cleaner air.

By a coincidence, the Mobil Company at just that time was about to make a most generous donation of one million dollars to the Corporation for Public Broadcasting for the presentation of a series of plays produced in England and to help cover costs of distributing the new *Sesame Street* magazine to preschoolers in the ghetto areas. For the gift, Mobil would receive donor's credit on the air for each of the plays and recognition in the press, since its program grant would be the largest yet made by an industrial contributor. The Corporation served this cause by calling a press conference for the announcement.

When Bill Greeley reported in *Variety* the coincidence of the grant and the delayed Nader program that would be taking to task a Mobil TV commercial, the petroleum company issued a statement denying that there was a connection. But there was no attempt to explain one further coincidence. The huge grant was secured for the Corporation by Stanford Calderwood, who was then president and general manager of WGBH, the very station producing *The Nader Report*. What made it a strange coincidence was that the grant was meant for the national service yet was negotiated at a local level, a highly irregular procedure. Most corporate grants to the network were arranged directly with officers of the Corporation.

The Nader Report premiered finally on November 13, but not with the originally scheduled program on deceptive advertising. That was postponed for several weeks and the Mobil Oil sequence retained, perhaps because its deletion would have been embarrassing after the publicity.

Concurrent with the grant from Mobil, Calderwood accepted a new position with the Corporation in a special area of fund raising, securing corporate underwriting for television shows. It was a good time for him to leave WGBH, since the station and he were under fire from the black community over a local series, *Say, Brother*, for allegedly imposing white standards on black expression. Calderwood had come to the station a few months earlier from an executive position with the Polaroid Corporation; negotiating with the business world for program grants was probably more in keeping with his cultivated skills.

Shortly afterward, on November 10, the FCC agreed to liberalize the rules governing on-the-air credit to industries which made program gifts to noncommercial stations. Where previously the donor was only entitled to his recognition (that is, his "plug") before and after the programs he provided, under the new provisions he could receive credit every hour for programs of longer duration. In addition, public stations were permitted to give greater identification of the corporations, noting for instance the separate divisions of the company that had helped pay for the broadcast.

There was a single dissent at the FCC to the new rules, and naturally it was by Nicholas Johnson, who viewed it as a step toward greater control over programing by big business. Johnson pointed out that commercial broadcasting rapidly developed into a selling medium, and he said it seemed "obvious" that public broadcasting "is well on its way down the same road."

Mobil's million dollars might have bought a single ninety-minute drama at CBS, perhaps two, although of course with full-length, bonafide commercials. Also, its total audience for a single CBS telecast probably would have exceeded the combined total of the thirty-nine *Masterpiece Theatre* dramas it was presenting. Still, the identification with programs of exceptional quality was a benefit that would accrue to the petroleum company from its public relations gift, and if by chance the British dramas were to gain a larger audience than anticipated the donation could have the approximate value of network advertising.

While it may seem innocent enough for a prosperous corporation to make a gift of money to public television for a program presentation, there are some dangers to the free system inherent in it. If a larger audience circulation would spur more gifts of the kind, the money-craving public television system might be drawn into the quest for rating numbers that had already made a rat race of commercial television. And if a patron corporation had a particular kind of program it desired to "provide" on public television, the network might abdicate its own programing judgment to accommodate the donor. The experience of commercial television contains evidence that only the rarest advertiser chooses to associate himself with controversial programs, so it would seem to follow that as the number of corporate patrons increased for public television the number of issue-oriented or controversial programs would decline.

With the government already taking part to an unhealthy degree, new concessions to fund raising in the private sector which would give big industry a deeper involvement in its affairs threatened to make a myth of "public" television.

Of all the organizations in the public television complex the one that appeared to have the best chance of remaining a free entity was the Children's Television Workshop. Supported by foundation grants for the first two years of its production of *Sesame Street*, the Workshop was determined to become self-sufficient by the most American of means, going into business.

An unquestioned hit with preschool children, *Sesame Street* could have been productive of vast subsidiary revenues if it had done what commercial children's shows had always done, licensed its name and television characters for product merchandising—toys, tee shirts, breakfast cereals, vitamins, toothbrushes, and all the myriad products that tots are prey to. As a matter of fact, there had been a single licensing agreement. *Sesame Street* gave its name, its songs, its lessons, and its characters to Time-Life Books for the production of books-and-records sets to supplement the programs, but the product went on the market at a price only the affluent families could afford, and after the first issuance of merchandise the agreement was terminated.

Joan Ganz Cooney, president of the Workshop and its founder, in effect the mother of *Sesame Street*, had worked to create an educational program for disadvantaged preschool children, and in her judgment it violated the aim of the program to spin off from it merchandise which either only exploited the show without adding to its instructional purposes or was out of the price range of her target audience. If there were to be *Sesame Street* products, she would not permit them to contribute to the ghetto child's sense of privation.

That made it necessary for the Children's Television Workshop to create its own products division, which would not be as profitable as outright licensing to private manufacturing companies but which was nevertheless expected to be a source of some revenue to keep the nonprofit company going. There was also some money to be made from the overseas sale of *Sesame Street*, both the American version to English-speaking countries and adaptations for other languages to be produced by foreign broadcast systems using some of the film and animation of the original. But the neediest nations had first priority at considerate prices, and the revenues were still not great enough to cover the budget for another new series of *Sesame Street* and a companion series for older children which would attempt to teach reading.

Aiming for a profit-making business to support the nonprofit company, Mrs. Cooney's Workshop took a fancy to cable television with, initially, a bid for the Washington, D.C., franchise. The city's resident Negro population had outstripped the white, and the Children's Workshop was primarily interested in penetrating the black urban pockets. If there was money to be made from CATV, Mrs. Cooney reasoned, why not by a noncommercial company whose principal interest and occupation was broadcasting and one which would be disposed to wiring the indigent households free of charge?

There was some precedent for the use of cable TV to support a public television facility. The city of Vincennes, Indiana, had awarded its cable franchise to the local junior college, which used the proceeds to build and sustain an educational TV station.

If wiring the nation for cable TV represented one hope for a qualitatively superior broadcast system in the United States—if that was to be the real second coming of television —how much greater the hope if the control of cable should be as accessible to broadcast idealists as to venture capital.

Short of dismantling the system and starting over again, which is of course unrealistic, the best that can be immediately desired for public broadcasting under the present conditions is that the earnest, caring communicators who are ambitious for the *medium*, who want it to be bold, meaningful, and uniquely expressive, do not desert it from frustration. With all its failings, the public system does afford opportunities for the breakthrough, and in television—commercial or otherwise—one shining example of program success invariably inspires attempts at more of the same.

Sesame Street had been rejected by the commercial networks before Joan Cooney raised the money from several foundations and put the show on public television. Within months it became the model for excellence in programing for the very young, and it drove all three networks to the creation of series for children that would be cultural and/or educational—and at the same time entertaining and commercial. NBC produced a delightful half-hour series, *Hot Dog*, which whimsically showed the young how commonplace things are manufactured. It would probably have been a more successful show in a late Sunday afternoon period than it was on Saturday mornings opposite the CBS cartoons. ABC spent nearly two years developing *Curiosity Shop* as a children's entry for the fall of 1971. As a direct result of *Sesame Street*, CBS began experimenting with one-minute newscasts for children, and NBC made a regular part of its Saturday morning service a raft of one-minute spots called *Pop-Ups*, which were designed to teach reading to preschoolers. Devised for television by the noted educator Caleb Gattegno, the *Pop-Ups* were developed as programing and sold to NBC by one of the network's own apostates, Paul Klein, the erstwhile nemesis of Mike Dann.

Public television had the ability to influence commercial TV and, in small ways, to raise the standards of content for the medium generally. Regrettably, however, the noncommercial system was not constituted to present a powerful challenge to the commercial industry; even if it were lavishly funded, it lacked the freedom, the spine, and the competitive spirit. It must be significant that the three most important shows in noncommercial television during 1970 were not products of the public TV establishment but rather came to PBS from outside sources, after having first been offered to the commercial networks. *Forsyte Saga* and *Civilisation* were from the BBC, and *Sesame Street* from an independent noncommercial production company.

I cannot believe that a permanent system of funding set up by the federal government for public TV would do anything more than make the existing mediocre system more comfortably secure. Money is not the panacea for what ails public television in America. It would be tragic, it seems to me, if the long-awaited funding were finally arranged without being conditional on certain correctives. If PBS is to be more than a charade of Britain's admirable (although imperfect) BBC-TV, it must, like the BBC, be made safe from government influence and the "magnanimity" of corporate donors. In addition, it must be delivered from the vested interests and petty fears of its member stations. If it is to be worth the taxpayers' money, the system must be free from fear.*

* Establishing a system of permanent funding for public broadcasting is by far the most difficult problem to be resolved if there is to be a healthy and meaningful alternative to commercial television and radio in the United States. Its source and the method of its distribution will inevitably be up to Congress, but it must be made to come without political strings, without, that is, the clear implication that it is an annually renewable reward for docility. To receive its operating funds, the public broadcasting system must not be asked to trade any part of its broadcast rights or obligations.

Ideally, the money would not come from the federal budget but directly from a new impost—perhaps a special excise tax on television sets, as the Carnegie Commission proposed, or perhaps a tax on the profits of commercial broadcasters—so that it would not be funneled through the legislature. The British Broadcasting Corporation owes its insulation from government to its source of operating revenues, which is from a license fee for individual households using radio and television of £6.50 (or $15.60 per year) administered by the postmaster general. Such a system is not recommended for the United States for three rea-

I advocate a single change in the structure of public television, one whose effects should not only move the noncommercial system into the vanguard of the medium (it is now well in the background) but also would reverberate so forcefully in the commercial sphere that it would compel the networks to raise their own standards for mass entertainment. What I propose—and it is not utopian—is a strong national network for public television that is augmented (but not controlled) by local service, a simple reversal of the existing priorities.

To be precise, I am suggesting that PBS become a full-fledged noncommercial correlative of CBS, NBC, and ABC —a head-on competitor, without the cash motive. I am not recommending that it join the Philistines, only that it give commercial television a run for its influence on society.

If the network came first in the public television scheme, it should be mandatory for all stations to carry its programs off the line. Not democratic? Okay, then make it as democratic as the commercial system. The stations would be paid compensation for what they carried off the line. The more they carried, the better they would be funded. A station in

---

sons: (a) Americans are not conditioned to paying for over-the-air television and would resent public TV if it did not come as free of charge as commercial television, (b) it would pose a hardship on those who probably need television most, namely the poor, and (c) the British are bedeviled by license evaders and are continually forced to track them down. After years of policing, the BBC in 1970 estimated that it had lost more than $18 million a year from families that were successfully evading their license payments. Still, there is much merit in a system that is not dependent on Parliament (or Congress) for its economic survival.

What is needed in the United States, as a first step to guide the legislature in its decision on how to provide funds for public television, is a conviction in the country that a national public TV network is vital to the quality of American life and thought. Indeed, a public lobby would have the carrot to dangle before the politicians, in that the independent and noncommercial TV system could offer free time to candidates seeking public office, an important consideration in a time of growing concern over the high cost of campaigning. In both national and local elections, public television is well suited to be the political stump.

the South that refused to carry a program with an integrated cast, then, would do so at a penalty; chances are, with money involved, it would not readily decline the show.

Besides, what is so democratic about the present public television system? When the board of directors of PBS is made up of local station operators, that is not democracy but oligarchy.

Of course, who governs the public TV corporation and the network is most important—who, in other words, undertakes as its inevitable responsibility the protection of the system from political and business interference, and who guides the network in serving the best interests of the complete society and not just of the craven and comfortable. To be sure, such appointments would not be easy to make, but an enlightened President might begin by eliminating two unpromising categories of candidates, career bureaucrats and professional fund raisers, who as it happens are prominent in the hierarchy of the present docile noncommercial system.

This new network, free and independent—and *then* well financed—must strive to be popular. Not elitist, not pledged to serve the minority audiences commercial television "cannot afford" to serve, not dryly informative for the academic world, but literally appealing to the people. That does not mean it must descend to foolishness, crassness, or vulgarity. Popularity does not diminish the quality of a book, a play, a movie, or a new song. Nor must popularity mean what it means in the commercial television game. There, if a show attracts 17 million people and gets a 25 share it is a failure. If a picture or a play should sell 17 million admissions, or a book 700,000 copies, it is successful beyond the most extravagant hopes. A recording of a song that sells a million copies is a smash.

I would ask for a public television system that shoots for 10 per cent of the viewership, say seven or eight million souls in a half hour of prime time, and then looks for 15 per cent. Not a 30 share that the commercial networks consider mandatory, but certainly not the 1 per cent share that public TV today is satisfied to receive.

The present public television leadership makes a virtue of being ignored. We program without consideration to ratings, they say. But on what philosophy? To prove what? To serve whom? To stay out of whose way?

Superior *television*, and not a self-congratulating cultural service, should be the goal of public television. It should try to show the commercial system what to reach for and prove it in the terms the advertiser-supported medium best understands, by creaming off some of its precious audience-for-sale. PBS must embrace light entertainment, if for no other reason than to attract the television multitudes and to give the lie to its being a snob service. An even better reason, of course, would be to demonstrate that light entertainment has broader possibilities and can be more imaginatively produced than the commercial industry permits, bound as it is to the time-tested formulas.

Britain's public television, the BBC, produced such national family hits as *The Morecambe and Wise Show, Dad's Army, Not in Front of the Children,* and *Monty Python's Flying Circus* during 1969, a year in which it also presented 600 television dramas, and numerous documentaries and talk shows, as well as operas, concerts, and coverage of sporting events. Granted the terms are different there, the BBC comprising two networks (one on VHF and one on UHF) competing with a single commercial service, ITV, which scarcely resembles an American network since it is a patchwork of regional stations, it is still interesting that in 1969 the BBC received a larger share of the audience than the commercial channel.

As mentioned earlier, out of BBC's light entertainment came *Till Death Us Do Part,* which inspired the CBS series *All in the Family,* and a new comedian, Marty Feldman, who was signed by ABC for a show in the winter of 1971.

If an American noncommercial network were to average

a modest 10 share of audience through all competitive periods with the other networks, the effect would be explosive. Commercial television would have to compete with it, if only to keep public TV from adding to its audience and growing into a still more potent force. Not only would the valuable Nielsen digits be affected but also the prestige of the three most powerful communications forces in the country.

It is easy to misjudge the commercial networks. CBS, NBC, and ABC are proud companies. Only the press of business and the demands on corporations which have gone public through the sale of stock have made them put profits before professional excellence. I doubt that they would passively accept usurpation of their pre-eminence in electronic theater and light entertainment or in electronic journalism. They would not let the noncommercial competitor steal the glory day after day as, in one arena of service, *Sesame Street* has done. The professionals in commercial broadcasting deeply believe in the superiority of their system, and faced with a proper challenge they would not cease trying to prove it.

A public television system that treated the networks as an opponent could not fail to induce healthy changes in American broadcasting. Such beneficent competition would serve the public interest in communications as it has never been served before.

But even if, unaccountably, the commercial networks were to decline the challenge and continue in the narrow, profit-seeking furrow, at least there would be one network in the United States working to realize the potential of the medium and willing to allow it to express not the neutral or noncommittal statements of corporations but rather what is on the minds and in the experience and hearts of human beings.

15

Quo Video?

Except that general business conditions hampered their economic progress, all three networks realized some measure of competitive success in the first half of the 1970–71 season. CBS did better in the ratings than expected and closed out December in a virtual tie with NBC; and ABC, largely on the strength of its Tuesday night line-up of *Mod Squad, Movie of the Week,* and *Marcus Welby, M.D.*, moved up in the averages to where it was two full rating points behind the leaders—not stunning improvement, but improvement nonetheless.

In some ways more significant than these statistical successes, however, were the networks' separate instances of failure during the season, for they pointed up an interesting truth about CBS, NBC, and ABC: that without intending it, each had over the years conditioned the audience to its own peculiar programing habits and thereby had formed a "personality." Each episode of failure had, in a sense, been an attempt by a network to step out of character. CBS could not put over "relevant" melodrama, because in the public mind it had low credibility with that genre; NBC again proved inept with program series of specific appeal to women and also with those of folksy character; and ABC was unable to establish programs of chic idiom or of an intellectual caliber the industry liked to refer to as "class."

The viewing public may not think in terms of networks when it switches on the set, but unconsciously it has come to know approximately what to expect in the way of entertainment on each channel in prime time. It seems to know intuitively that the station carrying NBC comes more naturally to anthology melodrama dealing with contemporary themes, and to sophisticated comedy; that CBS excels in situation comedy, rustic entertainment, and star-hosted variety programs; and that ABC deals most believably in action-adventure, family comedies, and the exploitation of new vogues in popular culture. These distinctions between the networks developed over the years through differences in traditions, continuity acceptance standards, success formulas, and image projection.

When CBS essayed topical urban melodrama with *Store-front Lawyers* and *The Interns*, and ABC with *The Young Lawyers*, they were dealing in a program type the viewers had been conditioned to accept on NBC. Similarly, NBC was in CBS's waters with Don Knotts, whose appeal was primarily rural, and in ABC's with such programs as *Nancy* and *Bracken's World*, both meant to appeal to women. The Neil Simon comedies, *Odd Couple* and *Barefoot in the Park*, were not the usual stuff of ABC and would have been more suitable at either of the other networks. It is entirely possible that Knotts would have averaged five more share points at CBS—the difference between failure and success in his case. That speculation derives some substantiation from the fact that Red Skelton's countrified humor made the Nielsen top ten at CBS but ran way off form when it switched to NBC. The success of shows is sometimes a matter of network environment.

Conceivably, NBC could have done a more convincing job than CBS of presenting Tim Conway as a sketch comedian. NBC's endorsement of the style and content of his comedy would have carried some weight, since NBC is associated with comedy-variety marked by uniqueness (*Laugh-In* and Flip Wilson), while CBS has traditionally emphasized star stature in that format, especially in the mid-America sense (Glen Campbell, Jim Nabors, Carol Burnett).

ABC's fast turnover in shows, the curse of the third-placer, apparently has identified that network with short-term and highly perishable programs, so that viewers do not normally look to it for the stable and lasting series but rather for the fads, like *Batman* and *Shindig*. Its effectiveness with straight action series like *The FBI* traces to the early sixties when Warner Brothers programed much of ABC's prime time with shows such as *Surfside Six, 77 Sunset Strip*, and *Hawaiian Eye*, and its tradition of family comedies dates to the years of *Ozzie and Harriet* and *The Donna Reed Show*. It was successfully carried on in 1970 by *The Brady Bunch, The Courtship of Eddie's Father, Nanny and the Professor*, and *The Partridge Family*.

The experience of self-discovery had little effect on the networks, for in their schedules for the 1971–72 season each would try again to make over its image.

In any good year, the buying activity is so spirited in November that by Christmastime the networks are practically sold out in prime time for the first quarter. But 1970 was not a good year, and in early December the sales outlook was so poor that CBS was driven to a desperate step. At the urging of sales vice-president Frank Smith, the network established that its minimum unit of sale would be thirty-seconds instead of one minute. The other networks had no choice but to follow, and within a period of days the thirty-second commercial became the new industry standard.

It had the immediate effect of lubricating the market, but even as purchasing activity became accelerated there was the melancholy sense at all three networks that the wave of business for the available network positions from January through March was a short-term enjoyment they would spend the rest of the year regretting. For the action that CBS initiated was like a department store sale that never ended, a two-for-one clearance sale that became a permanent part of the business.

For nearly two years, all three networks had held the line against the thirty-second standard against intense pressure from the advertising industry. While they had been accepting half-minute commercials since 1968, the networks required that the minimum purchase be one minute in each show. The advertiser had had the privilege of splitting it in two; if he bought *Laugh-In,* he could have two half-minutes, one at the beginning and one at the end of the show. Under the new procedures, he could buy a single thirty-second announcement in any show.

The troublesome aspect of the new standard was that advertisers were permitted to buy half-minutes at *half* the minute price, without being charged a premium. That was tantamount to the networks cutting their rates. The national magazines usually sell half pages at roughly 60 per cent the price of full pages, never 50 per cent. Part of the reasoning in changing to the thirty-second standard was to make network television more available to smaller advertisers who could not afford to buy full minutes, but those advertisers were notably absent once the policy was adopted. Mainly it succeeded in stimulating the regular customers who had been holding back their first quarter budgets. One who normally bought two minutes a week and placed them in two shows now could spread the same investment over four shows, giving him exposure to more of the television audience.

In the meantime, the networks' new concession to Madison Avenue exacerbated their relations with the affiliated stations, many of which felt they were victims of the networks' drastic measure to solve their sales problems. Under the old minute standard, every network had twenty-one available positions for sale each night; with the new arrangement, the availabilities doubled. Since the stations tended to get the leftover budgets of the national advertisers, once the choice network positions were filled up (those being the commercial breaks in the Nielsen top forty shows), they now had to compete with a giant unending sale which featured twice the number of choice positions that had been available previously.

The new commercial standard produced the flush of business that may have saved some jobs at the networks, but its long-term consequences were a source of grave concern to the managements. It took no genius to calculate that an advertiser who previously paid $50,000 per commercial minute to reach 10 million homes realized a cost-per-thousand of $5. At half the price with a thirty-second spot, he reached the same number of homes, so that his cost-per-thousand was only $2.50. Achieving essentially the same result in a single half-minute that he formerly achieved in a full minute, the advertiser might well decide to spend half the money in television that he had spent before. So instead of increasing network advertising revenues, the ultimate effect of the thirty-second standard might be to reduce them.

To cut back network time by thirty minutes each night must seem a small matter to those on the viewing side of the TV set, but in the television industry the FCC's three-hour rule broke long-established patterns of program service and created confusion on both the network and the station levels.

CBS and its affiliates, a number of Hollywood studios, and several stations independently went to the courts to contest the rule, but since the networks had to prepare their schedules for September 1971 well before the courts would consider the case there was no choice but to proceed with a shorter evening schedule for the new season.

Under the rule, the networks were allowed to program three hours a night in the four-hour period between seven and eleven. Since the least valuable period of the designated span was the half hour at seven o'clock, because the viewing levels were low then, the decision at the networks, practically speaking, was whether to program from 7:30 to 10:30, or from 8:00 to 11:00. Under the antitrust laws the networks were forbidden to confer on the question and decide upon a common course. Thus it was left to each network to declare the half hour it would surrender.

NBC initially chose for its three-hour span the period 8:00 to 11:00 (Eastern Time), except on Sundays, where the high-rated Walt Disney anthology hour dictated a 7:30 start.

CBS then announced that its new prime-time hours would be 7:30 to 10:30 seven nights a week. That left ABC faced with the decision of whether to oppose NBC or CBS in every time period. For several reasons, ABC chose to go up against NBC.

ABC's decision was in some ways a curious one, since it had a strong concentration of family situation comedies that were appropriate for the 7:30 period. The overriding considerations for a later start were (a) that the 10:30 half hour was generally a more desirable buy for advertisers than the 7:30, (b) that the Monday night football games needed the latitude to run past prime time, and (c) that a uniform designation of prime time seven nights a week was preferable to an irregular pattern under which the network might begin at 7:30 some nights and 8:00 others.

The football games, which began at nine in the East, ran overtime (*i.e.*, past eleven o'clock) an average of forty-five minutes per game during the 1970 season. At rates of approximately $65,000 per commercial minute, ABC was able to break even on the cost of football programing during the two hours of prime time it encompassed—the profits were all in the period the games ran over into after prime time. For the minutes after eleven o'clock, ABC asked around $45,000, and from those its net profits exceeded $100,000 per game.

If ABC had chosen to start prime time at 7:30, the games would have to be moved to that hour in order to be played entirely within the three hours of prime time. That would mean a 4:30 P.M. starting time in the Western time zone. Even worse, any game that might run beyond three hours would have to be cut off the air at 10:30, before its conclusion, and that would surely infuriate dedicated football fans. So there was no choice but to declare the 8:00 to 11:00 bloc.

Within corporate ABC, the later period was preferred for yet another reason—to feed audience to the eleven o'clock newscasts on the five ABC-owned TV stations, which in some of the larger markets had begun to overtake the local news on CBS stations. After years of running out of the competition, the ABC stations began to make inroads into the late news ratings with the concept *Variety* described as "happy-talk news." The basic format, widely known in the trade as *Eyewitness News* and employed by many stations, replaced the customary news reader with a team of news specialists on camera, each of whom had his moment to report and/or comment on a story. Upon this, the ABC stations embroidered a friendly interplay between the newsmen, encouraging them to josh each other in the intervals between news stories. Often, their gibes and wisecracks were written into the script. It was pure show business, but it got ratings that were worth millions over the course of a year, and ABC did not want to jeopardize those lucrative local gains by ending prime time a half hour before the newscasts began.

Whereas the three-hour rule was an annoyance to the other networks, it was a boon to ABC. For in reducing the size of prime time, the FCC had reduced the number of commercial minutes therein, so that ABC, with the third-ranked schedule, had less program inventory to lose money on and would be the beneficiary of any spillover in prime-time revenues from the other networks. In a three-hour league, ABC would be able to shore up its strongest shows to pit against the strongest of its rivals, and while CBS and NBC would be loath to part with certain programs they would have to drop, ABC had losers to spare. The abbreviated prime-time situation would put ABC on a more equal footing with its rivals.

It also stood to improve its program clearances. In numerous two-station markets across the country, ABC had been shut out and its circulation potential impaired. A city such as Macon, Georgia, for instance, had an NBC and a CBS affiliate, and either at its discretion could add several of the ABC shows, often in the fringe-time periods. In such markets, ABC might gain clearances on the CBS and NBC stations in the prime-time half hours in which they would no longer be receiving network service. That would give ABC a penetration into smaller cities it had never had.

But the networks' initial planning for the new prime-time conditions was to go awry, their affiliated stations were to be thrown into a turmoil, and *Variety* was to play an important part in resolving the absurd situation that followed. This is what happened:

Not long after the networks declared their three-hour blocs came the realization that if CBS was to start unopposed at 7:30 it would begin each evening with an immense rating and would probably enjoy the momentum through the night. Against only local and syndicated shows, a popular series like *Gunsmoke* might well deliver unprecedented 80 shares. Even an amateur could predict the CBS strategy: it would begin each evening with an hour-long show to overlap the eight o'clock starting time of the other networks, impairing their ability to get started. At the very least, CBS should have the top six positions in the Nielsen top ten, so that its participation "packages" for advertisers would be far the most attractive of the networks'. In self-defense, faced as they were with a possible massacre, NBC and ABC could not cede such an advantage to their competitor and were forced to declare that they would join CBS at 7:30. This meant that the prime-time evening would conclude in the Eastern and Western time zones at 10:30—but in the Central and Mountain zones at 9:30, just when the audience levels were at their peak. In time, this could result in a great erosion of circulation, since 9:30 was still early enough to leave the house for neighborly visits, late suppers, or to catch the last feature at the local theater. Left to their own programing skills, the stations had little confidence in their ability to hold the audience.

When NBC definitely announced a 7:30 schedule, its affiliates for the first time in the history of television rejected it and demanded that the network find some way to delay its service to the earlier time zones so that they, too, might have a 7:30 to 10:30 pattern. Not only would an additional delayed feed (there was already one to correct the three-hour time difference on the West Coast) add substantially to the cost of networking, but it would create havoc whenever network programs had to be interrupted for special events like Presidential speeches. Since different shows would have to be pre-empted in the different time zones, the make-goods to advertisers would become highly complicated. NBC was on the horns of a dilemma. One the one hand, a system of clock-time broadcasting across the country was both un-wieldy and fiercely expensive; on the other, it could not af-ford to risk giving CBS a strategic advantage that could make prime time a one-network race in September of 1971.

In the meantime, it was becoming clear that there would be no meaningful "access" to prime time for the independent producers and syndication houses—as the FCC meant there to be—if all the networks were to begin at 7:30. With net-work time ending at 10:30, the local stations would discover they could meet the program challenge simply by dropping their late newscasts down into the vacated half hour. Then at 11:00, which was outside prime time, the networks could resume with two-hour versions of their ninety-minute talk shows (Johnny Carson, Merv Griffin, and Dick Cavett). Per-haps for a year the networks would resist it to oblige the Commission in living up to the spirit of the rule. But inevi-tably, as long as the 11:00 half hour remained open, one network or another would seize it to gain a running start on the competition, and the others would follow in self-defense. A repetition of the 7:30 phenomenon.

The ironic truth was that none of the three networks really wanted to begin prime time at 7:30. That had always been their hardest half hour to program successfully, and the demographic make-up was poor, largely too old and too young. But as long as the option was open for one network to gain a head start on the others, one would grab it and the others would get sucked in defensively.

At the height of the confusion in early March, *Variety* observed that there was only one way the three-hour rule could be made to work remotely in the way the FCC origi-nally meant it to: the Commission would have to take it a step further and declare 7:30 off limits to the networks, establishing that network prime time was 8:00 to 11:00. Numerous broadcasters, including the head of the CBS broadcast group, Richard Jencks, then made just such an appeal to the Commission, and on March 11 all three networks received a hand-delivered letter from the FCC, stating: "It seems to the Commission that the particular hours of network occupancy of prime time may well have a significant effect in [demonstrating the efficacy of the rule]. Specifically, the Commission believes that the selection of an 8–11 p.m. time period would better serve the public interest as a general matter."

It was not an order, but the networks were happy to accept it as one.

At the same time, the FCC granted ABC a one-year waiver from the three-hour rule on Tuesday nights, allowing it to keep its powerful program order intact by surrendering an extra half hour on another night. Earlier NBC had asked for, and received, a waiver on Sunday nights. This meant that all three networks would begin at 7:30 on the waiver nights (ABC's *Marcus Welby, M.D.* going unopposed the last half hour on Tuesday nights and NBC's *The Bold Ones* likewise on Sunday nights) and at 8:00 the remainder of the week. The problem was partially solved.

What remained was how the individual stations would fill the gaping half hours that were being returned to them. Not many were able to draw from local resources, since most had long since given up the production of original shows. Business was shaky and money tight, and stations were not disposed to paying hard cash for eight half hours of prime-time programing every week. The field was wide open for the barter operators, who would place advertiser-financed programs on the stations in what was called a trade-out deal. The station received the program free for two or three minutes of advertisements, and it was permitted to keep all revenues from its sale of the remaining commercial breaks.

The three-hour rule was going to increase the amount of

commercial "sell" the viewer would be subjected to in the fall of 1971. The network code for prime time was three commercial minutes per half hour, but the local stations were allowed to log as many as six. With the fractioned spot, six commercial minutes could seem to equal twelve. Some stations would try to hold the prime-time limit to four minutes, but the barter shows in greatest demand were asking stiff terms—a few insisting on three sponsor minutes in the half hour—and this was driving many stations to the maximum commercial allotment.

In trying to solve the access problem, the FCC actually exacerbated the lingering and perhaps more serious problem of commercial clutter.

The FCC's three-hour rule was a travesty of regulation by a government agency that has never really understood the industry for which it is responsible. Inexcusably naïve, the rule failed to achieve virtually everything it was created for, and in the end it would not be the television industry but the viewer who paid the penalty.

By shrinking prime time, the Commission challenged the networks (which, after all, answered to their shareholders) to make the maximum profits from fewer peak viewing hours. According to that priority, everything venturesome or unproductive of ratings would be eliminated from prime time, or at least severely cut back, and naturally those would be the programs most in the public interest—news and cultural specials, and every series with a novel premise that might need time to build an audience. Because the rule ignored the networks' likely alternatives, it would leave television prime time a desert of formula adventure stories and contrived comedies, unredeemed by the nobler offerings which in the best times had been scant.

Another consequence of the new regulation was to cancel all hopes for an expansion of the networks' early evening news to a full hour. Indeed, by counting the networks' seven o'clock newscasts as prime-time programing, it drove that vital broadcast service from a period of high viewing to one of considerably lower viewing, 6:30 P.M.

Passed by the Commission in the belief that it would increase program access to the medium by production companies outside the cabal of New York networks and the major Hollywood film studios, the rule in fact led to the cancellation of shows by numerous independent suppliers who had been represented on the networks by only one or two series. While none was a loss to American culture, the fact was that their production companies lost their access to prime time and were made weaker by the law when the Commission's purpose was to make the independent suppliers a stronger force in television.

Hogan's Heroes, The Newlywed Game, Let's Make a Deal, Family Affair, The Bill Cosby Show, High Chaparral, The Andy Griffith Show, Mayberry R.F.D., The Kraft Music Hall, The Beverly Hillbillies, Green Acres, and the variety shows of Ed Sullivan, Andy Williams, Jim Nabors, and Lawrence Welk all were supplied by independent companies and were among those to lose their network mooring in the cutback of prime time. When the new schedules were devised for the fall of 1971, the major studios (Universal, Paramount, 20th Century-Fox, Screen Gems, Warner Brothers, and MGM) were represented by thirty-five hours a week of regularly scheduled film series and the independent firms by a total of only eight hours. Firms that lost all or some of their programs on the networks were the small ones, such as Filmways, Bing Crosby Productions, Talent Associates, and the production companies of Ed Sullivan, Chuck Barris, Aaron Spelling, Leonard Freeman, Don Fedderson, David Dortort, Red Skelton, and Danny Thomas.

The employment rate in Hollywood, which had been in serious decline through the business tribulations of the motion picture industry, was worsened by the FCC order which over-all eliminated about fifteen television shows weekly.

The toll was not only in acting jobs but in the technical and creative fields as well.

In a final irony, the FCC relented on its demands that the local stations fill their acquired prime-time periods with original programing not previously exposed on television. Accepting sympathetically the argument of local stations that one year was not sufficient time for syndicators to create a sufficient number of effective first-run shows, or for the stations to produce their own, the Commission quietly granted the stations one year's grace. They would not have to obey the rule until the fall of 1972. So what came of the FCC's good intentions was not more new programing but less new programing and a widespread use of cheap old film.

The disaster was born of the Commission's mistaken belief that everything wrong with television was the networks' fault. Although it licenses stations and not networks, the FCC habitually holds the networks responsible for the ways in which the system fails the American public, and invariably it excuses the stations. In truth, the local outlets are as much to blame as the networks for the caliber of prime-time programing. A chief reason that quality shows have failed over the years has been the unwillingness of stations to clear them; it was not that the shows were rejected by *people* but that they were prerejected by stations.

As a case in point, the ABC evening newscasts perennially trailed those of CBS and NBC in the ratings, seriously hampering the network's ability to recover through advertising support some of the $30 million that was annually budgeted for news operations. Indeed, the size of the loss militated against ABC expanding its news forces to the dimensions of its rivals, both of which were investing in excess of $50 million per year in the journalistic function for their radio and television networks. While it was true from the beginning that the ABC newscast attracted the fewest viewers in most markets where it directly opposed the *CBS Evening News with Walter Cronkite* or the *Huntley-Brink-*

ley Report (later, with Chet Huntley's departure, titled *The NBC Nightly News*), it was also a fact that the program's circulation was held down by the unwillingness of many ABC stations to carry it. Even when, early in 1971, the ABC news began to make strong gains in the ratings as a result of telegenic Harry Reasoner, from CBS, having joined as co-anchorman with Howard K. Smith, the network still trailed its competitors in station clearances. With the NBC news carried by 210 stations and the CBS by 202, it was impossible for ABC to be competitive with a line-up of 145 stations. The forty-odd ABC affiliates that declined to carry the national news (some of them owned by newspapers and some by powerful and prosperous station groups) for the most part offered their viewers instead movies, off-network reruns, and run-of-the-mine syndicated shows, presumably in the public interest.

But as to the three-hour rule, the saddest fact was that it was unnecessary. Had the FCC but realized what a powerful influence the member stations can exert upon their networks, it need only have held the licensed entities responsible for the narrow range of programing and the limited sources of supply in the prime viewing hours. Faced with such a mild threat to their right to hold a license, the stations would have forced the indicated reforms upon their networks.

The drastic change in the networks for the fall of 1971 actually was less an effect of the FCC's three-hour rule than of Madison Avenue's accent on demography. When the new schedules for September were drawn, they were less striking for what they contained than for what they had shorn away. For many devotees of the medium in the heartland, it would not seem like television any more without Lawrence Welk on Saturday nights, Ed Sullivan on Sundays, *Mayberry R.F.D.* on Mondays, and such other long-time favorites as Red Skelton, *The Beverly Hillbillies*, *Green Acres*, *Family Affair*, *The Virginian (Men From Shiloh)*, and Andy Williams. The new season was designed for a citified audience in the age range of eighteen to sixty-four; all others were welcome, to be sure, but except in rare instances they were not going to be expressly served in prime time.

Also purged, with the rural and the old, was relevance. None of the programs purporting to be "with it" in September of 1970 would be carried into the new season beginning September 1971, nor would any new offerings pretend to timeliness or social significance. The only survivor of the previous year's vogue—although technically a January starter—was *All In the Family* on CBS. The bigot comedy had surprised the trade by failing to create a furor, and although it had been a marginal performer in the ratings CBS renewed it for the fall believing that it had suffered from poor placement in the schedule, without benefit of a compatible lead-in. Network president Bob Wood had faith in the show—"It's got my name all over it," he said—and so that it might be bracketed in a new time on Monday nights with a series of comparable sophistication, *Arnie* was saved from cancellation to provide the lead-in.

Although CBS had generally run well in the numbers competition, its schedule for September underwent the most radical revision Black Rock had ever experienced, with every country bumpkin comedy ejected along with the vintage shows that had demonstrated a basic young-old popularity skew. Wood's "urban renewal" campaign was not going to advance in stages but would be realized in CBS prime time with the 1971–72 season.

Similarly, NBC, which had not seemed in need of extensive schedule alterations since it was leading in demographics as well as maintaining a tie with CBS in average audience, made a startling number of changes to rejuvenate the layout and persisted in trying to establish types of programs with which it had never enjoyed marked success. Three of its new shows were situation comedies, *Partners*, *The Good Life*, and *The James Stewart Show*, and one a musical anthology with distinct expectation of attracting women, *Marriage Can Be Fun*.

Numbered among the ABC casualties were Lawrence Welk, Pearl Bailey, and the hit of the previous January, *The Johnny Cash Show*, as that network stripped the schedule clean of variety programs to concentrate on half-hour situation comedies, hour-long action melodramas, and movies in its three-hour evening blocs. For this would be the third year in Elton Rule's three-year plan, and ABC was supposed to overtake its rivals, or at least catch them.

As early as March, the new season had a theme: Law and Order. More than twoscore series on the three networks would deal, in one fashion or another, with law enforcement. In place of contemporary involvement there was a decided swing to nostalgia for earlier, colorful American times—the Prohibition era, for instance, or the West in the early twentieth century. And far from diminishing in number, as Mike Dann had predicted in January of 1970, the movies had actually increased to ten each week and would probably go to eleven when, after the football season, ABC had a two-hour void on Monday nights.

The one remarkable thing about the new program designs was that they left the networks looking astonishingly alike. This was a natural effect of each network imitating the largest commercial successes of the season still in progress, after having dispensed with the old traditions. Everything was imitated, that is, but the *Flip Wilson Show*. Each network had its police: ABC, *Mod Squad*; CBS, *Hawaii Five-O*; NBC, *Adam-12*. Each had its father-centered situation comedy: CBS, Fred MacMurray's *My Three Sons*; ABC, Henry Fonda's *The Smith Family*; NBC, the new *James Stewart Show*. Each had its stylized Western: ABC, *Alias Smith and Jones*; CBS, *Cade's County* and *The Big Wheels*; NBC, *Nichols*. And each had its ninety-minute ersatz movie, begat of ABC's *Movie of the Week*, which predominantly were going to be mystery anthologies.

As NBC had a successful series with a crippled police investigator in *Ironside*, ABC would have a new one with a blind detective, *Longstreet*. As ABC had a hit with federal crime-busters in *The FBI*, CBS added *O'Hara, U.S. Treasury*. As NBC had its winning barristers in *The Bold Ones*, ABC added *Owen Marshall: Counselor At Law* and NBC another to its roster, *The D.A.*

Approximately 58 per cent of network prime time would be given over to escapist adventure in the law-and-order motif and to movies. Some 40 per cent would be made up of situation comedy, music and variety, and melodramas dealing with medicine and the occult. Less than 2 per cent would be devoted to news anthologies.

Both NBC and CBS withdrew their scheduled news features from Tuesday nights in order to cut down ABC's dominance of that evening. For its monthly newsmagazine, *First Tuesday* (which, of course, would be retitled), NBC selected Friday night, the least valuable night of the week in terms of its demographic composition; it thereby would reduce the program's financial losses. CBS moved its news magazine, *Sixty Minutes*, into Sunday night fringe time (six o'clock), as an economy measure, and there it was subject to preemption by football part of the year. But then, to keep from demoralizing the news division, the network capitulated to pressures from CBS News president Richard Salant and created a two-hour news offering, comparable to NBC's, which would replace the Thursday night movie once a month.

How many special news broadcasts might occur in prime time during the season would probably depend more on economic conditions than on the urgency of the news. News presidents have no access to television time beyond the periods regularly assigned to news. When there is an event that seems to call for special coverage, the news president must request the time from the network president. If the network president should deny it—usually from concern with fulfilling his revenue quota—the judgment of whether the business schedule should be pre-empted falls to the next officer up the line, the group or the corporate president. And it is he whose conscience must wrestle with the mandate to show larger profits continually.

The day after CBS announced its program schedule, Mike Dann called to observe that he had been wiped out of it.

"This is the first Fred Silverman schedule," he said. "Freddie's and Wood's. You ought to point that out—and also that most of the shows I brought to the network have been eliminated. And you ought to at least give the kid credit for a lot of guts. Freddie has taken the whole thing apart, and no matter how it works, it's got his personal stamp on it."

What Dann was saying was that CBS was probably going to lose, and Mike Dann had nothing to do with it. If it didn't matter to anyone else, it still mattered to him. He didn't want it charged against his own record.

During October, three months after he left CBS, Mike Dann addressed the Hollywood Television Society. He told the broadcasting and studio executives who attended that their commercial industry was in decline and that they had better look to raising the level of their service or suffer the consequences of becoming obsolete. It was not, at the time, a particularly original idea; others, in speeches and magazine articles, had been forecasting the doom of the old television system. But Dann had been a twenty-one-year practitioner and until the past July he had been the living symbol of network television.

A month later, NBC network president Don Durgin addressed the same group and had a easy time ridiculing Dann as one who in three months had "found religion in the world of colored chalk"—educational TV for children. For Dann, who had admonished his former colleagues to get honest, was the man who brought to CBS *Hee Haw, Gilligan's Island, The Munsters, Green Acres, It's About Time,* and other such masterpieces of banality.

Early in January I had lunch with him. It was the first time I had seen Dann since that speech, and I kidded him about how his remarks might have cost him a network presidency.

"When you went to the Workshop, I took it as a brilliant

step in the engineering of your career. Two years with *Sesame Street*, and a network with a problem looking for a president with honorable credentials would have grabbed you," I said. "Everyone would have forgotten that you wore the knife in your belt for CBS because you'd have soaked up the glory of *Sesame Street*. But you should have known that you don't make speeches attacking the industry if you expect to come back. They remember you for that."

After a pensive moment, Dann said, "Maybe I gave the speech to cut myself off forever. Maybe I don't want ever to be tempted to go back."

"You wouldn't want to be a president?"

"Not now."

"Really?"

"Look, what can a guy do who's president? A president doesn't make the system. The system makes the president. For now, Wood's the right man for the job. Durgin's the right man. Duffy's the right man. Once, I wished—well, believe me when I tell you I'm glad to be out of it."

Every few years the television system sheds its skin, and in 1970 it shed Mike Dann. Earlier it had shed larger men, Pat Weaver, Bob Kintner, Jim Aubrey, Lou Cowan, Ollie Treyz, Tom Moore, Fred Friendly. Once out, they never made it back. Each was the symbol of an era, and as each left the era ended.

The system seems to change but never really does; there are only modifications and changes in style. The president of a network can buy shows and set operating policies, but he is powerless to alter the machinery of his industry. Whatever their capabilities, however forceful they may be as leaders, the men in television are lashed to the system.

But the public is not lashed to it, and hope for the medium survives in that implicit freedom. The freedom of the public, in fact, is the time bomb in television.

Index